They Called It Peace

They Called It Peace

Worlds of Imperial Violence

LAUREN BENTON

PRINCETON UNIVERSITY PRESS

PRINCETON & OXFORD

Published by Princeton University Press
41 William Street, Princeton, New Jersey 08540
99 Banbury Road, Oxford OX2 6JX

press.princeton.edu

ISBN 978-0-691-24847-9
ISBN (e-book) 978-0-691-24848-6
Library of Congress Control Number: 2023945233

British Library Cataloging-in-Publication Data is available

Editorial: Priya Nelson, Emma Wagh, and Morgan Spehar
Production Editorial: Karen Carter
Text Design: Karl Spurzem
Jacket/Cover Design: Katie Osborne
Production: Danielle Amatucci
Publicity: Carmen Jimenez and Maria Whelan
Copyeditor: Jennifer Harris

Jacket/Cover Credit: Jacket image: *Charge on the Gwanga, Cape of Good Hope, on the 8th June, 1846* by Harry Francis Colville Darrell (1851). Prints, Drawings and Watercolors from the Anne S. K. Brown Military Collection. Brown Digital Repository / Brown University Library

This book has been composed in Arno Pro

Printed on acid-free paper. ∞

Printed in the United States of America

10 9 8 7 6 5 4 3 2 1

To ravage, to slaughter, to usurp under false titles, they call empire; and where they make a desert, they call it peace.

—TACITUS, *AGRICOLA*

We *will* go to war, but *not really*, because we don't want to and aren't allowed to, so what we're doing is in fact some kind of hyper-violent peace in which people will die.

—NICK HARKAWAY, *THE GONE-AWAY WORLD*

CONTENTS

ILLUSTRATIONS

PROLOGUE

In a speech on the Vietnam War in September 1967, President Lyndon Johnson listed reasons the United States should stay the course in the increasingly unpopular war. Among them was the claim that limited violence would prevent catastrophic violence, perhaps even nuclear war. The administration promised measured escalation. But by the end of that year, half a million American troops were in Southeast Asia, and the scope of death and destruction had erased any notion that the war could be a vehicle for peace.

I came of age in the United States during the Vietnam War. Like so many others in my generation, I thought the war was an abomination—a deep tragedy, in fact. Yet at the time I was also painfully aware of how little I knew about Vietnam and its history, and how impoverished our knowledge was about U.S. and European imperialism. I had only vague ideas about how to critique the claim that distant wars might be contained—or bent to some higher purpose.

By the time, years later, I began to study the history of European empires, I was working alongside many other historians striving to deepen our understanding of the imperial past. As I write these lines, I am surrounded by piles of recent books with "empire" in their titles. They analyze the halting origins of European global power and the troubled workings of imperial rule. They characterize the United States as an empire-state in the mold of European empires. They map a world of repression, while also documenting rebellion, persisting Indigenous sovereignty, and pluralism. Still, some of the puzzles of my youth endure. Small wars continue to multiply around the world, many echoing the logic and language of imperial violence. Governments still assert that waging limited war is both possible and necessary. And justifications for violence not classed as war remain both opaque and consequential.

This book places imperial small wars at the center of a new history of global order. It shows, first, how societies across the world embraced raiding and captive taking. Beginning in the fifteenth century, European empires mobilized these ancient practices on a novel scale. Conflicts in and on the edges of empires composed a global *regime of plunder*. Growing inequalities of power gave rise to new frameworks for violence in the eighteenth and nineteenth centuries. As Europeans asserted the right to set the laws of war and intervene anywhere to protect imperial subjects and interests, they assembled a sprawling *regime of armed peace* dominated by a handful of world powers.

As I traced these patterns, I was shocked by the frequency with which serial minor conflicts opened pathways to extreme violence. Wars that were billed as small and manageable exposed civilian populations to ferocious attacks by fighters suddenly released, it seemed, from any obligation to refrain from cruelty. Strategies that had appeared to enhance security just as often produced catastrophe. Like players in a game in which routine moves drop pieces to positions on the board where all is lost, participants in small wars were aware that utter devastation was a real possibility, but they could not prevent it. Empires and their agents, meanwhile, deftly combined pledges to check the ravages of war with authorization of spectacular violence.

In writing about this history, I had to reach for new ways of studying "small wars." Military analysts have tended to describe small wars as manifestations of insurgency and counterinsurgency. The bias has driven them to focus on questions about how and why global powers so often failed in the face of unconventional enemies. Typical of this tendency is the minor industry in the United States that aimed at assessing why American officials made so many wrong moves in Vietnam. But schooling sponsors of war to learn lessons from the past so they might do a better job next time is an odd, even chilling, objective. It also answers the wrong questions. Our aim should not be to help humanity master the art of war but to understand the arc of war—the logic and practices that move antagonists with exquisite precision from conflict to conflict, and from exercises in containment right up to the edge of atrocity.

If I couldn't rely on military analysts as guides, I also needed to cultivate a healthy skepticism of some common approaches to law and war. Followers of the German jurist Carl Schmitt, who began to ponder war when he was an enthusiastic member of the Nazi Party, have focused on the relation of imperial violence to states of emergency or exception. The approach has opened new ways of mapping the dynamics of imperial violence, but it also misses a great deal. Although empires frequently deployed emergency measures like martial law to sanction and systematize violent repression, their baseline condition was low-level violence organized in routine sequences. This ongoing violence and its many forms gave emergencies their logic and rhythm—not the other way around. The phenomenon also naturalized extreme violence. The slaughter and enslavement of civilians, starvation of whole towns, and campaigns of dispossession—these and other brutal projects were integral parts of the global imperial order.

The age of empires is in many ways still with us. In the twentieth century, international treaties and institutions sought to ban war, and it is tempting either to portray the proliferation of small wars as a sign of international law's failures or to regard parts of the world as descending into the unruly warfare of the premodern past. Instead, this book suggests many continuities in the mechanisms, justifications, and rhythms of war across global and international orders. When twentieth-century empire-states packaged their violence, for example, as an inside job—a work of policing, not war—they were drawing on an imperial repertoire. It is worth exposing such continuities rather than highlighting the novelty of contemporary puzzles about how to regulate and limit war.

Today's warmongers resemble agents of empires when they claim that "small" violence is necessary to keep and produce order. They deploy imperial languages of protection and peacekeeping to justify undeclared wars in far places. And they echo imperial sponsors when they assert that it is possible to limit the suffering unleashed by war. To be able to follow the underlying logic of small wars in the present, we need to understand the rhythms and rationales of imperial violence in the half millennium before the twentieth century.

It is fair to ask whether linking imperial violence to global order might shift attention away from the undisputed role of empires as engines of inequality and racism. The opposite is true. Imperial small wars deserve attention precisely because their histories help to illuminate the politics of difference and hierarchy, from racial exclusion to class and religious conflict. The analysis calls for care. The term "small wars" cannot be used or taken to reproduce the terms of European power by making Indigenous suffering seem like a minor phenomenon. The goal is emphatically not to support nostalgic champions of the greatness and civilizational gifts of past empires. The label "small wars" instead conveys something real and important about how imperial violence was organized—its staccato rhythm and its ad hoc justifications. The term reflects the insight that empires specialized in violence at the threshold of war and peace.

The suffering inflicted in imperial small wars was, of course, never truly small. Death in a skirmish or a desperate run to safety from a sharp, brief war was no less tragic for victims than losses in the context of major wars. It was also no great consolation to people caught up in wars to know about efforts to contain conflict. Yet writing the history of small-scale violence in all its forms recognizes the widespread preoccupation in the early modern world with defining violence between war and peace. The search occupied famous jurists and theologians, as well as obscure authors of diaries, logbooks, petitions, and reports. Unlettered warriors and captives also had their say. We would be hiding vital parts of history if we ignored the experiences of participants in small wars in empires and the swirling commentary, at all levels of society, about them.

Connections between the world of powerful European empires and the global order of the twenty-first century were very present as I was writing this book. Evidence of the imperial past swirled in news from global hot spots, and at home. In December 2021, the release of a cache of secret U.S. government documents about tactics in the "war on terror" revealed shockingly routine civilian killings in a program of so-called targeted strikes. On everyone's mind in reading those reports was the awful footage of the previous summer, when a drone had rained death on a Kabul driveway packed with children. Then in February 2022, Russia invaded Ukraine. Russian president Vladimir Putin drew on an imperial script to defend the invasion. He insisted for nearly a year on calling the war a "special military operation," as if its purpose was to discipline a recalcitrant region of greater Russia rather than to absorb another nation-state. News from Ukraine, meanwhile, pushed reports about another deadly conflict, the Tigray War in Ethiopia, out of the news cycle. By the time a truce was signed in November 2022, nearly half a million people had died in the fighting there, yet the war was coded as small and faded quickly from public view outside the region. War was everywhere, and it was everywhere echoing imperial themes and testing the contours—and the very idea—of global order.

Other conflicts will grab headlines and test our capacity to define violence between war and peace. Histories of imperial violence help to explain a persistent preoccupation with limited war and the strangeness of perpetrators of war crimes claiming the mantle of peacemakers. Writing this book has helped me, more than I imagined it would, to think critically about war in my own time. It has returned me, too, to the problems I pondered in my youth: what accounts for persistent magical thinking about supposedly limited war as a rough equivalent to peace and what explains the ease with which we minimize faraway wars and their effects by making them appear small.

The history that I tell here shows that we have long possessed a high tolerance for violence between war and peace. Perhaps something more radical is needed, like a genuine movement to banish violence in all its forms. The question is not just whether such pacifism is politically possible but whether it would render us helpless in the face of bloodthirsty regimes and overt acts of aggression. This is an old and familiar tension. It reminds us that history might not serve as any sort of useful guide for action. We can hope, at least, that the politics of the past can teach us by analogy about the politics of the present. At the very least, a global history of imperial violence warns us to temper our expectations about humanity's capacity to keep small wars small. It might also allow us to see the trapdoors to atrocity before we fall.

They Called It Peace

Chapter 1

From Small Wars to Atrocity
in Empires

A shopkeeper named Bremner in the region now known as the Eastern Cape of South Africa informed British troops in April 1847 that Xhosa men had stolen four of his horses. The lieutenant colonel of the local British regiment credited rumors that the raiders had taken the horses to a nearby *kraal*, a settlement and livestock enclosure controlled by a Xhosa group friendly to the British. Thirty cavalry and thirty infantry-men descended on the *kraal* in an unruly raid. The soldiers seized 155 cattle, killed a Xhosa man who refused to come out of his hut, and carried away two other Xhosa men as prisoners. The troops also captured four horses. They were not Bremner's horses.[1]

The small raid was part of a conflict that the British labeled the War of the Axe, so called because its immediate catalyst was an attack on soldiers escorting a Xhosa man to Grahamstown to be put on trial for stealing an axe. On the surface, there was little to distinguish this short war from the previous six frontier wars, or for that matter from the interlude of peace that immediately preceded it. Small-scale violence in the form of disjointed campaigns of marauding, cattle theft, and crop destruction had been business as usual in the region since at least 1779, when Xhosa outrage erupted over settler cattle stealing. In the decade before the War of the Axe, Xhosa chiefs decried settlers' systematic campaign to strip them of power and take away their land, while Dutch-descended and British settlers complained of Xhosa "outrages, so incessant and atrocious in their details as to surpass belief." The violent peace transitioned into a war of many fronts, and at times no front at all. Unstable alliances strained under mutual accusations of betrayal. When the War of the Axe officially ended, violence lingered, and soon two more frontier wars acquired the name, preparing the way for another series of wars, the Anglo-Zulu wars that began in 1878.[2]

These discretely labeled wars were part of a single, long-lasting conflict over territory, labor, and authority in the shatter zone of nineteenth-century southern Africa. The serial wars summed to violent dispossession of Africans, who regrouped again and again to resist settler incursions and strike back. This long phase of violence—more than a century of chronic warfare—resembled other arenas of frontier violence in which settler land grabs resolved into colonial state making. Yet we should resist the temptation to view the conflicts as a process trending toward nation-state formation or to suppose that the violence unfolded beyond the reach of law.[3]

There is more to the multiplicity of imperial small wars than first meets the eye. As they assembled repeating patterns of violence and peacemaking spanning polities and regions, small wars connected European justifications for imperial violence to wider—indeed global— projects aimed at defining limited war and allowing it to flourish. Repeatedly, the course of imperial small wars showed how grinding conflicts in the shadow of empires could suddenly, seamlessly, produce the worst kinds of unfettered violence. The repetition of these patterns inserted the logic of chronic violence into the heart of the global order.

Hannah Arendt described warfare as "from time immemorial the final merciless arbiter in international disputes."[4] Her words reflect a familiar story about humanity's long, gradual project to condemn and contain interstate violence. Eventually, according to that story, efforts to produce perpetual peace prefaced a twentieth-century diplomatic push to outlaw war by treaty and authorize international institutions to act to prevent it. Analyzed as residual violence seeping around barriers to war, serial small and "endless" wars of the late-twentieth and twenty-first centuries appear to result directly from nations' attempts to evade or change the contours of international regulation. From this perspective, the small wars that continue to plague the world seem to represent a return to the unfettered, extrajudicial violence of the age of empires.[5]

This book tells a different story. I show that serial small wars were endemic to the early modern world and I trace their evolution. The first of three interconnected arguments is that patterns of imperial violence composed truly global regimes. Despite variations in the way societies justified and regulated violence in different regions, imperial small wars followed similar rhythms and routines. Small-scale, chronic violence not only ticked along inside orderly mechanisms of an increasingly intercommunicating world. It also served to structure relations across religious, cultural, and political divides.

Second, I track how imperial small wars produced conditions for outbreaks of atrocity. For centuries, massacres and slaving were classed as lawful and just treatment of enemies who refused to submit. Aggressors represented their victims as peacebreakers or rebels, whether or not those designations matched reality. Widely shared practices of plunder were foundational to conquest and to empires' waxing power. Increasingly, as empires responded to proliferating calls to protect subjects and interests around the world, they authorized agents far from home to make decisions about when to engage in local violence, and in what measure. In the long nineteenth century, armed intervention was defined as a European right. Imperial sponsors and agents repurposed old arguments about preemptive defense and just reprisal to legitimize brutal campaigns of dispossession and extermination.[6]

Third, I show that Indigenous communities were integral to the regulation of violence. Conversant in arguments about the justice of war, they maneuvered to establish their right to go to war. And because the logic of violence was legible to all, Europeans and Indigenous people in empires deployed similar strategies. They alternated between representing violence as internal, akin to repression or policing, and external, a matter of war. At times parties claimed political autonomy and the capacity to fight as enemies, and at times they affirmed their status as subjects bargaining for protection. They manipulated markers of political belonging, in other words, and cultivated ambiguity about whether conflicts were wars or something else. Like their European interlocutors, Indigenous communities found reason to position violence at the threshold of war and peace.

These arguments run against some common ways of characterizing imperial violence. One familiar approach is to highlight the violent effects of deep, systemic clashes—of religious communities, civilizations, ideological orders, and economic systems. Another presents European empires as overpowering other peoples from the moment of first encounter and then quickly perfecting dominance. Meanwhile, a great deal of ink has been spilled on major wars and famous battles, and on changes in battlefield tactics, the rise of professional armies, the development of weaponry, and the relation of warfare to grand strategy. Some pitched battles did settle disputes or turn the tide of longer conflicts, and there is no doubt that religious difference and technological capacity influenced the progress and outcomes of war. Yet there is value in turning our attention to other varieties of warfare and to the framework that sustained small, chronic, and repeating violence.[7]

The reorientation should not keep us from seeing that imperial small wars produced lopsided suffering and consequential shifts in power. We know that some small wars—King Philip's War in colonial New England is one example—marked turning points in longer campaigns of conquest and colonization. We know, too, that the vast system of enslavement of millions in the Atlantic world was predicated on something very much like a permanent state of war between enslaved men and women and their enslavers. And we know that the imperatives of maintaining order—the "king's peace," as it was called in the British Empire—reverberated through colonies and served to justify violent oppression. As imperial small wars multiplied, they gave rise to new institutional gambits and experiments in revolution, reform, and repression.[8]

Far from arguing against these positions, I am building on them to point to the still broader effects of serial small wars. Many of the effects carry into the present. Together, the continuities belie the usefulness of familiar watchwords of international politics now and in the past century, from "asymmetric war" to "endless war" to "humanitarian intervention." From campaigns of targeted killing in the "war on terror" to proxy wars or cross-border interventions and invasions, echoes of the age of empires are everywhere. The threat of minor wars with cataclysmic possibilities has formed the background to domestic politics in nation-states while also hanging like the sword of Damocles over international affairs.[9] The imperial roots of the phenomenon come into sharp relief as we trace the global history of small wars in the five centuries between 1400 and 1900. Warriors and their sponsors, as well as political thinkers and anti-imperial advocates, grappled with a shared puzzle: how to define and structure violence at the threshold of war and peace.

On Small Wars

It is difficult to write about war of any kind without starting with Carl von Clausewitz, the Prussian general and military analyst best known for his widely translated and read book, *On War*.[10] Clausewitz focused mainly on major, formally declared conflicts and warfare in Europe. To the extent that he examined small wars, Clausewitz defined them as involving small detachments of irregular troops and regarded them as ancillary to, or integral parts of, larger conflicts.[11] Followers of Clausewitz emphasized tactics rather than strategy or deeper structural characteristics of small wars. They also studied small wars to provide advice to states and armies about how to respond effectively to insurrections and guerrilla campaigns.[12] Under the rubric of "asymmetric warfare," analysis of small wars in this vein continues to the present.[13]

In making distinctions between the orderliness of conventional wars and the relative looseness and improvisation of small wars, Clausewitz advanced a view of minor conflicts as chaotic, unpredictable, and exceptional. He imagined at least one kind of small war, popular uprisings, as emanating from political forces or entities other than the state. In doing so, he associated small wars with, as he put it, "the breaching of old artificial barriers."[14] For Clausewitz, fighting small wars in opposition to the state tracked a tendency among non-state actors to embrace primordial violence.[15] A corollary of this perspective was the view that small wars and conduct in them operated beyond the purview of the laws of war—in something like a separate realm in which conventional attitudes and routines did not hold.

That position intersected with another: the idea that the extra-European world occupied its own juridical space. Clausewitz referenced the distinction when he identified Spanish guerrillas resisting Napoleon's invasion in 1808 as the paradigmatic example of a small war. Extolling the fierceness of Spanish irregulars taking on the better-equipped French army was a subtle way for Clausewitz to critique Prussians' less dogged opposition to Napoleon's forces. But the position carried other significance. To call Spanish resistance the "first" guerrilla war was to adopt a studied ignorance of warfare beyond Europe. It meant writing out of history the armed opposition of local fighters to European imperial forces before the nineteenth century.

Writing about small wars in 1906, the British military officer-turned-writer C. E. Callwell seemed to solve this problem by associating the same definition of small wars—conflicts involving regular armies fighting irregular forces—with violence in the British Empire. For Callwell, campaigns of conquest and annexation, suppression of insurrections, acts of retaliation, and interventions in non-European polities to unseat dangerous enemies—these and other colonial conflicts qualified as small wars.[16] Callwell's account also pitted an empire rooted in morality against an external realm of supposedly lawless actors.[17] It repeated the old story of European force on the side of law and resistance as the origin of chaos.

In the twentieth century, the story of a sharp separation of European and extra-European warfare received endorsement from the German jurist Carl Schmitt. Writing as a member of the Nazi Party during World War II, Schmitt made the distinction a key organizing principle of global spatial order. According to Schmitt, the first global spatial order lasted for four centuries and divided the world into the "pacified order" of Europe and the "quarrelsome disorder" of extra-European space.[18] In Schmitt's view, the European legal order placed annihilating war outside its bounds, in lawless, extra-European spaces.[19]

Like Clausewitz, Schmitt regarded the Spanish irregulars resisting French rule as the first guerrilla warriors. Yet unlike Clausewitz, Schmitt was writing past the midpoint of the twentieth century and knew he had to find a way to explain increasingly strong and organized anti-imperial struggles. He did so by characterizing them as otherworldly events spawned by the marriage of guerrilla tactics and the lawlessness of the extra-European world. Anti-imperial fighters were "unmoored" from the forces containing war in Europe.[20] Once again, warfare beyond Europe made sense only as a deviation from practices in Europe. The irony of Schmitt, as an unapologetic servant of the Third Reich, relegating uncontrolled violence to spaces outside Europe is difficult to miss.

Particularly given the limited historical vantage points and the ideological biases of Clausewitz, Callwell, and Schmitt on small wars, we should reject the automatic association of small wars and guerrilla insurgency. The idea that small wars involved nimble, irregular fighting units arrayed against larger, state-sponsored armies flows, after all, from analytical choice (and the fixation on Spanish irregulars fighting the Napoleonic army) rather than broad or deep historical evidence. The category of "irregular" forces loses its meaning in eras when raids and counterraids dominated fighting on all sides. And later, when empires favored short strikes and empowered armed gangs of settlers to do their bidding, the term also makes an awkward fit with accounts of warfare. At different times and places, anyone might favor—or challenge—violence in the form of sharp, brief attacks. And even if combatants were labeled as stateless rogues or (more rarely) found advantage in representing themselves that way, they usually strained to maintain relations with legitimate sponsors and sought legal cover for their actions.[21]

For multiple reasons, then, it makes sense to define the category of small wars capaciously and flexibly. This book utilizes a broad definition of "small" imperial violence. The phenomenon encompasses raiding and other sporadic violence as well as conflicts that were small in scale, remained undeclared, or lasted for relatively brief periods. The "smallness" of many imperial wars is deceptive, of course, since they often repeated across long phases and extended over vast areas. Once we rid ourselves of the biases behind formulaic assumptions about conventional versus guerrilla warfare and shed ideologically charged representations of legal difference between Europe and the rest of the world, the value of a broad definition of small wars becomes obvious. It allows us to uncover prevalent patterns of violence and transcends fixed notions about small wars based on specific tactics or supposed lawlessness.[22]

The book will show that law, defined broadly, infused all forms of imperial violence.

Waves of imperial violence produced a messy assortment of names for war. I have decided, in part to recognize this confusion of labels, also to deploy a multiplicity of terms. I have kept the term "small wars," and I will describe some cases where that term helps to make sense out of serial campaigns of violence. I will also refer, at times, to "private" and "peacetime" violence. And I will describe a hidden theory of "limited war" comprising bits and pieces of European legal commentary. The phrase that works best to bundle these terms and phenomena is "violence at the threshold of war and peace." That is a mouthful, so I use it only where I think it offers clarity. The multiplicity of terms is intentional and designed to recognize a problem shared by legal writers, imperial agents, and Indigenous political actors: how to characterize the legal space for violence between war and peace.

The category of "small wars" in this book thus includes named wars like the War of the Axe and short conflicts with no name. It encompasses sustained campaigns of violence organized around discrete episodes of fighting and brief acts of violence such as attacks described as motivated by plunder, reprisal, or punishment. Although I pay close attention to justifications for violence, I do not impose a typology of forms of violence according to the rationales or tactics of participants and sponsors of violence.[23] Certain forms of violence, such as raiding, were more prevalent in some periods, but they also spanned centuries. Justifications for war arrived in clusters but also carried across eras and regions.[24] It is only by bringing these phenomena together that we can expose the role of small wars in global politics and law.

We can be sure that small wars in empires have not failed to attract systematic study because we lack sources. The historical record brims with sharp complaints about the agony and injustice of these conflicts, including vivid descriptions of the shock they produced for people who struggled to go about their lives without imminent threat of getting robbed, injured, kidnapped, or killed but who were swept up nonetheless in vicious and unpredictable fighting. Jurists and theologians puzzled over the legalities of small wars—and did so rather more often and at greater length than most historians have realized. Litigants also took notice. Although most plunder went unrecorded, some of it ended up as the subject of lawsuits that generated copious paper trails. Combat itself, whatever its rationales and legitimacy, inspired narratives by both victors and vanquished as they angled for political and economic reward and protection by powerful patrons or polities. Victims of raiding in every world region generated stories of captivity, and officials recorded truces, treaties, payments of tribute, and descriptions of gift ceremonies that reveal the machinations of peacemaking, security pacts, alliances, and other arrangements connected to repeating cycles of violence.

The record is so vast, in fact, that one can only proceed by focusing on select cases and themes. Rather than offering a comprehensive history of imperial small wars, I analyze exemplary conflicts in overseas European empires between 1400 and 1900 to reveal broader patterns. I have chosen to focus on small wars in regions that are typically less well integrated with global histories, especially Latin America and the Pacific world. That means that some other regions, including Africa and the Middle East, get short shrift. I include material from French and Portuguese empires but give special attention to conflicts in the Spanish and British empires. Some choices of wars to analyze were serendipitous; they came about when I found intriguing examples or followed promising sources. Others flowed directly from a desire to test or illustrate arguments about global violence. I do not always construct elaborate bridges from examples to generalizations, but the bridges are not figments of my imagination, either. The connecting sinews are made up of law—how people involved in violence thought about law, and how observers wrote about it in relation to violence.

The legal framework of small wars spans the realms that historians describe as theory and practice. I typically begin with conflicts in empires to show how the regulation of violence emerged partly from the actions and pronouncements of people far from Europe. Most histories of the laws of war start and stay in Europe and the United States, and they explain texts by analyzing the contexts in which they were made. The circle of context can be drawn tightly, for example, by focusing on a single writer, or it can be extended to encompass distant events and trends.[25] Here I take a different tack. Except in a few cases, I do not map the circulation of information or ideas between Europe and other regions. I instead enlarge the production of theories about law and war to include the whole world. At the same time, I analyze European writing on war and juxtapose it to histories of small wars. These moves break down the often implicit, artificial separation of theory (located in Europe) and practice (in events unfolding in or beyond empires). People in very different positions inside and outside Europe were grappling with similar problems of how to justify and regulate violence. We can think of my method as an exercise in refraction. It is like holding two objects next to each other to view each one in the reflected light of the other. I use imperial small wars as a prism focusing light on overlooked corners of European writings on war, and I look to European texts to illuminate more diffuse approaches to violence at the threshold of war and peace.

Strange Violence, Big Law

In 1504, a Dutchman penned an account of his voyage as a crew member on Vasco da Gama's second expedition into the Indian Ocean. At Calicut (Kozhikode) on the western coast of India, the Portuguese ships bombarded the port with cannon fire. After three days of fighting, the Portuguese took the prisoners they had seized and "hanged them to the yards of ships" within sight of the walls. They then pulled the captives down from the rigging and methodically "cut off their hands, feet, and heads" before piling the body parts in a ship and casting it adrift toward the town, with a letter on a stake. For good measure, they seized another ship in the harbor, set it on fire, and "burnt many subjects of the king."[26]

A casual reading of this account might give the impression that the Portuguese were resorting to theatrical violence to deliver their message across a stark communication divide. The context tells a different story. Gama already knew Calicut because his ships had spent three months there on his first voyage, when mutual distrust had colored negotiations. The two sides had exchanged hostages to cool the mood—a common practice—but, with the Calicut ruler and local merchants openly disdainful of Portuguese goods, trade was disappointing. Now, on his second approach, Gama had more fully embraced violence—both for the plunder it yielded and for its success in forcing trade and tribute. The display of mutilated bodies doubled as reprisal and an ultimatum to submit. Massacre and mutilation did not require exquisite explanation in a world where demands delivered at the gates of towns were deeply familiar and where extreme violence in response to perceived betrayal was common. The note among the corpses was there for emphasis, not explanation.[27]

The notion that Europeans fought with people who had fundamentally different ways of making and understanding war is common. It has also been much exaggerated. The idea of deep cultural misunderstandings in imperial wars can in part be traced to European chronicles written by men with a vested interest in extolling their own abilities to interpret foreign cultures and to translate exotic signs. The idea of misunderstanding—creative or otherwise—has also struck a chord with some historians of European-Indigenous interactions.[28] The impenetrability of violence has had eloquent defenders. The brilliant Australian historian Inga Clendinnen wrote that Spaniards in the conquest of the land they called New Spain were "baffled" by Mexica people's sacrificial killings and that locals puzzled over the invaders' odd "predilection for ambush" and their practice of killing enemies on the battlefield instead of taking captives.[29] In Clendinnen's telling, the conquest of New Spain was a "tangle of missed cues and mistaken messages." The destruction of the city of Tenochtitlan, on the future site of Mexico City, occurred because the Spaniards failed to elicit the Mexica people's surrender and the leader, Hernán Cortés, found himself heaping atrocity on atrocity to diminishing effect.[30]

This version of the story of conquest passes quickly over evidence of mutually intelligible diplomacy and violence. The Mexica rapidly adjusted to Spanish styles of fighting and accurately read Spaniards' intent. They also recognized that when the Spaniards and their local allies turned down their offer of tribute, fighting was imminent.[31] The likely consequences of refusing to submit were not lost on the inhabitants of Tenochtitlan. The clarity of likely consequences led some Mexica fighters to escape the city and join the Spanish side and persuaded others to refuse to surrender. For the Spaniards, unusual circumstances removed the possibility of half measures. They were not culturally opposed to captive taking, but in Tenochtitlan they found themselves "wandering men without a city."[32] They suspended an interest in acquiring captives in part because they had no way to keep them, a condition that would not last long. For the Mexica, meanwhile, the choice to fight to the death was informed by their own history of brutal punishment of the vanquished. They imagined, not without reason, they would be unlikely objects of mercy if they surrendered.[33]

The point is not to challenge the possibility of any degree of misunderstanding about violence but to begin from a different premise. We need not choose between the supposition that violence by strangers was incomprehensible to others and the assumption that violence was always transparent. Combatants everywhere interpreted the actions of enemies and adjusted their strategies in response, often very quickly. Historical actors knew that they lacked a full understanding of the violence of strangers, but they also recognized that by analyzing violent actions they could learn useful information about structures of authority, procedures for marking difference, and the strength of legal and political commitments. They were plainly aware that war and law were inextricably intertwined.

It is hardly surprising that groups of people who came into contact actively scanned societies for signs of how they worked. Strangers needed to know with whom to negotiate and, in contests for control, whom to seek to supplicate, incorporate, or topple. To make such judgments, travelers and locals looked for ways of ordering authority. They took note of routines of supplication and mercy, and anxiously sought to interpret acts of public punishment. Guided by experiences of unequal power in their own societies, they were alert to gradations of authority. Nearly everyone recognized a few broad categories of legal action: jurisdiction (the exercise of legal authority), protection (arrangements of security involving two or more legal authorities), and punishment (actions that announced and enforced legal authority). Together these rubrics composed a framework of "interpolity law."[34] As a convenient shorthand, we might use the label "big law." The framework of big law preceded the rise of international law, and it spanned political communities with very different legal sources and procedures.

To regard acts of violence as legal in this way means treating law as something much bigger than doctrine and less tidy than systems of rules or norms. The approach moves beyond a view of law as a constraining force. Operating instead as a social field, or framework, law set flexible parameters for conflict. It combined patterns of practice, which were lawlike because they shaped expectations about the regularity of behavior and its likely consequences, and trends in written or customary law that encompassed legislation, commands, and learned commentary as well as the pronouncements and strategies of a wide range of actors. Patterns of violence encoded and sometimes altered expectations about justice, cruelty, and mercy. They conformed to, while also shaping, law that stretched across polities and regions.

A further advantage of this perspective is that it allows us to bring Europe's interlocutors into the picture much earlier than usual and to treat them as active participants in making law across polities. Wherever possible, I pay special attention to non-elite, Indigenous actors' legal and strategic engagement with Europeans in small wars.[35] We know that in the nineteenth and twentieth centuries, local elites around the world used and altered European doctrines of international law in conflicts over sovereignty and self-determination.[36] But we can also find evidence of this intercommunication much earlier, in practices of violence and negotiation. Some legal approaches to war and diplomacy that we once thought of as exclusively European had clear counterparts in traditions and settings beyond Europe. Not just legal practices but also broader legal strategies were often mutually legible, and they were also often interactive. For example, just as Europeans represented warring imperial subjects as rebels or enemies, Indigenous political communities confronted with European aggression alternated between appeals for legal protection and assertions of their own capacity and right to make war. Moving nimbly between characterizing antagonists as enemies or subjects crudely but effectively marked out a space for violence at the threshold of war and peace. The process conjured into existence a framework of big law well before anyone was claiming the possibility, much less the authority, of international law.

Law and War

Traditional accounts of the history of war and law do not give a prominent place to small wars, or to the strategies they spawned. The usual narrative begins with Roman jurists' commentary on war, followed closely by medieval European political theologians selectively mining Roman legal sources to develop theories of just war. Sharing the view that only one party in a conflict could possess a just cause, these writers elaborated on the definition of just war as a response to injury or an act of self-defense authorized by a legitimate ruler.[37] The story then fast-forwards to the early seventeenth century, when Hugo Grotius, a Dutch lawyer, wrote *Mare Liberum (The Free Sea)*, a work commissioned by the Dutch East India Company to justify the Dutch seizure of the Portuguese ship *Santa Catarina* in the Singapore Strait. Grotius expanded the foundations for legitimate violence by arguing that both public and private actors could punish violators of natural law and that both sides to a conflict might possess a just cause.[38]

The next great turning point in the evolution of the laws of war, according to standard accounts, arrived in the eighteenth century. Marked by the publication and wide circulation of *The Law of Nations* by the Swiss jurist Emer de Vattel, the idea gained traction that states were the principal units of global legal order. Vattel's "dizzying array of rules" about war replaced just war theory as the centerpiece of European laws of war.[39] Building on this turn toward "Enlightenment rules of law," late nineteenth-century jurists, most notably Frances Lieber during the U.S. Civil War, codified standards of conduct in war. The tradition continued in other agreements, including the 1907 Hague Convention and the 1949 Geneva Conventions.[40] These efforts to codify the laws of war paralleled the formation of international institutions, including the League of Nations and the United Nations, and, we are told, foregrounded attempts to outlaw and "humanize" war in the twentieth century.[41]

Uncertainty and disagreement surrounded all these developments. Political theologians debated every aspect of just war doctrine, including who possessed the authority to sanction violence or declare war, what acts might constitute injuries that justified reprisals, and to what extent a war had to promote the common good to be classed as just.[42] Grotius's influential views remained open to interpretation, too, and posed new questions, for example about the variety of conditions under which private actors, commanders, or local officials might enjoy the same legitimacy as sovereigns in making public war.[43] In the wake of the wide circulation of Vattel's work, the consensus among European powers that "civilized" states were the responsible authors of the laws of war raised tricky problems about membership in this group. Increasingly, the widening participation by non-Europeans in debates about international law clashed with efforts to restrict entry into the international community.[44] Meanwhile, empires and micropolities persisted, even as nation-states proliferated and claimed their place as arbiters of international laws of war.[45]

In later centuries, creative interpretation of and selective deference to international law continued. International lawyers have repeatedly found themselves on the defensive, justifying the value of a kind of law that must operate without an effective authority—a world state, for example—to enforce it. With the UN Security Council unable to end many conflicts, small wars multiply and linger; they sometimes spread to engulf whole regions. Multisided proxy wars, like the conflict in Syria that erupted during the Arab Spring in the 2010s, have proven especially intractable. Actions against outliers, as in economic sanctions against Russia after its invasion of Ukraine, showcase the complexities of containing aggression without robust international jurisdiction to regulate war.

Past and present ambiguities of international law suggest the need for a new account that encompasses the regulation of war in all its dimensions: law-in-practice, including the actions of people outside Europe; institutions, defined in the broadest terms; legal and political theory, with attention to both legal writings and vernacular expressions regarding justice in war; and sequences of treaties or truces and outbreaks of violence not clearly labeled as war. This is a tall order. I approach the challenge in this book by beginning with local practices of violence in order to identify broad patterns that assumed the shape of global regimes. In the transition from one regime to another, I emphasize how decentered conflicts assembled big trends in violence and law. Only then do I turn to European texts and use the history of conflict to read them in new ways to uncover a theory of limited war.

The result is that some familiar topics in the history of the laws of war recede into the background. Common questions about law and imperial raiding—the status of pirates, for example, or whether to restore the rights and property of returning captives—become less salient.[46] In their place, I follow participants' commentary on raiding to highlight arguments about the punishment of truce breakers and about self-defense and protection in empires. Similarly, instead of tracking developments in *jus ad bellum* (the authorization of war) and *jus in bello* (the regulation of conduct in war) as separate phenomena, I show how participants and writers blurred these categories to describe lawful violence at the margins of war and peace. The approach takes us well beyond standard texts or common interpretations of the laws of war, and it points to the importance of inchoate theories of limited war.

It might seem counterintuitive to call scraps of analysis and patterns of violence a theory of anything, much less a theory of limited war. We find only rare explicit mention of limited war by writers whose commentary mainly referenced related phenomena, such as truces, controls on private violence, and the authority to contain violence by regulating conduct in war. But however unsystematic and obscure, commentary on law and war betrays a continual preoccupation with defining and justifying violence in forms other than open and unbounded war. Peacetime raiding, captive taking, punishment of rebels, short strikes against Indigenous polities—these and other varieties of violence prompted worried debate precisely because they threatened to provoke all-out war. Writers on law were painfully aware that they were operating with an impoverished vocabulary to describe violence at the threshold of war and peace—and to explain how it might be kept at tepid temperatures, somewhere between hot and cold war. The problem was especially salient in and on the edges of empires.[47]

It was not just Europeans, and not just law-trained elites, who were commenting on war. People planning and fighting in imperial wars on all sides made legal arguments, discernible sometimes through their actions or treaties, about the lawfulness of "small" violence. They were making law as they acted and wrote (or spoke). In most of the narratives of conflicts in this book, I give greater attention to European violence and European writings on small wars. There is no doubt that European imperial violence was especially consequential—for its victims and for the direction of global change. European sources are more numerous, and also more easily accessible to researchers. But the "small" violence that occupied the very center of successive global regimes elicited legal positioning and pronouncements from a broad array of parties. The actions of Indigenous groups in the Americas, Africa, Asia, and the Pacific world, this book will show, helped to create and alter the global legal framework for violence.

Empires and Global Violence

European conquest and colonization were not novel in the modes of violence they deployed, or in relation to the legal framework that sustained them. Empires everywhere relied on plunder, and they required ways of distributing it, including ways of integrating captives. Europeans were like other early modern peoples in their devotion to raiding and slaving. But they managed circuits of plunder that ensnared growing numbers of Indigenous peoples in the greater Atlantic, Pacific, and Indian Ocean worlds.[48] As European settlers pushed the boundaries of colonies, they intensified raiding and used common practices to turn opportunistic raiding into systems of enslavement and organized plunder.

A regime of plunder centered on raiding and captive taking expanded rapidly because its component parts were everywhere deeply familiar. Short strikes for booty, waves of raiding in advance of conquest, ultimatums at the gates of towns, and punishment of resisters to invasion—these and other practices composed an orderly choreography of conquest. Europeans did not invent these practices. They did not even perfect them. Conquest and colonization shared rhythms and rationales, and generated patterns of lawful extreme violence, including massacres in which perpetrators blamed the victims because they had refused to submit.

Captive taking was an elemental practice. The conversion from enemy to captive signified an act of mercy because warriors were forgoing the right to kill enemies. But slaving-through-war was only the first piece of a larger process. Captives had to be integrated legally into captor communities. There were mechanisms for their assignment to sovereigns or to the sovereigns' officers and delegates, for example, when captives labored in gangs on fortifications or other public works. Much more commonly, households and kin groups took charge of captives. We think of households as social units, but they were also legal entities, unusual in that they encompassed the most intimate domestic spaces, but commonplace as arenas where a recognized legal authority, the household head, possessed the right to restrict subordinates' rights. The relationship of households to sovereign power made sense out of captivity and war—and made both profitable. Sovereigns went to war to protect communities of households, and households continued war on behalf of sovereigns by holding and disciplining captives.

The first part of this book traces the way the regime of plunder worked in early European overseas conquests and in the militarized garrisons that advanced European imperial power. It first maps serial small wars as components of conquest and examines the logic of truces, truce breaking, and massacre. It then turns to households in early empires and their role in maritime raiding and captive taking. In uncovering concerted efforts to promote household formation and use communities of households to support a right to make local war in early overseas European empires, I highlight raiding's social and institutional effects and how they extended far beyond the actual routines of slaving and raiding.

In the nineteenth century, another regime of violence emerged. It is the subject of the second part of the book. As Europeans inserted themselves into politically complex regions, trading companies and settlers secured control over limited territories. They relied on networks of alliance, proxy wars, and collaboration with other empires to fight against

Indigenous polities and "rebels." In this context, imperial agents began to insist, with increasing force, on Europeans' authority to regulate the conduct of war. Instead of describing the Europeanization of the laws of war as a process that began in Europe and spread outward to the rest of the world—the usual story—I trace how conflicts in and on the edges of empires prompted new claims about European authority over war. As imperial agents debated standards of battlefield conduct, they affirmed Europe's power to regulate war and peace. In the process, they sharpened characterizations of Indigenous fighters as savage and increasingly labeled them as rebels.

Global militarization in the Seven Years' War and the Napoleonic Wars further altered these routines. Imperial navies and armies on patrol were authorized to make decisions about violence against groups located both inside and outside imperial spheres of influence. The practice established a new global regime of armed peace in which Europe and the United States claimed a right to intervene militarily anywhere in the world. It is tempting to pair claims about a right to armed intervention with the rise of ideas about humanitarian intervention. I emphasize instead how violence on patrol could preface colonial campaigns of dispossession and extermination. What I label "protection emergencies"— calls to shelter imperial subjects from harm—turned easily into broader programs to protect imperial interests and promote regional order. The shift encouraged colonial officials and settlers to redefine entire Indigenous communities as natural enemies who could be attacked and killed anywhere without need for further authorization.

Across these centuries, Europeans represented conquest, colonial rule, and intervention as projects of peacemaking. An element of pure cant was at play, but there was also more. Justifications for imperial violence routinely referenced peace and order. Campaigns of conquest approached the resumption of war after unstable truces as lawful reactions to even minor threats to peace on invaders' terms. Again and again, Europeans accused Indigenous groups of drawing them into war. Captivity was represented as punishment for refusal to make and keep the peace and defined as an act of mercy for defeated adversaries or rebels. Pledges of peacemaking also informed other visions of global order. In increasingly militarized empires, Europeans authorized violence in the form of measures short of war to protect not just imperial subjects and interests but also, more expansively, a vague objective: global order itself.

Some distinctive temporal qualities of imperial violence emerged. Small wars made for choppy violence, but just as they do today, they also operated against the backdrop of perpetual war.[49] Truces, cease-fires, and rituals of surrender—these and similar practices defined peace as transient and tricky, a mere interruption of an ongoing state of war. Staccato small wars permeated participants' everyday experience of violence and their expectations about future violence, while also presenting challenges to traditional justifications for warfare.

Spatially, small wars arranged violence unevenly, and at odd scales. The logic of violence centered on households, garrisons, archipelagic spaces occupied by armies and navies, and pluripolitical regions. The spatially complex conflicts of our own time appear less unusual in a wide and long historical frame. Corporate interests, religious and ideological solidarities, and shifting local-state alliances created kaleidoscope landscapes of war. Imagining terrorists as universal enemies with the capacity to cross borders, hide in plain sight among civilian populations, and transform with mysterious speed into battle-ready armies makes a hash of borders and other typical spatial referents of war. But wars with no fronts or with fractured fronts are not new. They find ample precedents in the imperial past—and not just because fighting in empires was often unconventional. In attending to phenomena at different scales and multiple sites, such as complexes of raiding, communities of households dependent on captive labor, and moving militias and squadrons authorized to engage in small violence, this book maps unusual landscapes in which scattered small wars assembled global regimes of violence.

Precisely because empires encompassed multiple political communities and had fluid boundaries, distinctions between internal and external violence were very blurred. Raids in which small bands attacked, scooped up booty, and withdrew provide quintessential examples. They could occur within the bounds of empires; continue in peacetime across fluid political boundaries; arrive in sets to form long campaigns of "quiet" warfare; and trigger major, formally declared wars. Like raids, various other types of small violence defied easy description because they challenged the distinctions between domestic and global or international order, and between war and peace. Small wars strained the legal and political vocabulary of binaries.

The history of small wars in European empires and global history is bleak—but necessary to tell. The hidden logic of limited war drove the pace and structure of conflicts across centuries and regions. It shaped and sustained vast empires and gave anti-imperial movements shared modalities. Never insignificant for the victims, series of small wars profoundly affected the lived experiences of people in a world of empires. The conflicts molded discourses of despotism, brutality, civility, and justice, and entered the daily workings of intimate spaces of households and the contours of public squares, real and conjectural. The imagination of perpetual war loomed in the background of extended moments of negotiation, accommodation, and unstable peace. Imperial small wars were, and perhaps still are, the beating heart of global order.

PART I

A World of Plunder

The sack of Constantinople, the battle of Lepanto, the clash at Diu between Portuguese caravels and the Ottoman navy, the fall of Granada, the taking of Tenochtitlan—we think of these and other major battles and events as turning points in long campaigns of conquest. But decisive battles were more than dramatic recalibrations of force. They took their meaning from the context of smaller, sequential episodes of violence and negotiation: raiding, captive taking, truce making, and the brutal punishment of truce breakers. In the early modern world, war raged, paused, or threatened; it hardly ever stopped.

Conquest advanced in fits and starts, with periods of unstable peace punctuating phases of low-level violence. Conquerors heralded their own supposed generosity in proffering peace, even characterizing themselves as victims of violence who had been drawn reluctantly into war and forced to perform acts of cruelty. Massacres were routinely framed as proportionate punishment for the betrayal of those accused of breaking truces. This trick of blaming the victims of violence smacked of hypocrisy, to be sure. But common legal arguments gave weight to the claim by conquerors that they were promoting peace by enforcing adherence to truces. It did not matter whether self-described peacemakers were earnest or insincere, and whether the injuries they condemned were real or imaginary. The legal framework of small wars of conquest presented opportunities for both accommodation and slaughter.

A global regime of plunder centered on key practices of imperial violence: raiding and truce making. Soldiers, many serving as part-time warriors and drawn away from agricultural or pastoral pursuits, drew their compensation in shares of booty. This fact made brief raids indispensable for recruiting soldiers to man longer and more coordinated campaigns. A familiar grammar of raiding, meanwhile, carried across disparate empires and polities. Raiders decimated rural hinterlands, and populations crowded for protection into fortified towns that served as coveted targets. Anticipating sieges, rulers offered tribute in exchange for guarantees of safety, often bargaining with raiders well before marauders arrived at the gates. Polities whose power was on the rise did not always press their advantage. They instead sought truces again and again to organize reliable and lucrative streams of tribute.

Repeated raiding did not produce anything identifiable as conquest for long periods. The allure of raiding motored vast economies of commerce and captivity. Merchants and slavers followed (and sometimes preceded) clusters of raids. Regional complexes of raiding and captivity transported large numbers of captives across political lines and across long distances, well before the rise of the transatlantic slave trade. When raids became very frequent or very destructive, they could turn the craving for plunder into a determination for permanent acquisition and rule. And when shifting alliances or other changes injected new possibilities of attack or parry, parties crossed the thin line separating raids from open war. But raiding also persisted alongside commercial interchange and the movement of warriors across religious and political boundaries to fight for pay or plunder. To recognize the ubiquitous nature of raiding is not to characterize the early modern world as a chaotic swirl of violence. There were patterns; there was law.

Small wars along unstable and fragmented frontiers generated serial truces, agreements to cease some kinds of fighting for a limited time. Truces often accompanied agreements to pay tribute, a benefit that came with few strings attached that could temper the appetite for conquest. Truces also set the timing and the terms for a return to war. A typical agreement specified a duration of years—the lifetime of the signees, for example—and spelled out conditions that either side might point to in accusing the other of violating the truce. Escalating raids entered this calculus as another source of ready-made grievances since raiding was technically banned in times of truce but usually continued, inspiring fear and prompting waves of counterraids.

The orderliness and familiarity of the complex of raiding, ultimatums to surrender, and truce making did nothing to make violence less terrifying or more predictable. Some of the most spectacular acts of brutality recorded in the early modern world took place in the wake of truces. The notion that violations of truces involved betrayal of hard-won agreements and equated to breaches of honor served as emotional escalators for the violence that followed their breakdown. Punishments that had been set aside by truce making—no-holds-barred attacks on women and children, indiscriminate killings, enslavement of vanquished populations—were unleashed with greater force in the wake of supposed violations of truces. Men claiming the mantle of justice committed acts of unmitigated cruelty. This juridically protected extreme violence stood in the background of political expansion by pact or force across the early modern world.

Captive taking was at the center of this regime of plunder. Raiding both produced captives as booty and created the problem in empires of where to put them—how to incorporate them into scattered communities that served as imperial outposts. In some cases, as in the seventeenth-century Mediterranean, it was more profitable not to integrate captives into captor societies but to hold them in limbo so they might be ransomed or sold. In early European overseas empires, dangerous sea routes linked fortified outposts and inserted captives into broader programs of turning garrisons into settlements. The challenges of forging stable political communities made empires reliant on the legal capacities of households to hold and discipline captives.

Households were essential pieces of the regime of plunder. The proliferation of households transformed imperial outposts into communities that could claim a right to make war in self-defense. Households could also turn any imperial enclave or territory into a place where booty might be converted to property. The authority of household heads to command and punish captives was interlocked with their lawful command over women, children, servants, and slaves. The institutional matrix of early empires extended from intimate spaces of households to networks of raiding to municipal governance. It recognized private violence as foundational to imperial rule, and to vast systems of slaving and enslavement.

The scale of the regime of plunder ran from the everyday exercise of personal power to efforts to create and sustain complexes of raiding and captive taking over sprawling regions. No one was safe in this dangerous world. Stories about maritime captures ensnaring wealthy pilgrims and merchants circulated in royal courts and in port marketplaces. Sexual danger, especially for women, together with the specter of forced conversion, hovered over prospects for any sort of travel. The pervasiveness of raiding, meanwhile, hardened communities to its realities, while possibilities for acquiring captives merged private profit and public legitimacy. Plunder made empires, and empires accelerated plunder. Raiding and the management of captives turned garrisons into colonies and warmongers into peacemakers.

Chapter 2

Conquest by Raid and Massacre

In 1513, in the wake of sharp debates in the court about whether the behavior of Spaniards in the New World was sinful, the Spanish crown approved a statement for its agents to read before attacking *indios*, as the Spaniards called Indigenous inhabitants of the Americas. Probably written by Juan López de Palacios Rubios, a jurist on the Council of Castile, the statement came to be called the *requerimiento*, or the requirement, and it authorized the crown's representatives to attack, imprison, and enslave *indios* who refused to submit to their authority. "If you [submit]," the statement read, "we . . . shall leave you, your wives, and your children, and your lands, free without servitude . . . and . . . shall not compel you to turn Christians. . . . But, if you do not do this . . . we shall powerfully enter into your country, and shall make war against you in all ways and manners that we can . . . as to vassals who do not obey."[1]

In Castile, the requerimiento became an object of brief but sharp controversy. Bartolomé de las Casas, the outspoken critic of Spaniards' treatment of Indigenous Americans, famously lamented that the statement was often read "to the trees"—directed at *indios* far away and in a language they did not understand.[2] Some historians have found the requerimiento odd, too. They have struggled to pinpoint its legal origins. One interpretation underscores the influence of Islamic jurisprudence in Castile and suggests that the document's authorization of violence against nonbelievers and apostates echoed jihadist doctrine.[3] Another approach locates the roots of the requerimiento in medieval adaptations of Roman writings on just war, in particular two well-established ideas:

that acts of violence not performed in self-defense required formal authorization by a sovereign and that enemies vanquished in a just war could be legally dispossessed and enslaved.[4]

Both interpretations—that the requerimiento had roots in Islamic law and that it reflected just war doctrine—may be technically right. But both miss a broader picture. The strangeness, and even the tight legal meaning, of the requerimiento recedes when we view its pronouncement as part of a bundle of common practices. Las Casas represented the requerimiento as strange in order to critique it. But the practices described in the statement would have been deeply familiar not only to jurists at the court in Castile but also to conquistadors and rank-and-file soldiers.[5] Framed as it was by other rituals and signs, the requerimiento would also not have puzzled Indigenous audiences as much as we might imagine. The statement gathered its meaning from routines of conflict that crossed political communities and legal traditions. Indigenous Americans, although not able to understand Castilian, were well equipped to interpret the actions of armed antagonists combining ultimatums and lists of consequences for failure to submit.

In the vast Afro-Eurasian world of which Castilians were a part and in the American regions they were invading, conquest followed a sequence in which demands for surrender implied threats of grave harm to anyone who hesitated to submit—and, of course, to anyone who mounted resistance. The requerimiento was unusual mainly in its economy. Its form and language also reflected the peculiar preoccupations of political theologians tasked with saving the souls of both perpetrators and victims in the Americas. But Spanish improvisation brought the requerimiento into a choreography of conquest that worked the same way with or without it. The logic behind the way war was staged began before and extended well beyond the fight for Spanish overseas dominion.

This chapter tells the story of conquest across the globe as a suite of actions of raiding, truce making, and truce breaking. Well-worn sequences of conquest and submission produced mutual intelligibility about warfare and its rhythms. Patterns of imperial violence also set up scenarios in which extreme violence became a set piece of conquest. Massacres of civilians fit into this sequence as a form of lawful punishment for truce breakers. Conquerors described warmaking as a burden; as much victims as aggressors, they thought of themselves as being pulled along, by the logic of truces and truce breaking, into the maw of war.

This chapter explores how sequences of raiding, truces, massacres, and conquest operated as a framework of global scope. European writings on law and war appear less singular in this context. The juxtaposition of theory and practice reveals a persistent preoccupation with defining routine and extreme violence in empires as responses to provocation. Warriors and jurists alike nominated violations of truces as keys to justifying serial small wars. The move worked to color spontaneous acts of imperial violence as predictable responses to provocation and to assemble acts of raiding and plunder into programs of conquest. Truces were crucial and irresistible elements of conquest. They structured breaks from war while also upholding war as perpetual, defining invaders as peacemakers, and prefacing cataclysmic violence.

A World of Raiding

To understand the grammar of raiding, consider a single small raid. In May 1306, a band of thirty-seven men, nine on horseback, ravaged the countryside outside Oriola, in Valencia. The attack was an act of vengeance, according to Oriola's mayor. The raiders hailed from the nearby town of Alcaraz, and their leader, Juan de Cato, was reportedly involved in a legal dispute with Guillen de Paratge, a resident of Oriola. The band rounded up 250 cattle and 1,000 sheep and kidnapped the shepherds who were guarding the flocks. After someone in Oriola sounded the alarm, a group of armed men set out from the town, fourteen of them on horseback, to give chase. The townsmen caught up with the raiders and managed to take back the stolen livestock and free the shepherds after a brief skirmish. Reporting on the raid to Jaume III, king of Aragon, the mayor of Oriola pleaded for royal measures to contain the opportunistic plunder and captive taking on the unruly frontier.[6]

This minor raid in Oriola was part of a broader pattern of frontier violence in fourteenth-century Valencia and its world. It had many of the classic hallmarks of raiding in a wider region. The attackers were

FIGURE 2.1. Skirmish to recover cattle stolen in a raid.
From Diebold Schilling the Younger, *Lucerne Chronicle*, 1513.

clearly operating with the benefit of local intelligence, and perhaps even extensive knowledge, about their targets. In Oriola, as in many raids elsewhere, the attack was connected to a private dispute. Also as in many other raids, the action against Oriola targeted poorly protected rural assets and areas, a pattern of violence that sharpened the contrast between protected towns and a dangerous countryside. In another typical practice, raiders in Oriola did not linger but quickly fled with the plunder they could carry or herd. Movable booty—in Valencia, that meant mainly livestock and some human captives—was coveted for the simple reason that it could be spirited away.

Raiding with these characteristics was deeply familiar to inhabitants of the Mediterranean region of which Valencia was a part. This way of war also extended much farther, encompassing violence in Eurasia, Africa, and the Americas. In Valencia, raiding was rife across porous frontiers typified by the interpenetrating zones of Christian and Muslim rule and residence, but we should not think of it as merely the vanguard of conquest across religious divides. As in Oriol, raiding structured relations among communities of co-religionists, and it shaped broad patterns of settlement and commerce as extensive raiding in rural areas pushed populations into towns and prefaced more organized assaults or sieges on fortified strongholds.

As one historian has pointed out, the contrapuntal rhythms of this way of fighting meant there was "no simple divide between full-scale war and minor raiding and skirmishing, for one led naturally to the other."[7] In many places, sides battled over the control of jagged lines of fortified footholds from which to watch over loosely controlled territories or launch further incursions. Ideal targets, places where capture could produce lasting wealth for raiders and their sponsors, were the largest urban centers. Information about towns' often inadequate defenses circulated in the written and oral accounts of travelers that lubricated raiding and counterraiding.

As the Valencian episode illustrates, raids in frontier zones often did not stay within the confines of cross-border violence. Some raiders attacked allies, and some targeted co-religionists. Because raiding depended on knowledge about targets of attack, it was common for bands to assail places they knew well, and to use perceived slights or ongoing feuds as rationales for plunder. Private disputes resembled and fortified public small wars; indeed, the boundary was difficult to locate. The violence of raiding was also spatially uneven. Fighting lurched into adjacent territories as raiders weighed down by their booty fled across friendly territories to reach home turf (or its symbolic equivalent) and defenders maneuvered to overtake or intercept them.

Raiding edged powerful empires as they formed. Accounts of warfare in the ancient Mediterranean feature the rise of professional armies, but raiding was also central to imperial expansion. Most soldiers fighting for Rome were motivated by the desire to obtain shares of plunder, and Roman armies devoted enormous energy to raiding, reprisals for enemy raids, and other small-scale engagements.[8] This pattern remained true even where Roman forces aimed at complete dominance and annexation, such as in the campaigns in Cisalpine Gaul and against Iberian and Thracian tribes.[9] Conquest could even escalate raiding. In the fragmented political landscape of the Iberian Peninsula, small groups combined forces to strike intermittently at Romans and their allies, and Roman soldiers conducted counterraids to make good on pledges of security to allies. As one historian writes, "Raid provoked counterraid to maintain a continuous cycle of plundering which might easily escalate into formal battles."[10] Raiding was also the modus operandi along Rome's frontiers, even and especially during times of peace. In the long peace spanning nearly two centuries that historians call the Pax Romana, Roman soldiers stationed in frontier garrisons routinely staged raiding expeditions into non-Roman territories. The grammar of raiding was familiar: a short strike against easy rural targets followed by a dash to return with movable booty to the safety of a frontier garrison.[11]

Other practices of warfare and writings on war paired elements of conquest with peacemaking. Roman campaigns against Mediterranean piracy were politically valuable because they represented the suppression of raiding as necessary to the protection of Roman citizens and peaceful commerce.[12] Conquest by agreement or pact did not signify a desperate act to avoid harm, although it might flow from that fear. It served as a recognition of the victor's promise of protection, indicated by the Roman term for surrender, *deditio in fidem*, which translates as "giving oneself up to the good faith or trust" of the victor.[13]

We can think of it this way: Roman war was singular in its success over a long period but not unusual in its modalities. Raiding, arrangements for surrender, and extreme violence flourished in strikingly similar patterns throughout the Afro-Eurasian world for centuries. Consider the practices of violence in the Arab conquests between the seventh and eleventh centuries. Historians used to describe the conquests as unusually fast and exceptionally far-reaching. They depicted Islamic-inspired fighters moving in waves from the Arabian Peninsula and cutting a wide swath of invasion and destruction across the Middle East, North Africa, and Iberia. Islam followed in the wake of conquest.[14] Recent studies teach that the conquests were less "Islamic" in character and the armies less "Arab" than historians initially thought, and they show the conquests as both relying on and engendering political pluralism. The conquests were neither "imperial" in the usual sense nor impelled by a singular group of interconnected bands and their descendants. Arabs joined an array of other peoples responding to opportunities for raiding created by a long "cold war standoff" of Byzantium and the Persian Empire and by weakening Byzantine, Persian, and Chinese power in the sixth century.[15]

Arabs' seventh-century advances deployed ancient Eurasian and Roman practices of raiding and truce making, as well as the distinction between conquest by force and by agreement.[16] Muhammad's coalition, for example, made peace agreements with a series of towns in Byzantine Arabia, Palestine, and Syria, concluding truces with local rulers rather than their imperial overlords. Truces depended on the threat of raiding, and raids for plunder could lead in irregular fashion to actual conquest. Raiders avoided fortified settlements at first and, pressed for provisions like other armies on the move, aimed initial attacks at easier, more quickly dominated settlements of lesser symbolic significance. When approaching larger targets, raiders demanded submission and tribute in exchange for a promise of securing lives and property. For their part, isolated and weak settlements anticipating an invasion could call for a truce and request terms. Pressures to submit in the face of the threat of

Arab raiders frayed imperial connections, as town rulers negotiated capitulations independently of Byzantine overlords.[17]

Towns suing for peace or agreeing to demands to submit did not necessarily consider themselves defeated or conquered. They sought to maintain some autonomy and often negotiated for a greater measure of it if they could offer military assistance to raiders. They were aware that submission, while saving lives, also preserved the possibility of a power reversal later. Peace agreements, whether implicit or explicit, had the quality of temporary truces. Sometimes, of course, raiders took their tribute or booty and withdrew. Conquest was more parry, partial retreat, and opportunistic return than inexorable movement of a line of control followed by administrative incorporation.

The lesson that escaped no one was that capitulating after a long phase of resistance could result in very severe treatment by raiders. After the Cypriot city of Lapathos surrendered in 650 following resistance and a siege, for example, the result was not just a thorough sacking of the city's goods and treasures but also mass enslavement and shipments of tens of thousands of captives to Syria.[18] Similar practices of submission and payment of tribute in exchange for the promise of protection permeated the Eurasian and African worlds into which Arab forces were advancing.[19] But even if a pact dictated the preservation of lives and property, agreements did not always hold. Decisions in the face of raids had life or death consequences, not just for warriors but also for their leaders, households, and whole towns.

The brutal calculus implied by these practices is especially clear in the history of the Mongol Empire, which expanded through the usual combined strategies of raiding and truce making but did so with a twist. Advancing armies relied heavily on their reputation for brutality against civilians in earlier attacks on towns that had refused to trade or surrender. When Genghis Kahn sent emissaries to open trade with Khwarizm, a then-powerful network of towns extending from the Silk Road entrepôts to Persia, an agreement to engage in peaceful commerce appeared to open the towns to Mongol trade. But a Mongol caravan came under attack at the town of Otrar, and the shah subsequently rebuffed Genghis Khan's demands for reparations. The episode prompted a full-scale

Mongol invasion. The campaign began, in classic form, with a series of seemingly disjointed raids on poorly defended rural settlements, attacks that pushed the population into a handful of walled cities. The Mongols offered terms of surrender to the major towns and mounted sieges in places that refused to capitulate. When towns that would not surrender were overrun, Mongol warriors—who liked neither sieges nor urban warfare—unleashed bloody reprisals, unchecked by Mongol leaders. The armies' reputation for unspeakable brutality then ran ahead of the next waves of conquest.[20]

Lest one imagine that raiding was a purely Eurasian affair that somehow spread as a practice with the advance of nomads against settled agriculturalists, it is useful to glimpse the familiar rhythms of raiding at work among polities in the Americas, sub-Saharan Africa, and parts of Europe far from Mongol or Islamic frontiers. Some historians and anthropologists suggest that Europeans brought unfamiliar forms of fighting to the Americas. They contrast, for example, the Spanish practice of killing on the battlefield with the Mexica aim of demonstrating dominance through captive taking and describe the bloody demonstrations by Spaniards in hand-to-hand combat as utterly bewildering.[21] They draw distinctions between the purposes of European and Indigenous armies on the move—the former aimed at laying down a grid for occupation, the latter focused on the "capture of women and ritual objects."[22] Or, more generally, they find in the raiding of non-Europeans—especially Amazon groups, whose supposedly late contact preserved earlier modalities of fighting—evidence of a "primitive" tendency to embrace perpetual fighting or vengeance that contrasted with Europeans' rejection of reflexive or ritual violence as a way of life.[23]

Sharp distinctions between European and Indigenous fighting do not hold up well when we place raiding in the foreground. Europeans raided for captives both at home and overseas, and European soldiers, like their counterparts in other regions, insisted on plunder. Observers sometimes expressed shock at the brutality of raids by non-Europeans, but we should read such statements as devices for galvanizing counterraids rather than as straightforward historical description. When Charles de Rochefort observed that Indigenous inhabitants of the Caribbean aimed to obtain "the spoils of their enemies" and "glory" by subduing them instead of angling "to become masters of a new country," the implied contrast with European behavior in the region was pure fiction.[24]

Raids were raids. If there were marked differences in rationales and tactics, they tended to fade as European and non-European raiders—for example in West Africa and the Indian Ocean—adjusted to prevailing regional patterns of violence, emphasized religious justifications for attacks, or gained the upper hand in armaments, for example by adding the firepower of cannons to ships. Raiding existed before European incursions but also intensified as a result.[25] Within Europe, too, raiding was ubiquitous, and it routinely accompanied siege warfare.[26] Armies mounted raids to despoil the surrounding countryside while engaged in prolonged sieges. In late sixteenth-century France, raiders fanned out from siege encampments to ravage the countryside at Orléans in 1563, Chartres in 1568, La Rochelle in 1573, Sancerre in 1573, Paris in 1590, Rouen in 1591, and Amiens in 1597.[27]

The ubiquitous nature of raiding in the early modern world did not translate into complacence about the practice. Raids could be terrifying. Intense fears of being overcome by marauders who would carry off property, rape women, seize children, and enslave civilians regardless of social status gave rise to flight, fortification, coalition building, preemptive attacks, and sometimes panic. Also shared widely were two sets of practices so routine that we might regard them as constituting law. One encompassed a variety of forms of peacemaking, including agreements to make one-time payments or pledge tribute. In a world of raiding, peace was temporary and unstable. Another involved actions marking the threshold to extreme violence. Most raiding, even when it involved the destruction of crops or other devastation to a population's capacity to live, did not compass slaughter. Yet in all cases, the possibility of indiscriminate killing stood behind even small-scale raiding. The threat of extreme violence surrounded small wars with rituals and rationales that marked the division between plunder and something much worse. Together these dimensions of small wars—the temporal rhythms of war and peace and the transition from raiding to massacre—converted conquests to series of truces, made and broken.

Truces

Powerful, expanding empires and vulnerable polities in their path habitually turned to truce making. A central part of the "politics of conciliation," truces marked a temporary halt to fighting.[28] Some agreements to ban violence were implicit and unspoken, and others were carefully recorded in writing. Signed truces typically stipulated the duration of temporary peace—for example, until the death of one of the signers. Pacts usually reflected the unequal power of the parties and contained specific, sometimes onerous conditions for one of them, including tribute payments. Together with the challenges of putting a stop to raiding, such terms made truces guarantees of future war.

Instability in truces also flowed from ambiguities about the agreements. Were they peace pacts of equal political communities or admissions of defeat? On the one hand, truces had the character of interpolity agreements; they were typically pacts between two political communities, each of which sought to retain its own authority beyond the signing. On the other hand, truces could contain language and terms recognizing subjugated peoples as vassals and laying the groundwork for their subsequent treatment as rebels or traitors. Some truces preserved authority *and* marked submission. To the extent that truces could be represented or interpreted as agreements establishing shared membership in a single political community, violations would signify acts of rebellion.

Chronicles of early modern war routinely describe massacres, destructive raids, and other sudden outbursts of extreme violence against civilian populations as retribution for broken promises to observe truces. The potential for extraordinary violence paradoxically increased incentives to strike first—and very hard. The common interpretation of violations of truces as acts of betrayal gave rise to furious attacks as combatants perceived that not just plunder or territorial gain but also honor was at stake.[29]

As an example of the way truces could engender violence, consider the dynamics of raiding and truce making in the long, multisided conflicts of the Iberian Peninsula from the ninth to the fifteenth centuries. Historians used to label these conflicts the Reconquista, or Reconquest, but have recently shown that the intricate politics cannot be accurately perceived through the lens of crusading Christendom or a clash of religions. Frontiers were fractured, and they were never defined simply by religious opposition. At times both Christian and Muslim rulers reached across religious lines to form alliances, and at times they attacked co-religionists or hired mercenaries without regard to religion. Some periods of intensifying religious zeal corresponded to phases of heightened violence and infighting among co-religionists. Not only did political solidarities sometimes straddle what we used to imagine as political or religious borders, but forms of alliance and warmaking also spanned these imagined divides.[30]

Between the ninth and fifteenth centuries, the fluid frontier was more hazard zone than battle line. Settlements were small and insecure sites exposed to predation, and raids in this fractured zone produced booty in the form of treasure, captives, and—of growing importance in Iberia—livestock.[31] Minor notables as well as commoners responded readily to the lure of such rewards, and royal sponsors of raids profited through collection of one-fifth of the value of booty.

Sustained campaigns of destructive raiding generated windfalls in the form of tribute. Rampant tribute taking by Muslims began in the mid-tenth century, when caliphate armies under al-Hakam wreaked havoc to the north, prompting dependent polities within a loosely structured Leonese empire to send peace embassies to al-Hakam and to agree to pay tribute. Under al-Hakam's successor, al-Mansur, Christian polities continued to recognize the superior strength of the caliphate, which in turn did not press to conquer them in part because tribute made uneasy truces so reliably profitable.

In the early eleventh century, continual civil war within the caliphate—there were fifteen changes in rule between 1009 and 1027—splintered Muslim political power. The multiple successor states to the caliphate, the *taifa* kingdoms, found themselves exposed to raiding and forced to pay tribute themselves. A resurgent Navarre under Fernando I in the middle of the eleventh century managed to extract tribute from *taifa* kingdoms in exchange for protection from attacks by Navarre's Christian neighbors in Castile and Aragon.[32]

Reversals of fortune continued to force adjustments of tributary arrangements.[33] After the Almoravids swept over the *taifas* in the twelfth
century, the states no longer had to pay tribute to Christians. But
in the early thirteenth century Muslim kings of Valencia and Baeza
declared themselves tribute-paying vassals of Fernando III, and the
caliph of Seville, Abu-l-'Ula, pledged to pay tribute to Fernando III
in exchange for a truce.

The flywheel political effects of raiding reached across the peninsula.
Royally sponsored raids supported political centralization, as occurred
in Aragon, where the king employed horse-riding Muslim mercenaries
called *jenets* to fight against Christian rivals and to display his reign over
polyglot communities.[34] Gifts of patronage in the form of land as rewards for military service supplemented windfalls from raiding and
padded household coffers of a rising warrior-nobility. The lure of plunder also permeated lower socioeconomic levels—its appeal rendered
more immediate and visible by opportunities for livestock stealing
across interconnected webs of transhumance. What made the saturated
violence tolerable was the frequency of pacts to suspend fighting, at
least notionally freezing political configurations and replacing (or sup-
plementing) irregular booty with regular tribute.

The centrality of truces to these processes becomes very clear in the
centuries leading up to the conquest of Granada by Christian forces in
1492. Muhammad I of Granada and Fernando III signed their first
tregua, or truce, in 1246, and it set the pattern for a long series of subsequent truces. In the 1246 agreement, Muhammad I declared himself to
be Fernando III's vassal, gave up his claim to the city of Jaén, and agreed
to pay the Catholic king annual tribute. Fernando III in turn recognized
Muhammad's authority within the emirate of Granada and nearby territories. The truce specified a duration of twenty years, although it rup-
tured in 1264, after eighteen years, when Muhammad helped to lead a
rebellion of *Mudéjars* (Muslims in Christian territories) and *Moriscos*
(Christianized former Muslims) against Castile in 1264.

The 1246 pact was followed by an astonishing seventy-four truces
signed between Catholic monarchs and rulers in Granada between 1246
and 1492.[35] The terms of later truces tended to reflect previous

FIGURE 2.2. Muhammad I of Granada (on dark horse at left) leading the Mudéjar Revolt of 1264–1266. From the *Cantigas de Santa María*. From the Picture Art Collection / Alamy Stock Photo. Original in the Library of El Escorial.

agreements. A truce signed by Alfonso X and Muhammad II in 1274 reaffirmed the earlier truce signed in 1264 and adjusted the tribute to be paid. A 1303 truce between Fernando IV and the representative of Muhammad III confirmed the tribute in an earlier agreement and recognized recent acquisitions of territory by both sides. Some truces merely extended the duration of existing truces, while others substantially altered the terms or added new categories of agreement. A 1320 truce signed at Baeza guaranteed the liberty of captives who fled across the lines so long as they were not carrying booty with them, and it stipulated that Moors and Christians should convert to the religion of the rulers if they remained in territories that had recently changed hands.

New truces were negotiated when signers died, and there were even stopgap truces to allow time to negotiate new agreements, as occurred in 1333, when the assassination of the Granada ruler brought a new king, Yusuf III, to power and a four-month cease-fire was signed to give time for negotiating the terms of a pact of longer duration.[36]

Ongoing raids formed the background to truces and often influenced their terms. Truces signed in 1375 and 1378, for example, renewed commitments to peace in the face of escalating frontier violence and a rebellion in Murcia. Enrique III and Muhammad VII signed a truce in 1406—after five months of negotiation and with a duration of only two years—that stipulated the release of Christian prisoners in Granada, the return of booty seized in raids on Christian territories, and the punishment of those instigating frontier violence. Raiding also continued during truces. An agreement signed in 1475 was followed by major attacks on the Christian towns of Villacarrillo and Cieza in 1477, reflecting a general pattern. There was not a single year between 1464 and 1481 without at least one recorded raid or counterraid; undoubtedly many other raids went unrecorded.[37]

Truces sought to quell violence without specifying its public or private nature. Vendettas, feuds, factional violence, and even intrafamilial conflicts at times spilled into interpolitical fighting. Because truces did not distinguish private from public violence, enforcement and violations were also broadly defined. Notifying his subjects of the recent truce with Granada, Juan II in 1450 instructed "all and every one" of his subjects "to keep the truce and make others keep it, and not to break it nor allow it to be broken." He commanded his subjects not to engage in raids or order others to undertake raids, and not to inflict damage "in the realm of Granada, or in the cities, towns, settlements, lands, and people . . . neither to their persons nor to anything of theirs during the said time."[38] The ruler or his agent signed the truce, but the agreement bound all members of the political community.

The counterpart of the truce was, of course, capitulation. The stuttering Christian advance was accompanied by ultimatums for towns to surrender and to meet certain demands. Across the Iberian Peninsula, many Muslims were sent into exile and instructed to leave all their property behind. Christian armies presented exile as a concession, the alternative to destructive pillaging. Fernando III agreed to terms that allowed the Muslims of Capilla, Baeza, Ubeda, Cordoba, Jaén, and Sevilla to leave and assured their safety, and even their possession of some property, as they traveled to Muslim territories.[39] Christian raiders did not always accept payments in lieu of attack, and, following practices familiar across the Eurasian world, they brutally punished townsmen who surrendered after long sieges or refused to submit.[40] Capitulation did not mark the end of anything. The challenges of governance in newly conquered areas made them legally and administratively distinct from colonizers' home territories, even though they were not labeled or ruled as colonies.[41]

When the Catholic monarchs' forces took Granada in 1492, the treaty signed with the ruler resembled the long string of prior truces that preceded it. The treaty stipulated the surrender of Granada to the Catholic kings, outlined terms under which Muslims might leave the kingdom, converted Granada Muslims to subjects who could be punished as rebels and traitors, and guaranteed the right of Muslims not to convert to Christianity. Strains emerged soon after conquest and erupted into war in 1499, after Christian officials began stretching procedures outlined in the treaty and not just interviewing but detaining Christians who declared they wanted to convert. Muslims claimed that Christians were abrogating the terms of the treaty, and Christians made the same claim about Muslim subjects, whom they accused of abandoning their pledges of loyalty as vassals. Anticipating a return to war, the treaty operated like the previous truces in pushing accusations of betrayal to the forefront of justifications for further violence.[42]

The constant threat of war accompanied claims by religious communities that the aim and duty of conflict was peace.[43] In and beyond Iberia, medieval Christian rulers regarded the categories of political, civic, and domestic peace as interconnected and crucially cultivated by the state of inner peace made possible through devotion and penance.[44] Imagery and texts from late-medieval Italy convey the emphasis on penitents' pacts to make peace. Here the "choreography of peacemaking" included the memorialization by notaries of settlements to public

FIGURE 2.3. Detail from "The Wolf of Gubbio," ca. 1437–1444, Stefano de Giovanni ("Sassetta"). Original in the National Gallery, London.

and private conflicts and cast peacemaking as the religious duty of whole communities.[45] An instructive story, celebrated in paintings and iconography, features Saint Francis making peace with a wolf terrorizing Gubbio. Merging religious, civic, and political peace, the story captures the form and logic of a truce: in exchange for the wolf's pledge to end its deadly attacks, the town promised to feed the wolf, and the saint formalized the agreement by witnessing the repentance of both parties.[46] As in the wolf's peace with Gubbio, signing a truce fused its terms with a divinely favored common good.

The same tendencies that merged private and public peace and linked its legitimacy to worship gave truce breaking its electric emotional charge. Truces were backed by the honor of the parties. Violations signified private ruptures, marked repudiation of the common good, and tainted piety. Not surprisingly, it was very rare for anyone to openly declare the intent to break a truce. Instead, the breakdown of a truce began at the moment of accusation that a violation had occurred. Retaliatory actions often served to announce such accusations. Aggressors could and did declare themselves to be aggrieved parties—victims of dishonorable actions who were stunned by betrayal. The vernacular registers of this discourse extended deep into everyday social relations. Friends, lovers, kin—anyone who might renege on an understanding of trust, however tentative—knew how to call out betrayal and urge vengeance, and to do so in terms that were culturally current, redolent with religious meaning, legally intelligible, and potentially deadly.

Timing mattered. Where one stood within the loop of destructive raids, truces, and tribute taking could mark the difference between life and death. Different positions in the sequence could place actors in contrasting moral and legal postures. The wolf that attacked in a fury—to kill for food or be killed—was not the same wolf that placed its paw next to St. Francis and swore to obey the peace. Anyone could enact civility by making a truce; only a rebel, an apostate, or a natural enemy would dare to break one. In this world, danger long outlasted fighting. Peacemaking changed some parties from enemies into subjects of uncertain loyalty—and into objects of suspicion and surveillance.

Conquest by Peace

Raiding and truce making belong at the center of accounts of the Spanish conquest of the Americas. Spanish chronicles, correspondence, and contracts about interactions with Indigenous people in the Americas described chronic raiding and explained massacres as reactions to the failure to make peace. The requerimiento repackaged common elements of truces and combined them with equally familiar expectations about the consequences of breaking agreements or rupturing alliances. The history of when and how the statement was read shows that Spaniards deployed a broad set of interconnected actions and pronouncements to legitimize violence. They fit the requerimiento within a repertoire of raiding, demands for capitulation, and proffers of protection in exchange for peace.[47]

An example makes the pattern clear. In 1512, the Spanish crown issued a contract to Juan Ponce de León, then resident in Havana, granting him the right to "discover and settle" the Island of Bimini, an undefined area that encompassed what we now call Florida, and appointing him *adelantado*, a term lifted from Iberia to signify an officer in charge of Christian territories seized from others who had responsibility for civil and criminal jurisdiction over an expedition and in any lands he might discover and settle.[48] The grant focused on the financial framework for Ponce's venture, mainly his commitment to finance expeditions and settlements to the region and his obligation to provide the crown with a share of "the gold and other metals and things of value that might be on the stated island." There was no explicit authorization of war against local inhabitants—only indirect references to sanctioned violence in the mention of *repartimiento* (forced assignment of Indigenous people as laborers), specifications about the financing of fortresses "for defense against the *indios*," and reference to Ponce's entitlement to exercise "full power" in the territory.[49] Two years later, the crown issued an addendum. Written after the passage of the 1512 Laws of Burgos placing constraints on the enslavement of *indios*, the second contract outlined the conditions under which Ponce might conduct an authorized war. In dealing with *indios*, Ponce should "make them understand" that they were required to embrace the Catholic faith and "obey and serve" representatives of the Spanish crown. The crown authorized war if *indios* chose not to obey or if they agreed and then later rebelled. Ponce's instructions included the text of the requerimiento.[50]

As this example shows, the use of the requerimiento came on the scene after decades of Spanish-Indigenous interactions. Once introduced, the statement was used unsystematically and in various unauthorized forms. On the long approach to Tenochtitlan, Hernán Cortés had the requerimiento read, but not consistently. On the island of Cozumel, off Yucatán, Cortés found deserted towns and sent emissaries to locate *caciques* (chieftains). When one came forward, Cortés explained that his only demand was "that the chieftains and people of the island should also owe obedience to Your Highnesses; and [he] told them that by doing so they would be much favored, and no one thereafter would molest them."[51] Meeting forceful opposition to a landing in Yucatán, Cortés had the requerimiento read three times and witnessed by a notary. When he wrote to the king to report these events, Cortés was careful to specify that he "did not want war" but that "the *indios* were most resolutely determined to prevent him from landing, and indeed had already begun to shoot arrows."[52] The requerimiento was read again the next day to another armed group; they, too, according to the account, were betraying a pledge to help the Spaniards because they were "attacking us with arrows instead of bringing supplies as they had promised."[53] Here and elsewhere, the mere failure to parley features prominently in Spanish justifications for violence.[54]

Ready declarations by Indigenous people of their vassalage pepper early chronicles. Cortés recorded frequently in his letters to the king that local rulers presented gifts and declared themselves "very well pleased to be Your Highness's vassals and my friends."[55] Historians have interpreted these reports as either willful misreading of gestures that were intended to signify the opposite—Indigenous communities' superiority over Spaniards and permission granted to them to remain—or as self-interested posturing by conquistadors establishing their worthiness for royal grants and titles.[56] Yet it is doubtful that Cortés was misreading or misrepresenting so many encounters in the same way.

Indigenous communities in the Americas were familiar with demands for tribute and keenly aware of the need to provide it in the face of superior military power.[57] Like Spaniards accustomed to the chaotic mixture of extended campaigns, staccato raiding, and limited truces in Iberia, Indigenous leaders made it clear that they also did not regard submission as marking a permanent end to warfare or a surrender of sovereignty. Cortés might have reasonably assumed, too, that his intended audience at the royal court would not find his accounts of pledges of loyalty by non-Christians either far-fetched or self-aggrandizing. Recall that Granada rulers had signed truces defining themselves as vassals of the Catholic monarchs for two centuries before the city fell into Christian hands.

Declarations of vassalage, real or imagined, would have matched Spaniards' expectations about the standard workings of a truce. Once Indigenous communities had supposedly declared themselves vassals of the Spanish king, any resistance could be styled treachery and rebellion, and brutally contained. Here again, the Spanish chronicles lay example on example. Prominent among these is the Mexica's supposed betrayal in repulsing Spanish forces from Tenochtitlan. The Mexica ruler's act of "treachery" followed several reported speeches in which Moctezuma supposedly promised his loyalty to the king and recognized Cortés's legitimate right to rule as the king's representative. Cortés might have invented or embellished the declarations. But the audience at the court in Castile would have read them, together with the string of evasive actions by the Mexica ruler, as a prelude to betrayal and to violent rebellion. Moctezuma's treachery grounded the rationale for every subsequent act of vengeance by the Spaniards and their agents, including the burning and destruction of the city.[58]

Betrayal was oddly linked to another set of rationales for violence connected with Spanish imperatives to trade and settle. Historians have noted the importance of Cortés's founding of La Villa Rica de la Vera Cruz (Veracruz), an act intended to remove the danger that he would be labeled as a rebel for disobeying Diego Velásquez, governor of Cuba, in undertaking the dangerous *entrada*. The maneuver was also intended to open direct communication with the king and to bypass officials in

Havana. From a legal standpoint, the founding of the town gave Cortés, appointed *justicia mayor* (chief justice) by the *cabildo* (town council) that he created and led, jurisdiction over a vast and still-unbounded political community of Christian and non-Christian subjects. In his judicial role, he could authorize specific acts of violence against Indigenous people classed as subjects.[59] When news reached Cortés in Tenochtitlan that *indios* in a coastal community had killed a delegation of Spaniards they had invited to their town, Cortés insisted that Moctezuma summon the chieftain at the place of the murders and investigate in order to name and execute those responsible.[60] This inquiry was on the surface a judicial act, but Cortés was also compelling Moctezuma to use his own authority over subordinate polities to uphold the terms of the truce to which the Mexica ruler had supposedly agreed.[61]

The same presumption that a truce was in play, together with flexible and overlapping rationales for violence, framed the most spectacular act of Spanish violence during Cortés's advance on Tenochtitlan, the massacre at Cholula. When the Spaniards occupied the town, they negotiated an uneasy, informal truce. In the next days, encouraged by Tlaxcalan allies who regarded the Cholulans as enemies, the Spaniards scanned the scene nervously for signs of danger. Whether the inhabitants were preparing an attack and whether Cortés was crediting self-interested reports and unsubstantiated rumors or simply reading too much into the dearth of provisions, he became convinced that the Cholulans were planning violence. Cortés ordered all "noblemen, rulers, captains, chiefs, and also the men of the town" to assemble in the temple courtyards.[62] Through an interpreter, he chastised them for plotting to harm the Spaniards and for having agreed to a false truce rather than engaging enemies in open battle. Ever careful to present a legal rationale for a resumption of violence, Cortés declared, according to the witness Bernal Díaz, that "the royal laws" dictated punishment for their "treasons . . . and that for their crime they must die."[63] The soldiers then slaughtered the unarmed Cholulans trapped in the temple courtyards.

In the Mexica account dictated years later to Fray Bernardino de Sahagun, the Spaniards' attack was entirely without legal foundation: "Nothing like this was in the minds of the Cholulans. Without swords or shields they met the Spaniards. Without warning, they were treacherously and deceitfully slain."[64] For Cortés, justification for the massacre came easily because it bundled arguments about the right to self-defense with implicit authorization to punish vassals who had submitted to the crown without laying down arms.[65] Cortés did not have the requerimiento read. The logic of truce breaking was enough. To Spaniards, Cholulans' submission and their promise to keep the peace were implicit in their reception of Spaniards in their midst. Still, the event pointed to the ambiguities of Cholulans' status. At one moment, they were cast as vassals plotting insurrection; at another, they were painted as enemies who had never given up the fight. Either way, Cortés could comfort the king that their massacre was justified.

The theme of violence as punishment of truce breakers or rebels continued to be useful in the widening arc of Spanish conquest. The term "pacification" entered the Spanish lexicon as a general description of armed actions against Indigenous communities across the region. Pedro de Castañeda de Nájera's chronicle of the Coronado expedition (1540–1542) in the region that now straddles northern Mexico and the southwestern United States is typical. In an early encounter, Spaniards attacked quickly after interpreters presented the requerimiento to a group of Indigenous warriors.[66] Word of Spanish aggression thereafter seemed to precede Spaniards as they moved. Some groups the Spaniards encountered, according to Castañeda, "accepted peace before any harm was done them" and produced gifts to mollify the invaders.[67] Some signaled peace by locking their hands or by taking the sweat of the Spaniards' horses and smearing it on themselves and then making "crosses" with their fingers.[68] Again and again, implicit truces did not hold. Accusations of betrayal flowed in both directions. Indigenous groups accused Spaniards of violating the peace after Spaniards seized two leaders they had invited to parley, and after they burned at the stake 200 local fighters who had surrendered on the promise of safety.[69]

After a long period of "daily skirmishes," an embattled, much-reduced Spanish force with little to show for its efforts limped back toward the safety of established settlements.[70] They did not wait for twenty raiders led by Captain Juan Gallego on a mission of reconnaissance. Peace was not on offer in that extended raid. The Spanish position was that the inhabitants they encountered should have held to promises of peace by other distant, unconnected communities and were therefore in revolt. The band of Spaniards repeatedly "forced its way into the pueblos, killing, destroying, and applying the torch, and falling upon the enemy so suddenly, with such swiftness and vigor, that they did not give them time to assemble or plan any resistance." The wave of terror produced quick submission in some places. But capitulation came with no guarantees of peaceful proceedings on either side. In one town, "Gallego killed and hanged a large number of people in punishment for their rebellion."[71]

Overall, the unsuccessful, violent *entradas* produced little plunder and failed to prepare the way for Spanish rule. But accounts of the expedition reinforced the legal fiction of conquerors as peacemakers and the arguments for punishing hastily declared vassals accused of peace breaking. Improbably, Pedro de Castañeda recounted, the "whole land was left pacified and calm" when the Spaniards withdrew.[72] This wishful thinking also signified more. Spaniards used "pacification" as shorthand for the rapid sequences of implicit truce making, accusations of betrayal, and brutal punishment.

Defining a Just Massacre

In another part of the New World, in a process less frequently labeled "conquest," truces played a similar part in structuring colonial violence. In the decades after the establishment of the Plymouth Colony and the Massachusetts Bay Colony in New England, English settlers' attention turned increasingly to the lower reaches of the Connecticut River. Motivations for settlement included the area's proximity to Indigenous producers of valuable wampum (shells used as currency), the control by competing Dutch traders from the Hudson Valley in the fur trade along the river, and the search by farmers in coastal Massachusetts for richer soil to farm. The region was home to the Pequots, who presided over a confederation encompassing various groups who paid tribute to them in exchange for protection. Initially, there seemed every reason to imagine that settler incursions in the area would be facilitated by trading and alliance on the model of interactions between English and Indigenous communities around the Plymouth and Massachusetts Bay colonies.[73]

Instead, relations devolved into a destructive war with the Pequots. Its opening was marked by a brutal massacre of hundreds of Pequots, including women and children, followed by attacks on civilians trying to flee the area. The facts of the massacre are undisguised and undisputed in English chronicles. In May 1637, a force of some ninety English soldiers with several hundred allied Indigenous fighters conducted a surprise attack on the fortified Pequot village at Mystic. After setting the wooden dwellings of the town and its palisades on fire, the soldiers posted themselves at each of two exits to kill anyone trying to escape. Between four hundred and five hundred Pequots were slaughtered, either in the fire or in the bloodbath surrounding the palisades. Only seven Pequots were captured at Mystic, and another handful escaped to join other remaining bands of Pequots, who were themselves soon attacked by settlers in pursuit. The captives were enslaved, and most were shipped for sale to English settlers on Providence Island.

The most detailed historical analysis of the Pequot War explains the massacre as an outcome of long-standing Puritan associations of Native peoples with Satanic forces. In this telling, the misreading of Pequot behavior amounted to a "profound incompatibility of cultures."[74] This explanation takes at face value English reflections on the war after the fact, when the victory itself could be interpreted as evidence of Puritan godliness.[75] Analyzing the conflict in a broader, comparative context shows instead that the events leading up to the war revolved around raiding and a failed truce. The logic of reprisal and punishment for the supposed treachery of Indigenous communities prepared the way for war.[76]

Both English and Pequots were participants in regional raiding that had intensified since the founding of the English colonies. Plymouth Colony settlers and traders had been enmeshed in a complex of French and Indigenous raids against the English, and counterraids by the English, in Maine. The Connecticut River Valley was, like Maine, an area of interimperial rivalry and a zone in which weaker polities paid tribute to more powerful groups in exchange for protection. Such arrangements held raiding in check, and settlers and Indigenous

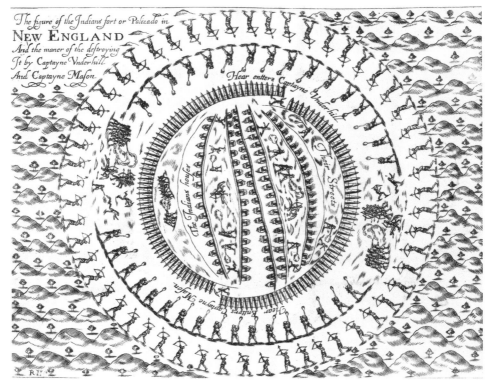

FIGURE 2.4. The massacre at Mystic, 1637. Engraving from John Underhill, *News from America; or, A new and experimentall discoverie of New England* (London: 1638).

communities alike recognized the importance of the fragile peace to trade. Pequots and Dutch made a formal peace agreement in 1633, one that allowed the Dutch to operate a trading post, the House of Good Hope, on the Connecticut River and upriver from Saybrook Fort, a small and underprovisioned English garrison at the river's mouth.

Raiding continually threatened the tenuous peace. Not long after signing the truce with the Dutch, a group of Pequots attacked and killed some other Indigenous men on their way to the Dutch trading post. The attack was probably opportunistic. It is possible that the Pequots reasoned that it would not be seen as a violation of peace terms since it was not a direct attack on the Dutch or their trading post. Dutch agents took a different view. In swift reprisal, they seized a Pequot sachem, Tatobem, when he boarded a Dutch vessel to trade, and they demanded a hefty ransom for his return. Tatobem's followers sent a bushel of wampum to free him—and were shocked to receive in return Tatobem's lifeless body. It was now the Pequots' turn for reprisal. A group of Pequots and western Niantics killed another trader, John Stone, when he stopped to camp on shore while traveling in a small vessel up the Connecticut River. Pequot representatives would later argue that they were avenging Tatobem's murder and had simply mistaken the Englishmen for Dutchmen; Europeans looked alike, after all. But the Pequots also had another reason to kill Stone. The trader had kidnapped two western Niantics, members of a group who paid tribute to the Pequots, to serve as guides on the vessel's upriver voyage. Niantics had stalked the boat from shore from the time the two local guides were seized, waiting for a good moment to strike.

Still, there was no straight line to war. The fur trade depended on the ability of trappers, buyers, and sellers to travel unharmed through the region, and there were plenty of precedents for peace to be struck following raids. Clearly betting that an English alliance would counterbalance Dutch incursions and force a halt to violence against them by English-allied Narragansetts, Pequot emissaries traveled to Boston in 1634 to negotiate.

The peace treaty proposed by the English, the text of which has not survived, contained two big catches. First, it was silent on a pledge for protection, which the Pequot agents had specifically requested.[77] English settlers did not want to be drawn into a war with the Dutch and would not pledge to oppose the Narragansetts, whom they regarded as their clients. Second, the colonists demanded that for them to ratify the treaty, the Pequots would have to fulfill some startling conditions. They would need to provide an enormous payment of wampum and furs, and they would have to surrender the men responsible for the death of Captain Stone.

In some respects, the conflict about Stone's killing was a classic jurisdictional dispute over frontier murder. Settlers who demanded punishment for men responsible for specific acts of violence encountered Indigenous legal cultures that recognized the right to reprisal, but not the punishment of individuals, for violent crimes.[78] Yet there was less cultural misunderstanding here than one might think. The context of raiding helped to make Indigenous and settler justice mutually intelligible. For the English and Dutch, the logic of reprisal behind Pequot violence was hardly opaque. Even John Winthrop Sr., leader of the Massachusetts Bay Colony, noted in his journal that he had found Pequot representatives very convincing when they explained that they had killed Stone because he had taken "two of their men and bound them, and made him show him the way up the river." Winthrop was "inclined to believe them."[79] It seems doubtful, too, that the Pequots would have found the English demand to punish specific individuals shocking, though they might not have wanted to comply. Pequot representatives were arguing, after all, that the killing of Stone was justified on several grounds, and they were not ready to concede that any penalty or punishment was warranted. They might also have suspected that the unusually high payment demanded by the English was a ruse. The English did not seem to be looking to end the cycle of raids and counterraids, at least not yet; if anything, a failed or even stalled discussion of peace would serve them well as a prelude to war.

In the months leading to war, rumor ripened quickly from Pequot intransigence to the idea that the Pequots were planning an all-out attack. The rumors were certainly encouraged by the Pequots' Indigenous rivals. Warnings of war accompanied confident statements in Boston about Pequot treachery, supposedly demonstrated by their bad faith negotiating and their unwillingness to meet the terms of the unratified 1634 treaty. Boston leaders then upped the ante. John Winthrop Jr. was dispatched to meet with the Pequot sachem with instructions to demand not only that the Pequots agree promptly to the treaty terms but also that they meet another onerous demand: sending the children of sachems to Boston as hostages to guarantee the peace. The communication took the form of an ultimatum and a warning; not unlike the requerimiento, it demanded peace on invaders' terms and promised war if Indigenous groups failed to submit.

We cannot know what the Pequots might have done or said if they had been given more time to respond. Escalating violence overtook negotiations. Indigenous bands not under Pequot control on Block Island raided a small English trading vessel and killed the trader. The English mounted a raid of reprisal that found unpromising targets on Block Island and so wandered into Pequot territory, where the English raiders killed more than a dozen Pequots and burned scores of wigwams. In Boston, Winthrop and others insisted that the English were seeking peace and that the Pequots were angling for war by rejecting terms of a truce.

The cycle of raiding and killing intensified. After the Pequots placed Saybrook Fort under siege, openings for diplomacy quickly vanished. In a parley with Lieutenant Lion Gardiner, Pequots asked whether it was common for the English "to kill women and children." Gardiner answered that they "should see." The Pequots present were "silent a small space" and then said that they were "pequits and have killed Englishmen and can kill them as musketoes" and would "kill men women & children."[80] A few weeks later, a group of Pequots, accompanied by some Wangunk men, raided the upriver settlement of Wethersfield. The Wangunk were former tributaries of the Pequots and were conducting their own reprisal for English settlers' refusal to honor an agreement to recognize Wangunk rights to settle on nearby land. The attackers in Wethersfield killed fourteen settlers, including three women, and captured two teenage girls. The Connecticut colony responded by formally declaring war on the Pequots, and a mere ten days later, on May 26, 1637, English soldiers with Mohegan and Narragansett allies descended on Mystic.

Alongside accounts of the conflict and its outcome as proof of God's favor, the English emphasized the right of reprisal for Indigenous violence and referenced just war doctrine. Connecticut settlers cited "just warre" in declaring war on the Pequots after the Wethersfield raid. On the eve of the expedition against the Pequots that produced the Mystic massacre, a sermon at Hartford described the conflict as a "just warre" and emphasized Indigenous "crueltie," calling on a God-bestowed "honour . . . to execute vengeance upon the heathen."[81] Yet just war arguments were invoked selectively and inconsistently, and they were only part of the framework for violence.[82] The defense of English violence also relied on judgments about Pequot behavior: not just the repeated raids but also their failure to ratify the peace treaty. Settlers emphasized Pequot treachery, intransigence, and inherent violence.[83] As with Spanish aggression, written arguments about the Pequot War as a just cause took its meaning from a broader logic that rendered Pequots as impossible subjects and English settlers as peacemakers.

Neither Peace nor War

European writings on law and war appear in a different light when juxtaposed with histories of imperial warfare. Bits and pieces of relevant commentary, rather than a coherent body of law, informed the case for legitimate violence in the form of raiding and in the wake of truces. It is easy to overlook European writers' preoccupation with these themes in favor of their focus on better-known controversies. But scattered discussions of legal rationales for routine violence provided a repertoire that conquistadors, settlers, and officials could draw on and reflected commonplace understandings of the rhythms of small wars.

Truces, so important in giving conflicts their structure and pace, had long drawn the interest of legal writers. Late-medieval civilian and canon lawyers struggled openly to define the nature of temporary peace. They promoted the idea of the Peace of God, the protection of certain classes of vulnerable persons (especially clerics) from the ravages of war, and the Truce of God, the suspension of fighting at certain times.[84] The peace movement reinforced representations of the Christian commonwealth as a community with a shared commitment to perpetual peace. The commentary also introduced the idea that war could be waged intermittently and the presumption that some violence could lawfully continue during agreed-upon periods of peace. Tilting against the Truce of God proponents (although not against the idea of Church oversight of war), the twelfth-century jurist Gratian argued that once a war had been declared just, it could be continued at any time, even during Lent.[85] Conduct of all kinds, including ruses and surprise attacks, was permissible once a determination had been made that violence was in service to a just cause. Just wars were fought by definition not by choice but by necessity, and canonical truces never prohibited violence performed in self-defense.

In the thirteenth century, the influential canonist Hostiensis reaffirmed the ban on most types of fighting during times of truce. But he also affirmed the legitimacy of unceasing warfare against people who had broken bonds with Christians.[86] His qualifications did little to overturn the idea that once declared, a just war gave cover to ongoing violence, including during negotiated interruptions to war.[87]

Political theologians wrote sparingly about truces and did not overturn this view. They offered some qualifications, taking up such questions as whether there were differences in short-term and long-term truces. Some writers—for example, the Italian jurist Pierino Belli—argued that a truce of long duration resembled peace and might require a declaration of war at the resumption of hostilities.[88] Ambiguities remained about whether truces lay closer to a state of peace or a state of war—or whether they perhaps constituted some third category.[89]

At the beginning of the seventeenth century, two writers, Alberico Gentili and Hugo Grotius, took up the subject of truces within influential treatises on law and war. Both Gentili and Grotius affirmed that a truce represented a break from war. Gentili argued that a truce did not put an end to war but merely postponed it and represented "a temporary and intermediate peace."[90] In his discussion of truces in book III of *De Iure Belli ac Pacis* (*The Rights of War and Peace*), Grotius quoted Gellius's second-century reflection that a "Truce cannot be called a Peace" because a state of war continued under a truce.[91] Both Gentili and Grotius sought to distinguish a truce from a peace. For Grotius, because a truce signified "a Rest of War," it was possible for either party to refuse a peace but grant a truce.[92] Gentili argued that whereas only sovereigns in most cases could make a peace, "commanders in the field" might grant truces. A very long truce could take on some qualities of a peace, but "a truce is never really the same as a peace."[93] According to Gentili, a peace pact settled all the issues in a war, whereas a truce either resolved some questions in dispute or merely suspended fighting without resolving anything.[94]

This characterization of truces solved some questions but raised others, particularly about the lawfulness of violence during and after truces. A key implication of the view that a truce marked "a Rest of War" was that violence could be resumed without a new declaration of war or any other rituals to mark the transition. Gentili regarded this conclusion as obvious, and Grotius cited a "Diversity of Examples," mainly from Roman warfare, to affirm that new declarations of war were not required if one party discovered that a truce had been broken. For both writers, this quality of truces opened a series of interpretive possibilities.

One vexing question was when one could conclude that a truce had been violated. For Gentili, it was clear that either party could resume hostilities as soon as the end of a truce was reached. The need for interpretation arose when violence erupted before that point. Gentili disapproved of manipulation aimed at a rupture. It was "corrupt and shameful," he wrote, to justify a return to violence by reading the text of a truce too literally, as the Thracians had done when they "agreed upon a truce for several days" and then attacked the enemy at night.[95] By the same token, war should not be resumed for a "slight, doubtful, or unjust reason."[96]

Such constraints left plenty of room for parties to justly respond with violence to provocations. It was always licit to act in self-defense, Gentili observed, and a violent response to the seizure of property—for example, in a raid—qualified as an act of self-defense.[97] And a truce, like any agreement, could be broken rightfully if conditions changed, or when "a new cause" arose.[98] There was also wide latitude for political communities to interpret actions as provocations that justified an early return to war. Since it was not necessary to announce the reasons for resuming hostilities, the line between temporary peace and ongoing war lay along a knife's edge.

Grotius agreed that truces could be dissolved without notice. But he paused to reflect on the fact that many combatants went out of their way to describe their reasons. Even though Romans had not been obligated to declare their reasons for resuming war, Grotius observed, they routinely did so anyway. In offering rationales, they were showing "how much they loved Peace, and how careful they were not to engage in War, unless for just causes."[99] The practice blurred the very distinctions between truce and peace that Grotius, like Gentili, had set out to clarify.

The fuzzy boundaries between war and peace were unsettling and unavoidable. Defining war as a "just and public contest of arms," Gentili noted that "raids and plundering" could not "rightly be termed war."[100]

He placed some pillaging, like the pirates or brigands who perpetrated it, outside the *ius gentium* (the law of nations). But some types of violence were neither inside nor outside, and they seemed to occupy a troubling middle area. Gentili approvingly quoted Paolo Giovio, chronicler of Italian wars, who described Hungarians and Turks as mired in "petty contests on the frontiers and disorderly raids" and suggested that when a full-scale attack brought a truce to an end, it pulled the low-level, unruly violence of frontier raiding into the more orderly realm of war.[101]

The bleeding edges of war and peace extended into the period immediately after victory. Gentili explained in book II of *The Wars of the Romans*, where he presented his defense of the justice of Roman wars, that many vanquished peoples refused to put down arms. Nominally defeated, they postponed warfare or sculpted it into phases. Romans redefined persisting conflicts as revolts, cast the periods between rebellions as implicit truces, and characterized rebels as savages inherently drawn to violence.[102] Against the persistence of war by other names, he concluded, Romans had been forced into ruthlessness. They found, in effect, that extreme brutality was the only way to achieve peace. Latins, Etruscans, Umbrians, and others were not "peaceful until they were utterly beaten down, received into capitulation city by city, and utterly subdued."[103] This logic placed the punishing phases of repression and violence following victory into a state suspended between peace and war.

Truces and imperial warfare were intricately related. Grotius wrote *Mare Liberum* (*The Free Sea*) specifically to defend the Dutch capture of the Portuguese ship *Santa Catarina* in the Singapore Strait.[104] Gentili's interest in describing the lawfulness of imperial violence was also not casual. Supporting the Earl of Essex and other leading Protestants who were urging English opposition to Spain, Gentili argued that preemptive war was just. It was not necessary to wait for an injury to occur; a "just fear" of future violence by an adversary was enough.[105] Although Gentili did not tie this argument explicitly to ending truces, he clearly implied that the fear of violence by Indigenous peoples would have provided sufficient justification for resuming war.

Although both Gentili and Grotius were writing after the events described in this chapter in New Spain and New England, Europeans in the Americas carried knowledge—some specific, some diffused in practices of war—about how truces worked. Puritans had set out for the New World in part because they feared that the end of the Twelve Years' Truce would prompt a return to war with Spain that would engulf the Low Countries and place them in danger. Spaniards, as we have seen, could reference decades of recent experience with truce making, tribute taking, and staccato violence.[106]

But the direct connections between European discourse on truces and the dynamics of imperial small wars should not detain us. The parallels of logic were significant on their own. In theory and practice, a clear sequencing of expected events coexisted with a hazy indistinction between war and peace. The confusion between war and peace was sometimes intentional and self-interested, but the ambiguity was also deeply structural. Wide interpretive latitude surrounded acts of violence during a truce and determined whether they counted as acts of war. Parties to a truce might simultaneously be tribute-paying vassals and dangerous enemies at rest. The drumbeat of raiding and other syncopated, serial violence sounded in a landscape between war and peace. And, in a twist that might have been ironic if it had not been so horrific in its consequences, extreme violence figured as the best evidence of a fervent desire for negotiation and restraint.

The tragic character of truces is difficult to miss. They were instruments for containing war that mainly worked to help stage transitions from grim choices—surrender or die, kill or capture—to grimmer outcomes. They were compatible with continuing raids, and they carried in their terms the promise of future wars, planned or unexpected. Truces invited paranoia, recriminations, accusations of betrayal, and frantic mass murder. The agreements were tragically associated, too, with durable and sharpening representations of Indigenous peoples as "savage" and untrustworthy. These tendencies, and the conduct of conquest as a sequence of signed and broken truces, were so well established and so pervasive that we can recognize them as key elements of a global regime of violence. One of its hallmarks was that small-scale, reciprocal, and chronic violence was readily paired with sudden slaughter—and both were imagined as operating in the service of peace.

Chapter 3

Private Booty, Public War

Bartolomé de las Casas was a child when he began thinking about the inhabitants of the New World. When he was nine years old, in 1493, seven Native American captives brought to the city by Columbus on his first voyage were paraded through the streets of Seville. Bartolomé's father, Pedro de las Casas, had been a member of Columbus's crew on that voyage. When Pedro returned from Columbus's second voyage in 1499, he brought a present from the admiral: a *Taíno* youth to serve in the Las Casas household.[1] The episode did not mark the family's last participation in the subjugation of Indigenous Americans. By 1516, Pedro de las Casas commanded four personal servants and sixteen laborers in Santo Domingo. On the first and second voyages that Bartolomé de las Casas made to the Indies, the future Dominican friar served as a soldier in raids on Indigenous communities in Santo Domingo and Cuba, where he received *indios* as his share of plunder.[2]

When Bartolomé Las Casas became an outspoken critic of the Spaniards' treatment of the people they encountered in the New World, he condemned both the permission for raiders to seize "as many *indios* as they wanted" and the subjection of captives to "infernal servitude" in households.[3] He emphasized the injustice of attacking peaceful *indios* and treating them as captives in a just war.[4] For Las Casas, chronic raiding and the "tyrannical servitude" of Indigenous inhabitants of the Americas were intricately connected.[5] Worried about the souls of Spanish slavers, he lamented that Indigenous captives were being cruelly treated and deprived of the possibility of having "households and property of their own."[6]

There are some reasons to contrast "domestic" captivity in Iberian households with the enslavement of Native peoples in the Americas for work in mines and on plantations.[7] But Las Casas and other contemporaries did not make this distinction. Indeed, Las Casas identified the household as the principal entity for holding and disciplining captives seized in war. Household heads exercised control and authority, *dominium*, over all subordinate household members, including women, children, servants, and slaves. Households, like the one headed by Pedro de las Casas, were the main repositories for captives in both Iberia and the New World.[8]

The principle that captives could be justly seized in war was cited regularly by slavers, often more as casual slogan than formal legal argument, and often as mere cover for unauthorized slaving. Many Christian raiders in Iberia labeled their captives "Moors" regardless of their origins or religion to justify keeping or selling captives seized in raids.[9] Iberian raiders did the same in North Africa, where early sixteenth-century raids became the main source for captives sold in Spanish and Portuguese cities. By one estimate, 60,000 women seized in Moroccan raids were sold in Spanish ports in 1522.[10] The links between households and raiding extended into distant sites of empires in the Indian Ocean and Atlantic worlds.

As sojourners, settlers, and soldiers jockeyed to seize women and children, they were driving to gain wealth and status for households. Factions of different status found common ground in advocating broad authority for household heads over their tiny commonwealths. Officials who opposed raiding or placed limits on the power of heads of household over captives faced harsh criticism, and even sometimes rebellion. Servants and captives, meanwhile, chafed against control over their own possibilities of forming families and households.[11] The political character of early settlements was deeply bound up with the politics of households.[12]

Nowhere is this connection clearer than in what I call "garrison empires," collections of fortified enclaves of early European overseas ventures. Metropolitan instructions or charters provided imperial agents in far-flung garrisons with incomplete and vague instructions about the political nature of these communities. Household formation represented not just a possible pathway for turning fortified outposts into settled colonies. It was in most cases the *only* pathway available. Imperial officials recognized very early the importance of encouraging household formation—to shore up the legitimacy of their rule, to enhance the viability of settlements, and to ensure Europeans' ability to ensnare or attract the coerced labor they regarded as key to profit taking through continued raiding.

Yet forming households in early empires was no easy trick. The demand for labor was usually high in imperial enclaves, but securing laborers, from dependent kin to servants to enslaved people, was irregular and costly. It also presented risks, from insubordination to rebellion. Even as raiding promised to secure captives for struggling households, it drew men away from garrisons and placed them outside the command of households. Again and again, incentives to promote stability and trade by containing raids clashed with local incentives to pursue plunder.

The close relationship between imperial violence and households found support among European political theologians and jurists. They regarded households as essential to the formation of political communities and linked them to settlements' right to make defensive war. Officials quickly figured out that arguments about self-defense could be stretched creatively to justify ongoing raiding, even against crown instructions to preserve regional peace. As raids produced captives, households completed the punishment of captives seized in raids. Consequently, at the heart of slaving and slavery was the idea that slave masters and enslaved people were locked in a permanent state of war.[13] Yet, there was nothing fixed or definite about authorization for raids and captive taking. While the demand for payment in booty by sailors and soldiers gave rise to opportunistic captive taking, early colonial policies were wildly inconsistent, at times limiting and at other times tolerating, or even actively sponsoring, the seizure and sale of captives. The profitability of trafficking in human beings depended on having someplace to put them. Imperial officials and community members in early settlements were acutely aware that armies on the move and jerry-rigged garrisons were less conducive to household formation than permanent colonies with municipal governments and stable religious institutions.

To show how households were foundational to complexes of raiding and slavery, this chapter begins with Portuguese enclaves in the Indian Ocean and moves to English garrisons in the Caribbean. In sixteenth-century Goa under the Portuguese Estado da Índia and in seventeenth-century English Caribbean colonies, officials encouraged household formation as a means of attaching footloose raiders to imperial enclaves, fashioning a colonial right to make war, and multiplying entities authorized to hold and discipline captives. In the same period and also later, European jurists and political theologians sought to define the relation of private violence to public war. Debating what conditions turned quasi-private raiding into legitimate public war, European writers sketched a legal framework for peacetime plunder. Their approach matched in its broad outlines (and some particulars) the logic of distant efforts to transform collections of colonies into empires. In both theory and practice, defining households as essential to the legitimacy of political communities helped to justify imperial plunder, and vice versa. Both European writers and officials far from Europe settled on households as the link between opportunistic plunder and organized violence and, ultimately, between ad hoc captive taking and slavery as an imperial institution.

Households and Political Communities

We miss the relation of households to violence if we regard them as only social units and not also legal entities. We also miss it if we accept a common, often implicit contrast between a public, male world of politics and a private, female sphere of apolitical domesticity.[14] Households were irrepressibly political spaces.[15] Their members struggled over limited rights to marry, reproduce, and live with kin.[16] Households were places where interpersonal turmoil intersected with broader conflicts over status, rights, and authority.

Political theologians in the sixteenth and seventeenth centuries addressed the relationship between the household and the political community (*civitas*) in some detail. The work of the Jesuit writer Francisco Suárez (1548–1617) is a good starting place for thinking about how European legal writers placed households and imperial violence in the same frame. It may seem odd to go looking for such connections in the writing of a solitary, bookish friar whose worldliness extended only as far as his itinerary through a series of posts in Castile, Rome, and Portugal. A late bloomer who was first rejected by the Jesuit order, Suárez never ventured outside Europe, unlike so many other important Jesuits, and he did not devote much attention to the problems of conscience raised by Spanish conquest in the Americas, unlike the Dominican Francisco de Vitoria. But Suárez's talent for synthesizing the views of other political theologians made him influential in the Spanish court and, after his death, throughout Europe. More clearly than many political theologians who belonged to the school of late scholastic thinkers, Suárez wrote extensively on both households and limited war.

Like other writers before him, Francisco Suárez cited Aristotle in distinguishing between perfect and imperfect communities. Perfect communities such as the city-state comprised citizens with "a mutual bond of a moral nature," and only those communities had the capacity of political government. Imperfect communities, of which households were a paradigmatic example, were not self-sufficient and depended on "diverse kinds of command." A perfect political community stood as the proper subject of human laws, whereas the variability of households made it impossible to legislate for one in ways that would apply to all. Legally, households were subordinate to perfect communities.[17]

For Suárez, households and political communities had a clear ontological relation. More natural in their origins than the civil community, households came together to compose *civitas*. Political power, Suárez observed, emerged when "many families began to congregate into one perfect community."[18] Because the very possibility of social ordering depended on the coming together of households, intrahousehold and civil peace remained inextricably linked.[19] At the same time, households did not have what today we would call foreign policy—they could not make war. Only a legitimate sovereign could go to war against another sovereign, and only to take up a just cause in response to an injury.[20]

FIGURE 3.1. Francisco Suárez, Spanish Jesuit theologian (1548–1617).

But households were also like other political communities in important ways. Suárez accepted the late-medieval view that both sociability and authority were natural to man, and it was sociability that brought individuals together to form political communities, whether perfect or imperfect. Political authority—including the authority of households—derived from the consent of members of those communities.[21] And for any political community, the pertinent question was to what degree the law promoted "justice or injustice" and existed "for the sake of the common good."[22] All political communities had to reference sources of law beyond natural law, within limits. The common good could never be subordinated to private good.[23]

The question of the proper relationship between private and public good was behind Suárez's approach to law and war, and to his take on the relation between households and violence. Implicitly, households supported the capacity for public violence. All scholastic writers, including Suárez, affirmed the legality of taking captives in a just war. Suárez clarified that this authorization might be withheld inside a political community, just as in Christendom—a single political community for these purposes—the Church had abolished the practice of captive taking in war between Christian nations.[24] A political community might also legislate against the authority of heads of households over captives, a power of *dominium*. But where a cause was just and there was no ban against captures, authority exercised by household heads over captives was legally unproblematic. By implication, enslavement represented the completion of actions begun on the battlefield or in raids, and it constituted part of a response to injury. It was also an act of mercy since captors were enslaving instead of killing their captives.

The household was a semiprivate site of semipublic punishment. In the case of enslaved people (as compared to other subordinates in households), their placement in households involved authorizing perpetual (or at least very extended) punishment. It is this logical extension of just war theory that Atlantic historians have cited in describing just war doctrine as the cornerstone of slaving in the Atlantic world—against both Africans and New World Indigenous people—and as the source of enslaved people's conviction that they remained in a state of war with their masters.[25] This point was not explicitly recognized by Suárez, or by most other scholastic writers.[26] To them, the *dominium* of household heads amounted to a right to restrict the rights of some persons, but it was not an *unlimited* right, and the violence of household heads in holding or disciplining captives was not the same as war. The arrangement of holding captives in households might have derived from war, but legal incorporation in households placed captives in a context where the authority wielded over them was subject to limits, both of natural law and of the sovereign.

The problems of defining the relation of households to political community and war paralleled another challenge taken up by Suárez: finding the mechanisms for converting private violence to legitimate parts of public war. Suárez condemned most private war as tainted by "the intrinsic wickedness of the duel," but he also acknowledged that there was nothing inherently wrong about a small war, even "one fought by two or by a few individuals." If condoned by public authority or if meeting the conditions of a just war, a conflict at any scale might have "the nature of war—at least, *war of a limited sort.*"[27] The main difference between a duel and a conflict with "the true character of war" was that the latter was undertaken "under public authority and for a public cause."[28]

It remained for Suárez to enumerate the ways in which a private contest might be "clothed with the conditions characterizing a just war." A small engagement might symbolize a larger armed conflict, as when a small battle was used to decide a war. Private violence might also serve as a legitimate way to weaken an enemy or strengthen the resolve of one's own soldiers. In these and other ways a small conflict might constitute "a portion of a war, justly undertaken and begun, which it is perhaps expedient to carry forward in this fashion." In other words, private actions— including, one must infer, the private violence of some raiders—could not only be subsumed under the public authorization to go to war but could attain the character of parts of a legitimate war. Participants could show that they were conforming to public resolutions or adopting positions consistent with arguments of "the possessor of authority."[29]

We now come to the relevance of these positions for justifications of violence in garrison empires. Violence by a collection of private actors might be made legitimate through careful attention to the ways that justifications aligned with public authorization to go to war. Unofficial actors as well as agents of sovereigns could promote this alignment. As nascent political communities, sponsors of violence, and holders of captives, collections of households supported the capacity to pursue war.

They might even claim the authority to make war on their own if their actions matched public or common objectives.

Francisco Suárez was writing decades after Europeans had founded archipelagos of garrisons and embraced raiding across the Indian Ocean and Atlantic worlds. His works never functioned as a manual for turning garrisons into colonies or mobilizing private interests for imperial goals. But we need not insist on finding evidence of circulating knowledge about the law to see that the problems engaging political theologians in Europe were also presenting themselves in distant settings and un-lettered circles. Puzzles about using households to forge political communities and coloring private violence as public war had surfaced in urgent and obvious ways centuries before, as Europeans endorsed raiding and pursued plunder in distant oceanic worlds.

Making Garrisons, Making Empires

Before founding towns populated with households and governed by imperial officials, Europeans had to mark protected enclaves. They also sought to turn collections of garrisons into the armature of empire. In surveying Portuguese ventures in the Indian Ocean, one historian has quipped that Portuguese ambition was "to trade where possible, to make war where necessary."[30] Usually, the Portuguese did both at once. From the earliest expeditions into the Indian Ocean, Portuguese commercial activities depended on violence.[31] With a dearth of highly valued goods to offer and armed with key military advantages—the ability to outmaneuver many Asian vessels in fast caravels, shoot cannon fire from carracks on coastal towns, and, under most conditions, over-power lower-lying galleys—the Portuguese threat of force created the mirage of peaceful trade. It compelled local communities to buy goods that the Portuguese or their allies brought to market, often at artificially high prices.[32] The Portuguese also famously sold protection in the form of safe-conduct passes to Asian ships carrying trade goods in or near Portuguese-controlled ports.[33]

Raiding was an integral part of this complex of trade-through-force. Portuguese captains were known to seize ships to obtain provisions and valuable commodities, and they sometimes attacked ships that had already paid for safe passage.[34] Some Portuguese crews ventured out without official backing to prey on local shipping, in effect becoming pirates.[35] Sea raiding received sanction at the highest levels, too, since the only way for the Portuguese to fully finance operations in the Indian Ocean world was through plunder.

The practice of fortifying ports to protect shipping and launch raids seems like a natural accompaniment to these strategies. The policy originated in Lisbon, where King Manuel instructed the first viceroy, Francisco de Almeida, as he departed for Asia in 1505, to build three fortresses at Indian Ocean ports already visited by the Portuguese and to scout locations farther east in Ceylon and Malacca. Almeida's instructions outlined the characteristics of a good site for a fortress: a strong defensive position and harbor, as well as access to water and proximity to trade routes.[36] He was responsible for the construction of fortresses in four ports: Cochin, Cannanore, Angediva, and Kilwa. But Almeida's enthusiasm for the project faded, and it was left to his successor, Afonso de Albuquerque (ca. 1453–1515), as governor from 1509 to 1515, to champion the program of fortification and develop it into something more: the armature of Portuguese commercial and military enterprise in Asia.[37]

The Portuguese crown had diplomatic and legal reasons to favor fortification schemes. The Treaty of Tordesillas had divided the world into Spanish and Portuguese spheres of influence by drawing a north–south line in the Atlantic. The treaty did not award sovereignty over the territories on either side of the meridian but instead conveyed "the right to navigate the said sea within certain specified limits and seek out and take possession of newly discovered lands."[38] In other words, it required Portuguese and Spanish agents to show proofs of discovery and possession in their sphere of influence. Settlements and fortifications were among other symbols supporting Portuguese claims.[39] Fortification projects extended Portuguese practices in North and West Africa, where some Estado da Índia officials had cut their teeth on service in military garrisons. In the Indian Ocean, Portuguese officials found that some coastal polities would not readily grant them rights to set up *feitorias*, or trading factories, without the threat or use of force. The need for fortification became especially clear after 1500, when local fighters attacked and overwhelmed the largely unfortified *feitoria* at Calicut.[40]

Despite support from Lisbon and conflict in the Indian Ocean, the fortification program was controversial among Portuguese in the Indian Ocean. When Albuquerque maneuvered as a captain to build fortresses, he encountered sustained opposition by other Portuguese officials and common soldiers. At Cochin in 1503, Albuquerque quarreled with his cousin, Francisco de Albuquerque, about the wisdom of building a fortress, and his cousin sailed out of the port and took his men with him. After failing to seize Aden as instructed by Lisbon, Albuquerque captured Hormuz in 1507, securing an important port strategically located between the Persian Gulf and the Gulf of Oman. Here he forced the sultan to recognize the suzerainty of the Portuguese crown and to agree to pay for the upkeep of a hundred Portuguese soldiers who would remain in the port and build a fortress. Once again, Albuquerque faced strong opposition from some of his officials and from soldiers to his plan to fortify the town.[41]

Rather than turning away from the program of fortification, Albuquerque embraced the project wholeheartedly and expanded it. One of his first acts as governor was to capture Goa, an island that he thought was well situated for the effective oversight of coastal trade. Some of his captains "told him how useless a place" Goa was and blamed Albuquerque "for wishing to hold on to it."[42] Opposition from his own men to fortification continued. At Malacca, where Albuquerque sailed with a large fleet in 1511, he "heard that some of the captains were saying that it was not in the king's interest to keep Malacca or to build a fortress there."[43] Albuquerque reportedly gathered the captains together and assured them that all expenses of building and maintaining a fortress would "be met from local taxes."[44] He then repurposed the mosque as a fortress and left soldiers there to man it, with strict instructions (mostly ignored in his absence) for them to stay in place.[45] On returning to the western Indian Ocean, Albuquerque found that the men he had left in charge at Goa had been spreading rumors that his fleet would not return and the king would name another governor. They had neglected the fortifications, and "a stretch of the old wall of the city, dating from Muslim times, fell down and nobody would mend it."[46]

The project of building fortresses depended on seizing existing towns and altering their layout and buildings. Defeated rulers were taxed to pay for fortresses. At Cochin, Almeida insisted that the king fund stone fortifications, and he made his point by setting a partially constructed wooden fortress on fire.[47] Often the Portuguese acquired stone for building by tearing down mosques. The symbolism was not lost on anyone: Muslims regarded the looting as a provocation, and an attack on Islam, while the Portuguese celebrated the desecration of the mosques for the same reasons. But there were other implications, too. Mosques in Indian Ocean ports owed their construction to investments by Muslim merchants for whom mosques were signs of the status and acceptance of Muslim communities in littoral societies. Built in a "commercial monsoon style" that reflected Hindu temple motifs, mosques were typically the most visible structures in port cities, often situated directly on the sea and at prominent sites. Cochin held as many as thirty mosques.[48] The buildings represented both the rise of Islam in the region and the dominance of Muslim merchants over trade routes coveted by the Portuguese.

Given the symbolic value of fortresses and the need for defensive positions in the face of militant opposition by some littoral polities, it might seem odd that Portuguese captains and soldiers were reluctant to support the fortification program. But time spent constructing and defending garrisons was time taken away from potentially lucrative raiding, and most Portuguese sought advancement and wealth through plunder. Whereas the highest officials in the East came from the landed nobility in Portugal and were positioning themselves for significant crown patronage on their return to Lisbon, most mid-ranking officials belonged to lesser noble families, and many were younger sons who had had no prospects of inheriting property in Portugal. They were in the East to make their fortunes, or at least to make their way, and they did not want to devote their energies to filling royal coffers, gaining royal recognition for Albuquerque, or defending outposts, however strategically located. Portuguese soldiers had even stronger incentives to raid. If it was received at all, payment to them for crown service usually arrived late, and it was rarely enough to keep them out of poverty. Most men had little chance of ever sailing back to Portugal since they required permission to return, and they found themselves permanently in a loosely structured empire starved for manpower. By 1516, there were about 4,000 Portuguese in Asia. Even in the 1530s, when voyages between Lisbon and Goa became more frequent, of the 21,000 Portuguese who departed for Asia, only about half returned.[49]

Men of all ranks had incentive and opportunity to go raiding. Unofficial attacks on Asian shipping were rarely recorded, for obvious reasons, but we get the flavor of how raids worked from official accounts, including Albuquerque's own letters to the king. On the first voyage against Aden, his men captured a series of small craft they encountered in the harbor, and they sacked both small and large coastal towns. At Muscat, the men "entered within the walls by force of arms and killed many men," and they held the town "until we had laden our ships with everything that was there." When Albuquerque's fleet captured Hormuz, "a great number of dead Muslims floated to the surface of the water" in the harbor, and Albuquerque's men spent a full eight days "harvesting" the valuables on the corpses, "during which time some of [the soldiers] gained much profit by what they found."[50] Captive taking, including by individual soldiers, was commonplace. Albuquerque described an attack on a village off the east coast of Africa during which fleeing villagers threw themselves into the sea. Besides nearly a thousand who were killed or drowned, he reported, numerous captives were scooped up by ship crews, "for the captain-major had given leave for every man to take as many as he liked."[51]

Albuquerque recognized the interdependencies—and the tensions—between raiding and his authority to govern. Portuguese fleets and factories, he noted in a 1512 letter to the king, depended directly on "whatever prizes and booty are captured from the Muslims."[52] The Estado da Índia had to organize raids—and to do so in a widening circle as peace agreements with various port rulers diminished immediate targets for lawful attacks. At the same time, the efforts of enterprising captains to lure able-bodied men to serve on vessels dedicated to private trade or raiding threatened Albuquerque's power and limited his ability to direct violence to advance crown objectives. Albuquerque parried with his captains over the service of soldiers and the command of royal ships. He intervened to seize the fleet of Diogo Lopes de Sequeira, dispatched from Lisbon with instructions to sail to Ceylon and Malacca, and led the planned expedition to Malacca himself.[53] And he complained to the king that at Goa, captains "put a gangway on shore and took from me all the good and healthy men that there were in India and left me with hospitals and houses full of sick. They also removed from me all my artisans and prisoners awaiting trial."[54]

South Asian polities presented another source of competition for labor and loyalty. Some men—it is impossible to know how many—left Portuguese-controlled ports and joined Muslim or Hindu communities, where some converted.[55] Marriage to non-Christians made their return unlikely. The threat became the stuff of official comment in a case reported to Lisbon involving one of Albuquerque's captains, João Machado, who had returned from long residence in a Muslim community near Goa. Machado brought his wife with him to Goa, and according to one account claimed that he had murdered his children before leaving the Muslim court where he had served as an interpreter. Whether true or not, the grim tale was no doubt intended to convince Portuguese officials of the sincerity of Machado's pledge to resettle permanently in the territories of the Estado da Índia.[56] There was no going back after committing such an act.

Fortresses had other military and strategic functions besides serving as repositories of soldiers in service to the Estado da Índia. Fortified ports provided protection to residents and placed ships and soldiers in positions from which they could launch expeditions against ships and other ports. Most fundamentally, fortresses served as points for receiving seized goods. In his instructions to Almeida, the king had directed that all prizes be "unloaded and delivered . . . in the fortress nearest to the region where the prizes were made."[57] Fortified ports were places where officials could report prizes and take the one-fifth share owed to the crown. More broadly, as Albuquerque warned the king in 1513, fortresses were necessary because it was impossible "to rule over a thing so vast as India . . . by strength at sea."[58] In doubting the permanence of sea power, Albuquerque acknowledged that many Asian traders could simply avoid waters near Portuguese-controlled ports. Their evasive tactics would undermine the military and commercial advantages of the network of forts.

Fortresses carried enormous symbolic value. Successive governors pointed to the forts constructed on their watch as strengthening bids for future patronage. The officials were reporting, after all, to a monarch who prized fortresses as potent symbols of Portuguese influence in the Indian Ocean. The association was represented in compendia of maps or views of fortresses of the empire. A short time after the union of the kingdoms of Portugal and Spain in 1580, an atlas of fortress maps was prepared for King Phillip II to detail the extent and character of Portuguese holdings in Asia. The *Livro das Cidades e Fortalezas* (book of cities and fortresses) gathered maps of fortified cities and factories on the Indian Ocean.[59] The images appeared with little text and spare labeling of key features of twenty-nine fortresses, some depicting towns within or alongside fortress walls, others sketching a few streets or buildings. The garrison views are ordered (more or less) from west to east, as if composing a tour of Portuguese holdings from Mozambique to Malacca.[60] The volume did not just convey information *about* the Portuguese empire in the East; it was a visual representation *of* the empire. In the same way that mosques had communicated the influence of Muslim merchants in Indian Ocean ports, fortresses made Portuguese power legible, at home and abroad. They projected both the permanence of the Portuguese enterprise and its capacity for regional violence.

Making Households

Command over a string of fortresses did not complete the foundations of empire. Portuguese officials maneuvered to promote its corollary: communities of households. Like the construction of fortresses, the policy of encouraging marriages of Portuguese men to local women initially issued from the crown. The king warned Almeida to keep vigilant about "the men keeping company with the women of the land" because "this is a thing that causes great offense to the natives."[61] It was a short step from here to encouraging marriage, also with the goal of promoting order. In 1507, the king wrote to the captain of Kilwa that if he got local women to marry the *degredados* (convicts) assigned to the fortress he would make "the land more peaceful and have better service out of them."[62]

As governor, Albuquerque soon identified the formation of households as crucial to effective Portuguese power in the region. With encouragement (but few specifics) from Lisbon, he put in place incentives to encourage Portuguese men to marry local women. First at Cochin and then at Goa, Albuquerque offered soldiers direct payments if they married, and he distributed patronage accordingly, by appointing married men to lucrative positions, for example as fortress commanders, and assigning them plots of land. Designated as *casados* (married men), heads of household became eligible to participate in municipal governance, and their presence gave garrisons the formal character of Portuguese towns.[63] Marriages also created instant Christian communities of respectable size, as wives were expected to convert, along with household servants and slaves.[64] Christianization was a goal intimately connected to security— and to the larger objectives of creating stability in garrison towns, transforming them into pieces of the Portuguese realm, and reinforcing the authority of imperial officials over commerce and plunder.

As with his fortification scheme, Albuquerque's marriage policy met with the opposition of captains who were competing with him for the labor and loyalties of Portuguese soldiers.[65] At Goa, he complained, a "rebellious counsel" of men had set out to "wreck the whole enterprise" while Albuquerque was in Malacca. In the face of this "evil," Albuquerque called for the king's full support for "the entire mixed marriage project."[66] He warned that there were plenty of Portuguese in the East who would "do their utmost to spoil and obstruct" his sponsorship of marriages. And he bluntly declared that opposition to the marriage policy was "the worst vexation that I have at present in India."[67]

Albuquerque's vexation jumps off the pages of his letters to the king. He raged about a Dominican friar who was inserting himself into marriage matters and undermining Albuquerque's authority over the assignment of local women to Portuguese men. Writing to the king, the

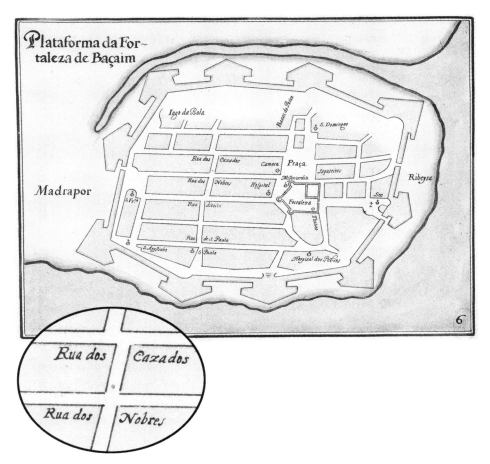

FIGURE 3.2. Portuguese Fortress of Baçaim (Vasai) with inset showing street labeled "Rua dos Cazados" ("Street of Married Men"). Redrawn from João Teixeira de Albernaz, *Plantas das cidades, portos, e fortalezas da conquista da India Oriental* (ca. 1650).

governor described the case of a woman "seized in Goa" who had been sold to a Portuguese physician, identified only as Afonso. Because Albuquerque "had not authorized the match," he confiscated the woman and had her "instructed in the Christian faith and married to a man who was asking for her hand." Here and in other cases, we find Albuquerque personally directing the assignment of women to Portuguese men. This case took a twist when the friar conspired with Afonso to reclaim the woman by having her declare in church that she had married involuntarily. Albuquerque ordered the arrest of Afonso but explained to the king that he refrained from punishing Afonso "because he was a physician and said that he intended to marry in India, and especially because the *casados* asked me to."[68] Albuquerque was trumpeting his role as the protector of local order, in contrast to the unruliness and impropriety encouraged by the friar, who "constantly preached against the marriages of the *casados* and against me."[69]

No amount of detail about conflicts over women seemed too petty to be left out of Albuquerque's letters to the king. Albuquerque wrote that while he was in Malacca, he had "arranged the marriage of a woman of good repute and appearance from Goa with a certain nobleman." When the woman's husband died, she married another Portuguese man, and at the ceremony, yet another man "fell in love with this woman" and bribed the same corrupt friar to annul the marriage and install the woman in a residence where the smitten man "visited her to take his pleasure with her."[70] The emphasis in Albuquerque's account was not on the plight or suffering of the unprotected woman but on the disruption and impertinence of the men's actions: the unseemly lusting after the woman at her wedding, the illegal bribery to annul the marriage, and the complicity in passing her from man to man, whether through marriage or not. Irregular marriages and disorderly households made for unstable settlements.[71]

The point was to assert the legitimacy of imperial power over local liaisons. Albuquerque specifically addressed the dangers of Portuguese subjects forming relationships with local women without Estado da Índia approval. He explained, in this case without providing details, that at Cochin he had to "put an end to certain evils that were being committed" as Portuguese men sought out local women. The dangers did not end with the formation of households, since unwieldy and unregulated households could be sites of religious contamination, and even robbery. Albuquerque lamented that some "newly converted Christian ladies had ten, fifteen or even twenty people in their households, cousins and brothers and other relations, who were not

Christians but had dealings with them, and there were other heathen houses where the Moslems of Cochin came to sleep with the Christian women." Large, religiously mixed households were an entry point for thieves and spies, according to the governor. They "gave shelter to heathen and Moslem men from outside the city, whose occupation it was to entice male and female slaves to rob their masters and flee." Such households were described as magnets for Portuguese men who, "weary of sleeping with Christian women, have gone to live with these heathen women."[72] Albuquerque was certain that the threat of disorder was real and systemic. The "misdeeds and sins" had "many times caused Cochin to be burned and reduced to ashes."[73] Seeking to contain the problem, Albuquerque proposed restricting Portuguese households to one area within the town.

Attempts to control the movements of Portuguese subjects and local women complemented household and marriage regulation. At the same time that Albuquerque claimed that the "business of the *casados*" was going well and that many Portuguese artisans were marrying in Goa, Cannanore, and Cochin, he reported that he was still battling to control a lively market in women and had received frequent complaints from *casados* about "how many women have been taken from Goa without my permission and by certain men who have held them."[74] In contrast to these men, he had "never handed over a woman to anybody except on condition that, if he wishes to marry her, he should make some provision for her," and he declared that "nobody should take a woman out of Goa without my permission." Albuquerque presented as an obvious conclusion that the king should "order the natives of the island of Goa to be evicted and the *casados* to be given the land." [75] Controlling women and composing households would establish Goa as a settlement of Christians firmly under Portuguese rule.

The practice of placing women "of good repute and appearance" with high-ranking men sustained Portuguese networks of patronage.[76] It also conformed to patterns of practice in the wider region. The circulation of elites and their insertion into local societies through intermarriage were common in the littoral societies of the western Indian Ocean.[77] So was the taking of war captives, with women generally outnumbering men as captives and being incorporated into households as slaves, non-slave servants, and wives—fluid categories.[78] Across the region, gifts of women occurred in exchange for concessions and as a means of solidifying loyalties.[79] As one historian warns, it is a mistake to regard Indian Ocean slavery as purely domestic or, for that matter, as an institution; instead, "slaving was regulated alongside marriage and conversion."[80] Somewhat unoriginal in aligning policies on captive taking, control over women and marriage, and the extension of regional power, the Portuguese were assimilating into an Indian Ocean complex of slaving and slavery, not inventing or imposing a new regime.[81]

The number of captives seized in raids and subsumed into Portuguese households is difficult to measure. Most marriages were with women who were living in and around Goa.[82] But there is no doubt that Albuquerque regarded the control of women as key to turning Goa from a garrison into a town and as essential to securing his authority over freewheeling raiders. Albuquerque complained that women were being "taken from Goa without my permission by certain men who have held them," while he bragged to the king about his success at making marriages not only for many "gentlemen" but also for "blacksmiths and carpenters, turners and gunners." He urged the king to facilitate more permanent settlement in Goa by providing land to Portuguese household heads.[83] Repeatedly, he explained to the king that the only way to avoid a permanent state of war in the East was to construct and maintain fortresses, send "plenty of troops and good weapons," and encourage men to come to Asia for life.[84] These measures in turn depended on the ability to hold men in the service of the Estado da Índia. Albuquerque's most strident conflicts in India were with captains and middling nobles who wanted to control troops, ships, and war captives independently from the Estado da Índia or the crown. At one point, in a telling phrase, he remarked on the urgent need for men to "sell their property" in Portugal and commit to a career of service in India, "and not for the sake of turning gentlemen's private houses into fortresses."[85] India, Albuquerque informed the king, "must of necessity be settled."[86] Fortresses had to be converted into governed towns, and that meant making them into places where subjects held residence and the responsibilities of household and community governance.

Attention to the triad of commercial objectives, military projects, and settler interests continued after Albuquerque's death in 1515. By the 1520s, the Portuguese were at war with Mappila Muslims in the western Indian Ocean, and they were making uneven commercial inroads in the Bay of Bengal through the awkward, private diplomacy of Portuguese *alevantados*—traders indifferent to the authority of proximate crown officials. The Estado da Índia exercised relatively little authority over Bay of Bengal Portuguese communities and traders, who collaborated with royal agents without answering to them.[87] Meanwhile, the Estado da Índia struggled to extend territorial control or effective rule over lands to the north of Goa surrounding Chaul, Daman, Diu, and Baçaim, where Muslim and Hindu residents vastly outnumbered Portuguese subjects.[88] The status and political role of *casados* evolved, too. Officials began to regard them as not fully Portuguese and increasingly questioned their loyalty to the crown.[89]

Tensions roiling Portuguese operations in the Indian Ocean in the late sixteenth and early seventeenth centuries gave rise to a common characterization of the empire as divided into "formal" and "informal" (or "shadow") components.[90] Certainly the split, already visible in Albuquerque's time, between centralization, championed by royal officials, and decentralizing forces created openings for self-interested maneuvering by middling nobility who favored plunder, trade, and improvisation. But the formal-informal distinction is somewhat misleading. Private and public spheres intermingled in overlapping networks of Portuguese nobility, officials, and Muslim merchants.[91] Public and private capacities for violence were deeply intertwined. In the next century, the shifting relationship between captive taking and imperial authority kept women, raiding, and local governance at the center of the global Portuguese empire.[92] As repositories for plunder, households held the key to turning booty into property and integrating captives into communities. Calls for the protection of households colored private raids as parts of defensive small wars.

An Army or a Colony

A similar process unfolded in a very different place: the seventeenth-century Caribbean. British ventures into the Atlantic world outlined sharp, repeating tensions between planting and plunder. A proven strategy of enrichment through attacks on Spanish shipping in the days of Francis Drake and John Hawkins inaugurated a private and public drive for maritime raiding, and early colonizing to a large extent centered on the goal of creating bases from which raiders could reach Spanish sea lanes.[93] Yet it was impossible to establish viable footholds from which to mount raids without both planting and fortification. Like the Portuguese in the Indian Ocean, the English in the Atlantic and Caribbean sought to root households in place and to construct and maintain fortifications while pursuing opportunistic raids on foreign shipping. As with the Portuguese, these projects competed for labor and embroiled small communities in sharp disputes over the regulation of households and the distribution and defense of property.

Colonial officials haltingly worked to assemble a *local* right to sponsor violence. Raiding continued even (or especially) in the context of interimperial peace. Officials promoted raiding in concert with a litany of strategies centered on household formation: distributing land, seeking new sources of servants, encouraging immigration by families from other colonies, and sponsoring trade in enslaved Africans for sale to planter households. It is not an exaggeration to say that the legal underpinnings of plantation slavery began with measures to expand the size and viability of households in English colonies.

The centrality of households to early English colonizing was on bright display in the puritan colony of Providence Island. Located off the coast of what is today Nicaragua, Providence Island was a tiny outpost in a vast Spanish sphere of influence. Its brief history as an English colony, from its founding in 1629 to a devastating attack by Spanish forces in 1641, highlights the limitations posed by the presence of households headed by free men who were dependent on servile labor—and on the strategy of depriving servants, and later slaves, of the capacity to form households.[94] Unsure of the colony's viability, Puritan sponsors in England decided not to send families in the first wave of Providence Island settlement. But their inability to envision a structure other than one based on household units led the Providence Island Company directors to group free men and servants into "artificial families" composed of about seven men, one to serve as a head of household authorized to draw goods from the company.[95] The "families" were charged with responsibility for the good order of their members and for contributing to the protection of the island by building strong houses and contributing labor to the work on fortifications. The liberal terms offered to servants, who stood to receive land of their own to work after only two or three years of service, represented one of many ways that the island's sponsors sought to address the problem of manpower.

It quickly became apparent that the system was unworkable. By 1632, island settlers were in near revolt, complaining about the burden of laboring to build fortifications and the dearth of women. Settlers also petitioned the company to curb the recklessness of the military men who had endangered the island by Spanish raiding. The Providence Island Company agreed to abandon the system of artificial families and allow the colonists "to sort themselves as they shall see good."[96] At the same time, the adventurers began planning a new infusion of colonists to include families and, especially, more servants—lured, they hoped, by the promise of high status through association with benefactors' wealthy households. As one historian explains, the new recruits were effectively "extensions of the grandees' families."[97]

Providence Island's life as an English colony was cut short by a successful Spanish attack in 1641. But it continued to feature prominently in the imagination of English Atlantic colonizing—not only as an experiment in puritan planting but also as a close approximation, in its final years, of what the historian Stephen Saunders Webb called "garrison government." Increasingly in English colonies, governors-general exercised unified authority over military and civil affairs, embodying, as Webb put it, the awkward reconciliation of "the rules of law and of force."[98] The concentration of political and police powers in the hands of royal officials was matched by the opposition of colonists to infringements on their liberties, a resentment that found its focus in laws imposed by crown or parliament.[99]

On a much bigger scale and in a setting where military command was firmly in place at the start, the conquered island of Jamaica illustrates the pattern very clearly. The English scheme to capture a significant Spanish site in the Caribbean formed the centerpiece of Oliver Cromwell's "Western Design," dreamed up in 1654 and touted as a response to Spanish attacks on British shipping in the western Atlantic and Caribbean. The man chosen by Cromwell to lead the expedition and to command its ground forces, General Robert Venables, was authorized to seize any "Territories, Dominions, and Places belonging unto, in the possession of or claymed by the Spanyards in America."[100] The main target was the island of Hispaniola.

From its inception, the Hispaniola expedition depended on plunder. It began with a chaotic recruitment process that stuffed the ships not with trained soldiers but with men Venables called "raw fellows" and an observer described as "common cheats, thieves, cutpurses, and such like lewd persons."[101] The order to embark came so suddenly that ships carrying stores for the huge army were separated from the fleet and soldiers who sailed without officers "concluded that they were thither brought to be sold to some foreign prince."[102] Conditions worsened at Barbados, where the army, still without sufficient provisions, took on several thousand more recruits. The fleet left Barbados with a huge force of 8,000 soldiers and another 1,000 sailors.[103] The men hoped to profit from the capture of ships and the plunder of conquered ports. Venables's instructions enjoined him to "seize upon al ships and vessels which you find in any of [the Spaniards'] Harbors, and also upon al such goods as you shal find upon the land."[104] At Barbados, the fleet seized sixteen Dutch ships in the harbor, an act that angered island residents trading with the Dutch. The initial haul yielded little of value—most of the trade goods had already been offloaded—until the capture of a Dutch ship carrying 211 slaves, who were sold to island residents.[105]

Conflict over the distribution of booty was already roiling voyage politics. The navy commander, General William Penn, pressured Venables to sign a commission appointing Penn's nephew as prize agent, an arrangement that made it easier to siphon the proceeds of ship captures into private pockets, Venables later charged.[106] The question of shares in plunder became still more hotly disputed in Hispaniola. Three commissioners accompanying the fleet prevailed in the view that Venables should impose strict limits on the booty that soldiers might keep. Just after landing on Hispaniola, the invading army learned that plundered goods would have to be surrendered to the public store for redistribution. Venables agreed to deliver the bad news to the men on shore but also warned the commissioners that the soldiers "had both pay and Pillage" in England and that the order would likely strip their enthusiasm for the fight.[107]

The limit on plunder was just one of many factors that set the conditions for a disastrous outing. The army was set ashore far from its target and without enough fresh water and food to sustain a cross-country march. With as many as a thousand English soldiers dead in just a week and many more ill, the army scrambled back to the ships and the fleet ran for Jamaica. The decision to abandon Hispaniola was one of a string of doubtful decisions that would later land Venables in the Tower of London, imprisoned for abandoning his army.

At the time of its conquest, Jamaica was a sparsely populated, mostly agricultural, and weakly fortified island. It seemed like a very poor substitute for the rich prize of Hispaniola. The conquest itself was a cakewalk. Hoping that the English would take on water and whatever goods they could find before leaving, the Spaniards negotiated a quick surrender in the main town and began carrying their goods and livestock into the hills, where they would begin to organize a vexing guerrilla campaign against the ragged invaders.

In a fantasy of orderly transition, Venables presented the Spaniards with a treaty that affirmed Spanish households' possession of all property—except slaves—and provided transportation off the island for household heads and their dependents, if requested. Venables informed the Spanish that the English "came not to pillage, but to plant." It was a strained argument with a plunder-hungry army at his heels, but Venables had brought his wife with him and testified that his own plans were to set down roots and plant. He could barely assert his authority over the famished army.[108] Pressing again to control raiding and, now, to prevent his soldiers from being picked off by Spanish guerrillas, he issued an order that no soldier should wander into the countryside alone, even just to hunt wild cattle or search for provisions. To the starving soldiers, the order seemed like a continuation of the ban on plunder sprung on them in Hispaniola.[109]

There was very little to pillage, in any case. Soldiers who knew "how to do little else except to Plunder" were soon wasting away.[110] A Council of War ordered plantations distributed to the soldiers by lot, but they had few tools for planting and almost no knowledge about what to do. Venables wrote to London begging for "Brandy, Bread, Meal, Pease, and Rice."[111] His officers proposed that they might pay out of their own pockets for servants to be sent to the island, possibly from Scotland.[112] London officials agreed that the island needed settling, and they tried various measures to send laborers. They debated how and whether to offer an allowance to each of "1,000 Irish girls . . . to be sent to Jamaica."[113] Wives would be encouraged "to go to their husbands in Jamaica," and soldiers would be offered payment of back wages for transporting wives and children there.[114] Already in 1655, London officials were proposing incentives in the form of grants in land for the resettlement of colonists from New England and Nevis.[115]

There was no recipe for constructing an economically viable colony. After six months, only half the great army that had invaded Hispaniola remained alive. Near death himself, Venables sailed home, where he would be arrested. The soldiers who stayed in Jamaica ate through the cattle "within neare twelve miles" of St. Jago, the main town, and moved on to eating their dogs. Visitors found the town and its surroundings dotted with shallow graves.[116] When Colonel William Beeston arrived in 1660, he described Jamaica's residents as "an Army but without Pay."[117] In London, the Committee of the Council of Foreign Plantations came to the same conclusion. Jamaica was neither "an Army, nor a Colonie" and its English inhabitants were men "neither fit to defend, nor improve" it.[118]

A series of commanders, governors, and deputy governors in Jamaica continued the struggle to promote planting. They found that even if they succeeded in assigning land to men willing to plant, they faced the continuing problem of how to recruit labor for planter households.

Initially each free person on the island above the age of twelve was offered thirty acres of land by patent—a measure intended both to lure
new recruits to the island from other colonies and to turn soldiers into
planters.[119] There were repeated calls for more servants to be sent to do
the work of planting, a request always balanced against fears that Jamaica
was too unstable to receive them. In London, the Committee of the Council of Foreign Plantations fretted that white servants would have to be
"drawn out of gaols and Prisons" and that Blacks would prove "trecher-
ous and unsteadie people." In Jamaica, officials worried that the dearth
of stable households ready to receive dependents made it likely that servants who reached the island would join the ranks of the unfed.[120]

Raiding for captives in Spanish colonies or Indigenous communities
represented another potential source of unfree labor. English invaders
in Jamaica were entering a region where seizing plunder in the form of
human beings was a well-honed practice. The English had engaged in it
since Elizabethan times, when Drake, Hawkins, and others had seized
enslaved (and some free) people in Spanish ports to ransom, sell, or
hold in slavery.[121] Like other European seafarers in the region, English
crews also captured slave-trading vessels and sold their human cargo.[122]
As the English angled for contracts to trade slaves to Spanish ports and
imagined Jamaica as a future node of circum-Caribbean slave trading,
they continued to search for opportunities to organize raids and capture
enslaved people from other colonies. On the Mosquito Coast in Central
America, they took Indigenous captives while stimulating raids by Indigenous groups to generate captives for purchase.[123] Privateers sailing
with commissions from Jamaica, as we will see, also carried off captives
for sale in English colonies.

The push to create planter households developed in close connection
with raids for captives and with policy shifts to enable people to be
traded as property. English law provided only indirect mechanisms for
enforcing contracts for the sale of persons, so early exchanges in the
Caribbean involved transfers of land—with people attached—rather
than agreements to transfer ownership of people.[124] Privateers could
work around the lack of clear mechanisms for establishing property in
people by trading humans for goods or by contracting in advance for

captives secured in raids.[125] But raiders and merchants were not operating on their own. The crown had a clear interest in cultivating households capable of holding captives as property. In Barbados and Virginia, the crown directly tied grants in land to grantees' importation of servants. As Holly Brewer has shown, the association between owning land and owning people took shape as a matter of royal policy.[126]

Trends in Jamaica solidified the link between landed property and enslavement. Governor Thomas Modyford was instructed to grant thirty acres of land to household heads for each servant and family member imported to the island. Modyford urged the crown to go further and award land beyond the initial grant "to such as have good Estates, & doe ingage to bring on more people." The king and Privy Council agreed.[127] The creation of large plantations in this way in effect reversed the terms of the equation. Instead of granting land to facilitate the peopling of settlements, the crown was making ownership of human beings a prerequisite for acquiring large tracts of land. Legal change was not just creating households but also establishing a framework for household property in land and people. The framework was also built, not incidentally, for war.

A Right to Make Local War

Narratives of English piracy in the Caribbean tend to pass quickly over the story of the army's crisis and the struggle to turn the garrison into a colony. Many accounts highlight, or even begin with, the period's richest prize, the 1668 capture of Portobelo by Captain Henry Morgan, and most emphasize the exploits of footloose men who collected in Jamaica's Port Royal and created a raucous culture of privateering.[128] A series of spectacular Jamaica-based raids of the 1660s and early 1670s represent, in this telling, a colorful beginning to the "golden age of piracy." Opportunities for plunder drew impoverished men to Port Royal, where raiding, officially condemned, was unofficially sponsored by colonial officials sharing in the profits. We arrive, then, at two stories of early Jamaica: one focused on English privateers' search for booty and another on the rise of a plantation society centered on sugar and slaves.

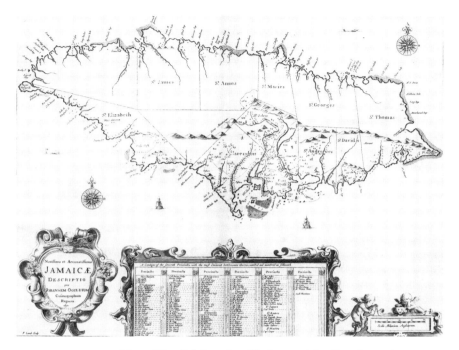

FIGURE 3.3. Map of English Jamaica. *Blathwayt Atlas*, London, 1671.

But these two stories should be merged. Households bridged these phenomena and sketched intricate links between Jamaica as a plantation colony and Jamaica as a pirate nest. Both trends activated attempts to recast private raiding as legitimate public war.

As they did for the Portuguese in the Indian Ocean, households in Jamaica served as the nexus between the continued allure of raiding and growing interest in planting and property in human beings. Men sought plunder to support their efforts to build planter households, and officials regarded opportunities for plunder as essential aids to island order and to the vision of Jamaica as a settled place prepared to receive captive labor. The connection was at its most direct when raiders targeted concentrations of enslaved people in Spanish and Dutch colonies and transported them to Jamaica or other colonies for sale. The proliferation of households also fortified arguments about the right to sponsor raiding and make local war.

As directives from London to rein in raiding gave way to tolerance and active sponsorship of privateering, Jamaican officials claimed a local right to make war. Some arguments for local war—or peacetime violence—invoked the principle that European treaties did not apply "beyond the line."[129] But commentary on the lawfulness of raiding often mentioned this principle only in passing, while highlighting other arguments about the colony's right to defend itself against attack. As occurred with the Portuguese in the Indian Ocean, the logic of self-defense was rooted in the colony's constructed reputation as a community of households. As in the Indian Ocean, too, the possibility of plunder grounded visions of colonial order.

In Jamaica, officials recognized raiding as an outlet for disgruntled and impoverished former soldiers. When a regiment mutinied in 1661 and the soldiers declared that "they would live no more as an Army," English officials reported that the only way to quiet the mutineers was to allow them to plunder the dead officers' houses.[130] The first governor of Jamaica, Edward D'Oyley, received orders to "disband the Army & encourage them to settling the country" in 1662. But he soon pivoted to sponsoring attacks on Spanish ports.[131] Later, Governor Modyford noted that offering commissions to privateers allowed men to resist the lure of French privateering. The Council of Jamaica conjectured, too, that profits from plunder would enable "many to buy slaves and settle plantations."[132] In general, Colonel Beeston observed, hungry men, "being Por & wanting conveniencys to settle," joined in raiding to get the resources they needed to turn fledgling plantation households into growing concerns.[133]

A colony of "composed families" looked to raiding as a means to gather unfree labor.[134] An early ban on the sale in Jamaica of captives seized from Spanish colonies was overturned in 1662. Increasingly dwarfed by the trade in African captives, the profits from plunder in human beings were nevertheless significant, and regional slaving continued alongside growth of the Atlantic slave trade.[135] Attacks led by "privateers"—the word coined to distinguish sponsored raiders from pirates, or entirely freelance raiders—created opportunities to seize captives, including many who were probably free in Spanish colonies, alongside treasure.[136]

For obvious reasons, few documents tally the proportions of enslaved and free captives taken in raids or note whether or where captives
were ransomed or sold. But English and Spanish records provide revealing glimpses of a robust trade. In 1661, for example, a conflict erupted
over the right to profit from the sale of captives seized by a British naval
vessel in the Port Royal harbor with 180 slaves on board. D'Oyley sold
the captives to a Quaker merchant and a Spanish ship, claiming that his
authority to make the sale derived from his role as general and reminding
the Council of Jamaica that he answered only to the crown.[137] In 1666,
Edward Mansfield, sailing with a commission from Tortuga, recaptured
Santa Catalina (the Spanish name for Providence Island), seized "150
negroes"—the label disguised the capture of some free subjects as
slaves—and carried them to Jamaica.[138] Profits from taking captives were
hardly negligible. When Henry Morgan took Portobelo in 1668, his crew
seized enslaved and free inhabitants of the town and held them for
ransom.[139] In 1670, Morgan and his men sacked Panamá and carried off
between five hundred and six hundred captives to sell in Jamaica.[140] A
decade later, a handful of those captives managed to escape on a French
sloop. We learn from testimony they gave when they sought sanctuary
in a Spanish port near Cartagena that they had been enslaved, alongside
other seized captives, on a Jamaican plantation west of Port Royal.[141]

The English had already adopted a flexible approach to justifying
local violence. In 1654, when Venables inquired about the legal foundation for his expedition against Hispaniola, he was informed "That either
there was Peace with the Spaniards in the West Indies, or not. If Peace,
[the Spaniards] had Violated it, and to seek reparation was Just. If we
had no Peace then there was nothing acted against Articles with
Spain."[142] A series of officials enthusiastically took up the search for legal
cover for violence against Spanish targets. They were motivated partly
by self-interest since they stood to share in the profits from raiding. But
private violence had to be given a public spin. In 1661, on the same day
that D'Oyley received news from the governor of Cuba of a British
peace with Spain, soldiers brought in a hundred enslaved people captured in the mountains and claimed them as prizes. D'Oyley called a
council of war that declared the peace to be inapplicable to raiding in

and around Jamaica. Not only was the raiding "beyond the line," D'Oyley recorded, but it was also essential to the livelihood of so many who were living "only upon spoil and depredation."[143] In a similarly creative response to a command from London to shift Jamaica from raiding to planting, Deputy Governor Charles Lyttelton offered his understanding "that the war with privateers was not intended to be taken off by the King's instructions, so [he] has not thought it his duty to call them in."[144]

Some governors went still further to assert their independent right to make war. In 1662, Governor Thomas Windsor declared "a Warr with the Spaniards on this Ground." In defending this extraordinary act, Windsor could point to his instructions, which had directed him to pursue peaceful commerce with Spanish settlements but also "to endeavor to settle such trade by force" if the English were refused the right to trade.[145] He held the "power in himself to make eithr Warr or Peace," he asserted, because the Spaniards had refused to welcome him to trade in Puerto Rico and Santo Domingo on his voyage to Jamaica.[146] Windsor's declaration of a local war had real and immediate effect. It led to the assembly of a fleet of eleven ships and 1,300 men to attack St. Iago on Cuba, a raid that yielded a rich booty whose distribution on the men's return "made the people quiet."[147]

Under Thomas Modyford, the rationale for local war, or for violence in defiance of the peace with Spain, developed greater sophistication. Modyford began his tenure as a committed slave trader seeking to advance regional peace to further the crown's interest in expanding commerce and profits from slave trading through peace with Spain; in Jamaica, his tune and tactics changed.[148] In 1666, the Council of Jamaica, operating under Modyford's influence, openly defied crown instructions when it issued commissions for attacks on Spanish targets. Modyford trotted out some familiar—and some new—arguments, emphasizing the duty to defend "the interest of the island."[149] He creatively stretched this logic several months later, when he authorized more privateering against Spanish targets on the strength of rumors that France had declared war and the probability that a war with France would prompt Spanish attacks on Jamaica.[150] Modyford was claiming the right to authorize preemptive strikes to keep the colony safe.

The argument that raiding was essential to the island's security gave cover to privateers' most lucrative raids. When Henry Morgan sailed against Portobelo in 1668, he was instructed by Modyford to collect evidence of Spanish intentions to invade Jamaica. In 1670, with news in hand of the coming peace with Spain, Modyford gave Morgan a commission that allowed him to attack Spanish ports if he discovered information about a planned attack on Jamaica. Unsurprisingly, Morgan obliged.[151] Here and in less celebrated cases, the rationale for raiding fit with representations of Jamaica as a settled colony—a community of households—with a right to self-defense.

Jamaica was increasingly being represented as a political community composed of white households commanding Black labor.[152] The racialization of language about households is reflected in William Beeston's accounts of the kidnapping of women in the 1670s. Beeston's narrative, not unlike Albuquerque's letters to the king, devoted lengthy passages to the plight of individual white women seized in Anglo-French raids while he mentioned only in passing the continuing practice of seizing many more enslaved men and women in the same raids. When the English landed "Men of Warr Sloops" on the coast of Hispaniola, Beeston reported, they met with a Frenchwoman, the wife of an Irishman who had joined the French in raids. Beeston claimed that the men "would have left her there where they found her but she Earnestly desir'd to go with them & be quit of her Husband." Later the husband landed with a small force at a "lone house at St. Elizabeth" that belonged to a minister's widow, Mrs. Barron, and he "Plundered all the Negroes Household Goods & all she had Tortur'd her to Confess if she had any Money & then took away with him her Maiden Daughter." At about the same time, a group of privateers on the north side of Jamaica seized a couple, Major Terry and his wife, and "strip'd her to her shift & beat her at length for Ransom."[153]

These acts of violence against a few white women raised for Beeston questions about the rules of war under which the privateers were fighting. He considered the kidnappings "inhumanities beyond the common customs of War amongst Christians," even as he promised retribution in kind. After Mrs. Barron appealed to him to aid in the return of her daughter, Beeston sent an envoy to the French commander, Monsieur

Ducass, with a flag of truce and a demand for punishment of the offenders. If Ducass did not comply, the envoy was to "tell him that I would make satisfaction to ourselves on any of their People that we met with." The mission to Ducass made little impression; the envoy's boat was seized and plundered, and everyone on board was taken prisoner.[154] When the French later landed in force, Beeston made special note of their violence toward women, some of whom the French "suffer'd the Negroes to Violate and dug some out of their graves so that there was never more inhumane barbarities Committed by any Turks or Infidels in the World." The French, he reported with much less concern and without comment on the law of nations, also carried off "about a thousand three hundred Negroes."[155]

By the time Beeston was writing about these raids, a rapid expansion of the trade in enslaved people from Africa was making sugar plantations powered by slavery a grim reality. Island and metropolitan elite interests were moving into closer alignment. The influx of enslaved captives would not have been possible without earlier local and imperial actions combining to establish households as legal entities authorized to limit the rights of human beings under their command and to hold captives as property. The same moves lent legitimacy to continued raiding. Crown and colony worked together to convert Jamaica from a garrison to a colony. As with Portuguese garrisons in the Indian Ocean, Jamaica's viability rested on the constitution of households as repositories of soldiers, receptacles for captives and property, agents for the command and disciplining of enslaved people, and elemental units in political communities with their own right of self-defense.

Spaces of Violence

As Europeans struggled to define the political and legal properties of places far from imperial centers, they confronted the limits of legal imagination. Called on to justify violence, they improvised, and they relied on analogies. War built imperial households by packing them with captives subordinate to the will of petty sovereigns. Protecting property in empires also required more: fusing private violence and public authority. The alignment took place in part through the reorganization of imperial space to defend communities of households.

At the beginning of this chapter, I noted the lengths to which Francisco Suárez went to specify the ways that private or limited war could form part of public war. Later European writers delved further into questions about the relation of private violence to war. In *De Iure Belli ac Pacis* (*The Rights of War and Peace*), published in 1625, the Dutch legal writer Hugo Grotius argued for the right of private parties, as well as public entities, to use force. He had already published *Mare Liberum* (*The Free Sea*) in 1609 arguing for the lawfulness of the Dutch seizure of the Portuguese ship *Santa Catarina* because the Portuguese were injuring the Dutch by violating their natural right to travel freely on the seas.[156] Grotius was building on scholastic arguments, in particular Francisco de Victoria's assertion that Spaniards' legitimate title to the Indies was based on the refusal by *indios* to recognize Spaniards' rights under natural law to travel and trade. A political community (*civitas*) could act to limit and channel those rights but could not extinguish them. Grotius pushed the logic further to define as legitimate *private* actions to punish violators of natural law.

Not all violence by private parties was legitimate, Grotius clarified. The right to punish violators of natural law was activated in places where no civil authority was present, "as on the Seas, in a Wilderness, in desert Islands; and any other Places where there is no Civil Government."[157] Authorization of war varied depending on location and on warmakers' relation to political authority. Piecing together Grotius's logic, the historian Annabel Brett refers us back to the opening sentence of *De Iure Belli ac Pacis*, in which Grotius described two categories of people "bound by no common civil law."[158] One group comprised those "of different nations among themselves," a designation that placed private war squarely within the *ius gentium*, the law of nations. The other, more significant in relation to raiding, encompassed "those who have not yet come together into a nation."[159]

While identifying the limits to civil controls on violence, Grotius sought to narrow the definition of formal war. What he called *bellum solemne* (solemn war) was a declared war in which one side had a just cause. Like Suárez, Grotius avoided a contradiction between his focus on solemn war and his analysis of possible justifications for violence that fell short of solemn war. Suárez had written of "limited" war; Grotius referred to the possibility of "a publick war not Solemn." Such a war might "be made be made both without any Formality, and against mere private Persons, and by the Authority of any Magistrate whatever."[160] In various circumstances, violence might acquire the character of legitimate war by approximating the conditions of a solemn war.

Households came subtly into play. A collection of families might not always cohere to form a *civitas*. Grotius avoided this problem by turning to a spatial definition of political community. Only in a solemn war could captured goods be lawfully acquired by bringing things (or people) within the borders of a place under some authority. Practices of marking off territory were therefore important aids to constructing a right to wage war. Fortifications might mark a controlled territory very effectively. So might the presence of an army, which itself could stand in for the *civitas*. By implication, designating raiders as members of an army or marking spaces as under military control became symbolic acts in support of the right to make war. Whereas Suárez emphasized the adherence of participants to public goals in legitimate limited wars, Grotius pointed to the way space constructed, as Brett puts it, the "juridical exoskeleton" for war.[161]

A place where armies massed or a fortified place could stand in for home territory. It became a space where booty could be converted to the legitimate spoils of war—and private violence could shade into public war. Suárez, Grotius, and other writers were grappling with the problem of defining the political community to be defended through waging war. They were also describing the way conflicts authorized by private parties might acquire the character of war.

Limited war and the defense of community and property—the themes commingled and collided. As they worked to justify the violence of conquest and colonization, European writers were defining just war in relation to the defense of both physically bounded political communities and more widely distributed rights to property, travel, and trade.[162] Yet we should be careful not to equate empire with the protection of individual rights. Corporate entities and households limited the rights of members and claimed ownership over property.[163] The authority of household heads over others—including women, children, servants, and enslaved people—might vary by time and place, but it was never in doubt as an element of political community. Empires of private-public violence necessarily had households at the center.

Europeans in empires were not *following* Suárez, Grotius, or other writers. Very few had theological or legal training, or for that matter access to legal tracts. And there would be obvious problems of timing if we wanted to trace influence. The Portuguese were acting in the Indian Ocean before Suárez and Grotius were even born. I am suggesting something different than a relation of influence. Imperial agents were confronting versions of the same problems as they sought to encourage household formation and regulate war, and they were producing analogous solutions.

In the Portuguese Estado da Índia and in the English Caribbean, officials improvised to address uncertainties about the legal character of imperial outposts. Portuguese officials were closely attuned to the symbolic significance of fortifications, important not merely for the defense of the empire but also for projecting the very existence, and potential durability, of a Portuguese empire in the East. In Jamaica, the dissolution of the Cromwellian army posed a double threat to English power: it represented military defeat and signaled the impermanence of English footholds in a hemisphere where Spain claimed dominance and Indigenous polities persisted.

Fortified garrisons put empires on the map, but they were not enough to project imperial power. The legitimacy of colonial public authority depended on the constitution of political communities capable of governance, and municipal governance relied on households. In alignment with existing, widespread practices of captivity, households composed civic communities from which officials—Estado da Índia governors and English governors-general—drew their authority. The very existence of communities of households provided officials with reasons to make supposedly defensive war. When governors in Jamaica declared a local war against the Spaniards, they were not just acting in self-interest as sponsors and beneficiaries of lucrative raiding. They were also affirming claims that private raiding served the public good by warding off future attacks and by solidifying English rule in conquered territories. Similarly, Portuguese officials' tolerance for private raiding was more than instrumental; it recognized private actors as arms of the state.

Concern about households permeated early European empires. When Albuquerque wrote to the king about his conflicts with a friar over specific marriages or when Beeston wrote pages about the fate of a single French-born woman taken captive, they were doing more than using colorful details to enliven dull reports. Control over women, servants, and captives loomed large in governors' reports and company deliberations. Albuquerque described opposition to his marriage policy as his "greatest vexation," and he devoted considerable political capital to encouraging the marriage of Portuguese men to local women. On Providence Island and Jamaica, Protestant leaders and military men plotted to root soldiers and servants in households or household-like units, to settle new families from Britain and from other colonies, and to incorporate or assign captives, servants, and land to household heads. In Lisbon and London, king and company followed distant struggles surrounding such issues with interest, and they issued their own series of instructions about the formation and regulation of households, often alongside directives about war.

Piracy—that well-worn and often romanticized phenomenon—took much of its energy and meaning from the legal politics of households. Collections of households bestowed the rights of limited, local war on distant outposts of empire. Imperial and colonial officials assembled their power, and their capacity and right to sponsor war, by seeking to convert garrisons to towns, and armies to colonies. Such strategies cast households as foundational to imperial violence and turned private raids into commonplace elements of public war. Tragically, there was more. Households as legal entities made sprawling garrison empires into prison archipelagos built on dominance over women and the enslavement of Indigenous people, Africans, and their descendants. Entities ostensibly defined by intimacy and limited authority became foundational to a vast system of publicly approved, perpetual violence.

PART II

A World of Armed Peace

The world underwent a series of significant shifts between the middle of the eighteenth century and the end of the nineteenth century. Accounts of global transformations in the period often feature a new vision of international order, one predicated on the dominance of the West within a system of sovereign nation-states. Global order arose, the story goes, out of Enlightenment ideas of secular governance blended with great power diplomacy at the end of the Napoleonic Wars. The Congress of Vienna in 1815 encapsulated the vision of a European balance of power, which then served as a template for international order.

Against this story, part II places conflicts far from Europe at the center of shifts in global law and order. European participants in small, distant wars began to formulate claims about Europe's unique capacity and right to regulate conduct in war. Interventions in the form of strikes by European-sponsored forces multiplied, supposedly aimed at protecting imperial subjects and interests. Older justifications for imperial violence still circulated alongside new assertions about European empires' special role in making and regulating war. The emphasis on European legal authority altered the form and frequency of imperial violence and gave rise to a global regime that I call "armed peace."

The first piece of this new framework involved the Europeanization of the laws of war. Chapter 4 tracks how European claims to authority over conduct in war emerged from the pens of commanders in the field who were enmeshed in multisided conflicts. Navy and army officers were not just military commanders but also legal agents. Even as they improvised, imperial agents narrated their actions in ways that they hoped would impress superiors and sponsors. Their interventions carried broad authorization but also posed the risk of exciting anxieties in Europe about the costs of imperial expansion. Paradoxically, muscular assertions of a right to regulate war debuted in places where European forces found themselves deeply dependent on local allies and fighters. Violence coexisted with pledges of interimperial peace. In some places, multisided proxy wars broke out; in others, imperial alliances produced coordinated campaigns to oppose Indigenous revolts or support settler incursions. Indigenous communities were far from being mere objects of imperial experiments in the use of force. European authority over the laws of war was a story that Europeans told themselves. Their actual political power was often tentative and partial, eclipsing Indigenous sovereignty in bits and pieces, if at all.

New regional orders proliferated. As European agents wrote letter after letter to decry the savagery of Indigenous fighters and the untrustworthiness of imperial rivals, they were also commenting on the legitimacy of a wide array of political communities. Their world was thick with competing jurisdictions. Corporate groups within empires—from town governments to religious communities to trading companies—retained some legal authority, and it could cut against or enhance imperial power. Local groups opposed to empires, or seeking alliances with them, still controlled vast areas. Europeans found it necessary to insist that the regulation of violence was an interpolitical affair. And it had to be.

Some imperial projects brought real change to the arc of war. From the time of the Seven Years' War, between 1756 and 1763—the first global conflict—Europeans were engaged in a race to militarize sprawling empires. They expanded navies, organized new armies and militias, hired mercenaries in greater numbers, intensified efforts to strike formal alliances with local polities, and dispatched armed patrols to regions where they projected commercial advantage and political influence. This new trend of global militarization centered on routines for lawful violence. Patrolling armies and navies carried permanent authorization to engage in small wars, so long as they stayed small.

As commanders and captains decided how much force to use, and when, they gave new meaning to the category "measures short of war." Many or most imperial interventions were described as responses to what I call "protection emergencies"—crises of real or imagined danger to imperial subjects. Commanders acted as legal agents, self-appointed judges, and quasi-diplomats. They punished individuals or groups supposedly responsible for endangering imperial subjects. Their violence was defined and described as limited. But series of small clashes and acts of reprisal surfaced arguments in favor of long waves of extreme violence against subjects redefined as natural enemies.

As with the global regime of plunder analyzed in part I, the regime of armed peace opened the door to atrocity. An orderly legal sequence moved from limited violence to protect subjects to sustained campaigns to protect imperial interests and, in some places, to open-ended crusades to protect order. Just as accusations of truce breaking in early empires facilitated both small violence and indiscriminate slaughter, the conversion of small wars into campaigns of dispossession or extermination in the nineteenth century had a settled, familiar logic. It did not require declarations of martial law, though they often created the conditions for accelerating violence. The regime of armed peace mapped clear pathways from lawful interventions with modest objectives to brutal campaigns of dispossession and extermination.

Imperial agents and European political theorists contributed to the new regime in different registers. In conflicts far from Europe, the shift from protecting imperial subjects to protecting regional order involved a move from treating individuals as criminals to defining whole communities as natural enemies. The ease of alternating between labeling opponents as rebels and defining them as enemies—a switch that was already part of the legal repertoire of empire, as part I showed—found new appeal and even more spectacular effect in the nineteenth century. European writers eagerly reworked protection talk to integrate new modes of imperial violence into programs to sponsor capitalist investment across borders and advance campaigns for free trade.

Indigenous polities did not go quietly into this new legal world. Nor were they ignorant of its possibilities and implications. As Europeans toggled between labeling opponents as rebels and classing them as enemies, anti-imperial militants made their own distinctions between war and rebellion. Some insisted on defining imperial violence as interpolitical in nature—as war, not policing—because it reinforced their claims to sovereignty. Others sought to negotiate with colonial officials by presenting themselves as loyal subjects seeking imperial protection under the law. Still others alternated between these strategies. Strikingly, many Indigenous elites quickly adapted European terms and arguments of the emerging field of international law. But their long and continuing immersion in interpolity law ran deeper and produced uncanny parallels. Repeatedly, anti-imperial mobilizations defined violence as limited and as a means to restore order to a world turned upside down.

The regime of global armed peace generated new tensions. The practice of placing whole groups of non-Europeans outside the frame of the laws of war clashed with the project of reimagining regional ensembles of states as the required framework for regulating war. The practice of declaring people protected subjects one minute and enemy aliens the next revealed, at minimum, an embarrassing sleight of hand. Defining interventions as acts to promote order required other legal and rhetorical contortions. New pathways from imperial small wars to atrocities shocked a metropolitan public already trained to mistrust claims about the benefits of empire and to bemoan its costs. As with global practices of raiding and captive taking, the regime of armed peace reflected both the allure and the tragic consequences of "small" violence.

Chapter 4

Bad Conduct in Far Places

In the spring of 1754, an ambitious twenty-one-year-old colonel named George Washington led forty-four settler-soldiers and a group of Indigenous allies into the Ohio Valley. In a skirmish with French soldiers, the British lost only one man. The contingent killed thirteen French soldiers and took twenty-one captives. One of the Frenchmen who died in the skirmish was the commander, Ensign Joseph Coulon de Jumonville.

Reports of the skirmish prompted a dispute about the rules of conduct in war and whether they had been violated. The French protested that the British, engaging in an offensive war during peacetime, had murdered the officer. They claimed that Jumonville was functioning as an emissary and had been on a peaceful mission. The British complained that the French were acting as if Jumonville "had been killed by a Soldier firing at him, whilst he was reading some kind of Declaration by the Governor of Canada to a Party of English," whereas he was "actually commanding the French Party & was killed in the Skirmish" with the "hostile orders" still in his pocket. The French portrayal of the killing as an "assassination," according to the British, served as a smoke screen for "unprovoked Hostilities" during a time of peace.[1]

This episode, together with the British and French debate that ensued about the legality of the fighting and of the killing of Jumonville, took place when the French and British were nominally at peace in the period after the Treaty of Aix-la-Chapelle was signed. The conflict served as prelude to the global Seven Years' War.[2] Disputing everything else about the episode, the British and the French could agree that the skirmish represented violence short of war. Both sides carried instructions to avoid open war as well as authorization to use force when needed to expel and oppose rivals.[3] Everyone recognized that peacetime violence and imperial militarization went hand in hand. The British plan to build forts was supposed to counter French claims to possession "without the appearance of Hostility or We being considered as Aggressors."[4] The French had found "by Experience they are able to make greater and more sure Advantages upon their Neighbours in Peace than in War."[5]

The Ohio Valley standoff illustrates a pattern of peacetime violence that informed debates about law and war in the mid-eighteenth century. We know more about broad changes in the laws of war than we do about how imperial violence figured in that history. References to natural law and just war faded as positive law and treaties gained importance.[6] Historians frequently point to one touchstone of this shift, the publication of Emer de Vattel's *Le Droit des Gens* (*The Law of Nations*) in 1758 and, in the wake of its influence, the growing importance of the idea of a European balance of power after the 1815 Congress of Vienna. New approaches to the laws of war crystallized with the publication of Frances Lieber's code in 1863, during the American Civil War.[7] This story misses almost entirely debates about peacetime violence in eighteenth-century empires. The French and British clash in the Ohio Valley sometimes gets noticed, but it is rarely placed in the context of other imperial small wars around the world.

Yet imperial conflicts did influence the timing and content of debates about the law of nations. They troubled the idea of a smooth transition from natural law to positive law foundations for global legal order, tested meanings of statehood, and challenged European powers to define the limits of their authority over politically fractured regions or systems of states.[8] The conflicts also did more. Wrangling over conduct in imperial small wars cast company and colonial officials as diplomatic agents conducting state business. Concerns for proper conduct made representatives of rival empires and some corporate groups into illegitimate actors and labeled Indigenous polities as incompletely sovereign.

For Europeans, this position was not consistently born of strength. Global empires were operating in pluripolitical regions where they had weak authority and spotty territorial control. In insisting on their right to regulate violence, European imperial agents were projecting power over regions they did not rule—or even clearly dominate. The exclusion of some political communities from debates about legitimate violence narrowed membership in imagined regional state systems that were often treated as the proper regulatory framework for commerce and war.

Indigenous communities had their say about this new legal world. They sometimes insisted on the interpolitical nature—rather than the imperial character—of violence, claiming the role of sovereign polities. At other times, they pressured empires to uphold commitments to protect them as subjects or subordinate polities with some autonomy. As they forcefully challenged Europeans through warfare, diplomacy, and assertions of sovereignty, Indigenous forces pushed Europeans to assert a right to engage in peacetime violence for the sake of establishing and preserving order. Together, Europeans and Indigenous actors were creating and preserving spaces for violence at the threshold of war and peace.

This chapter examines these processes in two small wars during an interlude of interimperial peace at midcentury. In both conflicts, European empires engaged in intense rounds of negotiation about battlefield conduct. Their actions prefigured the Europeanization of the laws of war. In the Second Carnatic War, on the Coromandel Coast, in what is now southeastern India, French and British company officials threw themselves into a quiet proxy war. They furiously lobbed accusations back and forth about battlefield infractions and tested arguments about self-defense and the right to aid allies against rebellions. In the Guaraní War in the Río de la Plata region of South America, fighting followed directly from terms of a treaty signed by Portugal and Spain in 1750. After the Treaty of Madrid directed a territory swap and the relocation of tens of thousands of Guaraní living in seven Jesuit mission towns, Spanish and Portuguese officials overturned the regional order by delegitimizing not just Guaraní authority but also Jesuit power. In both conflicts, Europeans insisted on imperial authority to use and judge legitimate violence.

Imperial small wars were redefining politically fractured areas of incomplete dominion as European-dominated regional regimes of armed peace.[9] The chapter's last section uses the conflicts to reexamine the contributions of the eighteenth century's most influential writer on the law of nations, Emer de Vattel. His approach to the law of nations was wholly consistent with the interimperial regulation of violence in distant, politically fractured regions. Vattel's writings, disseminated after these midcentury conflicts, charted a new way to imagine limited warfare as the centerpiece of regional and global order.

War by Proxy

On the Coromandel Coast, conflict in the wake of an imperial peace treaty gave rise to a cacophony of law talk. French and British company enclaves were perched on the edge of a region in turmoil. The fragmentation of Mughal power had led to what was already a multisided military contest involving a constellation of forces: local rulers, or nawabs, once appointed by the Mughal emperor but by now exercising authority of their own; Maratha armies to the west; forces sponsored by Hyderabad and Mysore with their own designs on the region; and the followers of Nizam-ul-Mulk, the regional Mughal official operating with much-reduced power. In this mix, as the Europeans would soon learn, shifting alliances could suddenly recalibrate the balance of power.

The initial strategy of French and British companies was to behave much like other polities and factions. They concentrated on fortifying as best they could a small number of enclaves, and they attempted to deploy limited resources to secure allies who could offer protection, or even modestly advance their commercial interests. When news of a tentative peace signed in Europe between the French and the British reached the Coromandel Coast in November 1748, it seemed reasonable for company officials there to hope for a quick return to peace and profitable trade.[10] Fighting between the two powers on the coast during the War of Austrian Succession (1740–1748) had not gone particularly well for either side. The British East India Company (EIC) had begun the war with its regional headquarters at Fort St. George (the seat of one of

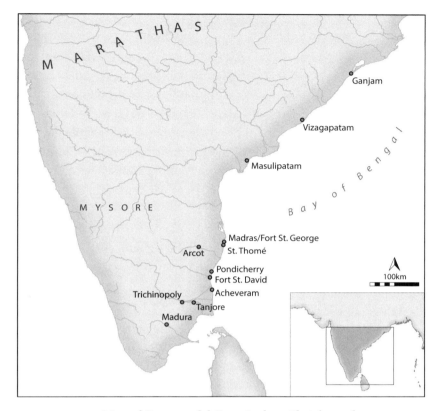

FIGURE 4.1. Map of Coromandel Coast in the mid-eighteenth century.

three presidencies of the EIC) and the adjacent town of Madras, but they had lost Madras to the French in September 1746, forcing the EIC president and council to decamp for Fort St. David, uncomfortably close to the regional headquarters of the Compagnie des Indes Orientales (French East India Company) at Pondicherry.[11]

British efforts to strike back at the French had also failed. Complaining that they had been all but abandoned by the company, which was increasingly turning its attention to Bengal, EIC officials found themselves forced to seek protection from the forces of the nawab of Arcot. The council lamented, "We have nothing in our power but to let [local forces] act as they think proper and secure from them as much protection as we can."[12] The conquest of Madras was symbolically important for the French, but apart from gaining that prize, they had not fared much better. It had proven difficult to induce merchants to resettle or trade in French Madras, and the danger of capture by ships bearing British commissions during the war had brought French shipping to a virtual standstill. To make matters worse, the commander of the French squadron that captured Madras, Bertrand Mahé de la Bourdonnais, had quarreled with the ambitious governor at Pondicherry, Joseph-François Dupleix, over who should take charge of the captured city. When the French squadron was damaged by a monsoon, La Bourdonnais left the region for good, stranding 1,200 French troops at Madras and adding a new drain on French company coffers.

Peace brought fresh challenges. In January 1749, the British at Fort St. George got news of the signing of peace preliminaries at Aix-la-Chapelle, and Dupleix at Pondicherry received orders to end hostilities. Both sides soon learned that the Treaty of Aix-la-Chapelle would return the region to the status quo ante bellum. That meant, among other things, that the British would get Madras back, though EIC officials worried that the French would maneuver to delay the handoff.[13] In July 1749, French and British company officials signed their own local treaty, the Treaty of the Evacuation of the Town of Madras, to establish rules for the transfer.

The contested return of Madras took place against the backdrop of a more consequential set of maneuvers by the companies to secure local allies. Already during the war, the British had formed an alliance with Muhammad Ali Khan, recognized by the Mughal emperor as nawab of Arcot after his father was killed by French-allied forces. Soon a French-assisted army led by another nawab claimant, Chanda Saheb, opposed Muhammad Ali Khan and forced him to take shelter in the fort of Trichinopoly, south of Madras. His alliance with the British made a desperate kind of sense; besides the immediate threat posed by French-allied forces, the fragmentation of the Mughal Empire had left the region badly exposed to Maratha raiders.

At this point, the French seemed to have the upper hand and were poised to install their candidate as nawab. But momentum in the contest swung the other way as a small force led by Robert Clive, in what

Nabob Omdut il Mulk.
Seragil Dowla Anaverden Caun.
Behauder Delaver Jung.
Nabob of Arcot and the Carnatick.

FIGURE 4.2. Portrait of Muhammad Ali Khan (1717–1795). Victoria and Albert Museum, London.

biographers would later celebrate as an impressive debut as a military commander, took and held Arcot and went on to rout Chanda Saheb and French forces. Muhammad Ali Khan's diplomacy was in fact more important than Clive's acumen in turning the tide toward British victory. The nawab bought Mysore's alliance with the promise to surrender Trichinopoly, then reneged on that promise and forged a timely alliance with Marathas to accelerate the defeat of Chanda Saheb.

A few lessons of this little war have, for a long time, seemed obvious. One is that Europeans were fighting as auxiliaries or mercenaries to local or "country" governments.[14] Another is that the subordinate position of the companies and their search for funds to sustain their military forces thrust the French and British into a new and consequential mode of operation. Through their joint actions with local forces, both French and British officials began to grasp the rich possibilities of trading military assistance, or simply promises of protection, for rights to revenue collection. A third often-repeated claim is that the fighting on the Coromandel Coast revealed to Europeans how to fight effectively against South Asian cavalry.[15] The usual story, in sum, is that the war brought the companies closer to asserting military dominance and political authority, as the French flirted with the idea of assuming the office of nawab themselves and the British had their first taste of directing a land campaign and a glimpse of the benefits of local military alliances. The search for the origins of European imperial power in the Carnatic conflicts mark an improvement over older narratives of British empire in India that entirely left out the Coromandel Coast and began with Clive's army's victory at the 1757 Battle of Plassey.[16]

There is much more to the story of conflicts on the Coromandel Coast than their service as preamble to imperial rule in Bengal. Voluminous French and British correspondence about the war reveal that contemporaries saw it as central to defining the legal framework for European conflict across the region. Precisely because the French and British were fighting as "auxiliary" forces to local armies, both sets of European officials felt obliged to justify their increasingly open and direct participation in the war. Both sides took pains, too, to point to actions that appeared to violate the treaty. And both characterized specific acts of war as violations of the law of nations, while sharpening distinctions between European and non-European fighters. Despite their position as marginal powers in the region and despite their mutual enmity, the two European companies and their sovereign sponsors were advancing the idea of a European legal framework for regional violence. They were also inserting into the structure of a colonial proxy war the permanent possibility of direct European military action.

Constrained by orders not to cause the outbreak of another war and consumed by the objective of returning company activities to profitability, French and British officials claimed they were adhering to the terms of the peace treaty and characterized their role in fighting as merely auxiliary to local forces. In doing so, officials were following clear instructions not to engage directly in fighting. In January 1751, the EIC in London directed Governor Thomas Saunders at Fort St. George to take "no part . . . in Country Government disputes unless the Company's interest absolutely requires it."[17] Later in the same year, Dupleix wrote to d'Auteuil, the French commander, "Against the English you are auxiliary troops, in the pay of Chanda S. and Salabat J."[18] Instructions on each side made it clear that the goal was to try to do as much damage as possible to the interests of the rival company.

The pretense of being auxiliaries in a local war produced a correspondence rich in accusations of violations of the peace treaty and the law of nations. Dupleix was an especially prolific recorder of supposed violations. Compared with only 112 preserved letters written by him between 1742 and 1748, he dashed off an astonishing 3,813 letters between 1749 and 1754. Most of Dupleix's letters were directed to Paris, but he also often lodged complaints with local EIC officials—so often, in fact, that we find one EIC official warning another against replying so as not to stimulate "a tedious correspondence to little purpose."[19] The British were not shy about composing their own protests. EIC officials drafted pointed responses to Dupleix, and they recorded their own objections to French misconduct or perfidy. French and British company communications freely combined references to notionally accepted principles of the law of nations even as they upheld their commitment to improvisation. Correspondents cited the peculiar demands of local conditions—both to justify violence and to determine the legalities of conduct on the battlefield.

In the years before the peace, Dupleix rehearsed arguments about the use of force in peacetime. Initially focused on his own enrichment through trade, Dupleix was a late but enthusiastic convert to interimperial legal controversy. When he took up the position as governor of the French company in Pondicherry in 1742, he found the place "dilapidated beyond all expression" and the company deeply in debt.[20] His inclination was to find a way to get along with the British and operate on the premise that "peace is best suited to the Company's interests"—by which he meant his own interests, too.[21] As the situation tipped toward open war with the British, Dupleix rehearsed justifying warfare in peacetime. When the French commander La Bourdonnais asked in 1746 for a ruling about whether he might legally attack a British ship taking refuge in a Dutch port in retaliation for the British having seized a French ship under Danish protection, Dupleix replied that the council in Pondicherry could not authorize an attack on such ships, "but neither do they order you to desist from attacking them. They simply wish that your conduct should be most circumspect and that in destroying the enemy you do not infringe on the treaty between France and Holland." Dupleix noticed that the British had claimed self-defense to justify attacking a French ship in Danish waters, and he advised the council that British behavior "should serve as a guide."[22] The council deliberated again and, betraying either cynicism or humor, decided that "the extent of Dutch neutrality was to be decided by the range of their cannon."[23]

Self-defense was soon on offer as a convenient exception to the prohibition against direct Franco-British fighting. In August 1751, the EIC was instructing Saunders to act to preserve the company's rights and privileges through "all proper means" in opposition to the French, authorizing violence "short of acts of hostility in breach of the Treaty *except in self-defence*." In the same letter, the company promised to send more troops to "enable the English to act upon the defensive."[24] Sometimes carefully, sometimes without much finesse, British and French officials related the right of self-defense to a broader right to use force—virtually anywhere. EIC officials at Fort St. David decided to caution one captain "to be particularly careful how he acts with regard to the French flag" but added that if the French offered "any offense" to the British flag, he should present a formal protest. Then, "if no regard is paid," the captain was authorized to "protect [his forces] to the ultimate of his power against any enemy that may attack him."[25] Dupleix drew an even clearer connection between the right to act in self-defense against specific acts of aggression and the right of the French to fight the British anywhere, and at any time, in the region. In a letter to his military commander, d'Auteuil, Dupleix began by cautioning that the French were fighting only in an auxiliary role. But then Dupleix continued, "You are *partie principale* also, in both cases, for you must attack the English if they oppose your operations." And he added, "It would be extraordinary if they had the right to fire on us as much as they pleased and we, all the while, must hold ourselves back out of respect for them." There was nothing ambiguous about Dupleix's conclusion: "You can attack [the English] anywhere."[26]

Even the threat of aggression by rival Europeans justified the use of force against them. French and British commanders were clearly aware of the elasticity of self-defense arguments. In his memoirs about the campaign, Colonel Stringer Lawrence described the moment when a messenger from d'Auteuil crossed battle lines to deliver the message that the French commander had no "design or inclination, that any European blood should be spilt" but that he would also not be held accountable if the French happened to harm British soldiers. Lawrence's response was to inform the French that he was "carrying the English colours on my flag gun" so that French soldiers could see "where the English were posted." He went on to assure the French commander that he did not want to spill European blood, either, but that if the French fired on the British, even by accident, his troops would fire back.[27] Military men on both sides were preparing legal cover for killing other Europeans while formally at peace.

Self-defense was a useful and effective argument, but it was not the only justification for peacetime violence. Both French and British officials offered a second rationale: they stated that they were lawfully assisting allies in putting down rebellions. The two sides, after all, were backing different claimants to the title of nawab, and by definition one of the candidates had to be a fraud. The British referred to Muhammad Ali Khan as "the lawful prince" and the French-backed contingent as a "rebel government."[28] Dupleix wrote, in turn, that Muhammad Ali Khan was a "rebel and traitor" and the British were "favourers of his rebellion."[29] When the French produced a document from the Mughal emperor recognizing Chanda Saheb as nawab, the British derided it as a work of forgery by an illegal pretender. Like the principle of self-defense, accusations of rebellion created expansive cover for peacetime acts of war.

These two legal arguments—self-defense and the need to assist allies battling rebellions—underpinned a broader and more overtly political rationale for the use of force. A defensive war not only might respond to immediate and specific harm but also might aim at preventing harm in the future. Even if French and British commanders did not explicitly make this assertion, it was implied in the combination of protests about individual acts of aggression and references to the threat of future aggression. Similarly, there was no defined limit on what one might do to protect an ally from rebellion. If aiding a legitimate government against rebellion was a just cause for war, then any act of force against the ally's enemies was also justified.[30] Colonel Lawrence interlaced these arguments when he reflected that "it was necessary to put a stop to the progress of the French, whether in justice to assist the lawful prince against rebels or as an act of self-defence." France was "an oppressive neighbor" clearly bent on the destruction of the company.[31]

Such European positions reassembled well-established ideas about law and war. But fighting as "auxiliaries" and with no declaration of war presented novel complications—and some new opportunities. It was unclear whether Europeans in the region had standing to make agreements to end an undeclared war. When Dupleix wrote to Saunders in June 1752 to let him know that the French would recognize Muhammad Ali Khan's possession of Trichinopoly in exchange for a cession of hostilities, British officials remarked that they were "in no way certified of M. Dupleix's power to treat on this subject." At the same time, they warned the nawab that he should "enter into no treaty or agreement whatever with Mr. Dupleix without the knowledge of and concurrence of the

English."[32] On another occasion, the French lodged a formal protest with the British when their forces seized the fort at Virudhachalam, which was flying a French flag. On what basis did local British forces claim the right to take French territory during peacetime? The French, meanwhile, were seeking a peace agreement directly with Muhammad Ali Khan and refusing to recognize his alliance with the British. At still another moment, Dupleix claimed that Muhammad Ali Khan had asserted that he was "no longer the master" of his forces, implying that he was little more than a puppet of the British.[33] Proxy warfare by companies upset clean arguments about the right to make war in a time of peace. The same conditions complicated questions of battlefield conduct.

Subjects and Prisoners

Alongside French and British officials' correspondence about justifications for violence, a barrage of letters focused on the conduct of war. The exchanges played a role in constructing a permissive framework for company-sponsored violence in peacetime. Repeated protests about bad European conduct worked, oddly, to sharpen characterizations of Indian fighters as uncivilized and untrustworthy. Formally fighting as auxiliaries, Europeans who were accused of unlawful battlefield conduct could and did label local combatants as the authors of barbarous behavior. Meanwhile, in excluding locals as correspondents, French and British letter writers reinforced the claim that European laws of war established standards for multisided violence far from Europe.

The chatter about law and wartime conduct began almost as soon as the ink was dry on the evacuation treaty at Madras. Admiral Edward Boscawen, in command of a British squadron recently arrived in the region, took possession of Madras for the British. He quickly warned company officials that the Catholic priests in Madras were sympathetic to the French and could not be trusted.[34] British forces seized two priests and two merchants suspected of aiding the French and took possession of the houses belonging to the merchants, Quentin de LaMettrie and Francis Barnewall. The priests and merchants were to be sent to Europe, a reverse exile designed to protect the region from further discord and shift the sensitive question of their punishment to London. The British also announced plans to confiscate the church and hand it over to Lutheran Danish missionaries. The extent of British anti-Catholic sentiment was captured in a letter from Admiral Boscawen in which he proposed "that an Order of Council be established that no person under the Protection of the Company permit their slaves to be perverted to the Roman Religion and all who are so perverted be forfeited to the Company."[35] Tensions ran particularly high when Boscawen's forces seized St. Thomé, the Portuguese enclave only about five miles from Madras. The priest there was a relative of Dupleix's wife, and the British viewed him as "a secret enemy and a stimulator of the animosities already too notorious between the French and us."[36]

French protests about these actions focused on the question of who might be classed as a prisoner of war.[37] Dupleix repeatedly complained that the two merchants were being held in flagrant violation of the Treaty of Aix-la-Chapelle and the evacuation treaty, both of which provided protection for the lives and goods of residents of Madras.[38] It was months before Boscawen supplied the rationale for their imprisonment: LaMettrie had "not only resided under protection of the French after the capture of Madras but proceeded to Pondicherry at a time when we were at actual war with that nation," and Barnewall had acted "as Quarter Master to the French troops under the command of Monsieur dela Bourdonnais."[39] The men were not being charged as traitors—at least not yet—but the British view was that their switching sides during the war had removed them from the protections of the peace treaties. That argument worked both ways, of course. The prisoners themselves pointed out that if they were English subjects, then they retained the rights of Englishmen. Francis Barnewell wrote that he was entitled "by birthright, by the known law of my country and the rights and privileges of all Englishmen" to know his crime, and LaMettrie reminded the council at Madras that there were "courts superior to yours to which I can appeal."[40] Dupleix pressed relentlessly for their release, going so far as to claim that because LaMettrie owed the French company money the British would be responsible for his debt if he was sent back to Europe. French protests continued to flow about the imprisonment of the priests at Madras. Detaining Father René, Dupleix asserted, was a direct violation of both the Treaty of Aix-la-Chapelle and the Anglo-French treaty on the evacuation of the town, "on account of his being a subject of the King of France."[41] EIC officials responded that Father René had lived for a long time under British protection and "we can't but esteem him a subject of the King of Great Britain, [and] as such we have made him prisoner."[42] If the French took anything away from this episode it was perhaps that repeated protests might have some effect; the British resolve to punish the two men, and to hold the priests in custody, slowly evaporated, and all were freed.

Slippery subjecthood was at issue in desertions, too. The council at Fort St. David learned that Samuel Warral Cornet had admitted to having corresponded with Dupleix "with the intent to desert the Honorable Company's service and enter in that of the French," apparently resentful that he had been passed over for promotions. Cornet had used burnt cork to blacken his face and disguise himself as a local to cross over to French territory. Once he was caught, the EIC board wanted to cashier Cornet, but they realized that would only make his move to French allegiance easier, so they recommended sending him back to England, where the company could determine what to do with him.[43]

The French and British had already tangled over the case of two British deserters seized from a French garrison. Dupleix called the action an "insult to the [French] flag." When apprehended, the sailors "were in the [French] Company's bounds, where the right of princes afforded them a security . . . a natural right which has been established and acknowledged time out of mind."[44] The French even submitted the depositions of two witnesses—described as British "peons"—showing that the sailors had been within French company territory when taken into British custody. The British made two counterarguments, one referencing the law of nations and the other based on a more general view of law guiding territorial claims. The Fort St. David council president remarked that the French were clearly "unacquainted with the Law of Nations," which recognized the right to pursue deserters "not only into the territories of other powers, but even to the very garrison gates."[45] More generally, the fluidity and indeterminacy of territorial claims by

Europeans in the region made it impossible for the British to agree that the French, merely by "putting up a white flag close to our bounds" or by winning a skirmish might establish that a particular place belonged to the French company. The EIC had no intention of recognizing territories merely marked by the French, or to "suffer them to mark out ours."[46]

Dupleix's rhetoric in these cases established a precedent that he would follow in other disputes over prisoners. The British were endangering "the whole Christian world" by violating "so authentic a treaty."[47] The British argument against this view was that the treaty did not alter British (in reality, EIC) authority over its own subjects, and the right "to administer justice according to the tenour of the laws."[48] The approach became even clearer in the case of a soldier captured by Clive's forces as one of "22 Englishmen deserters." Kelsey was a British sergeant who had served as an officer under the French after deserting; Clive had him "instantly hang'd."[49] When Dupleix objected, the a British scoffed at the idea that Dupleix would think he had any standing to object. The council at Fort St. David suggested that "the question be put to him whether a subject of France that robs and deserts his colours and is afterwards laid hold of . . . is not according to their Laws Military liable to suffer death."[50]

Such exchanges became especially heated when they centered on a British or French soldiers captured on the battlefield. The a British delivered a sharp complaint about the treatment of military prisoners transported to Pondicherry. The prisoners had been subjected to "some very cruel and unhuman actions," including being cut by swords while sick and weak. These acts, the Fort St. David Council observed, were "more becoming of the character of barbarians than those who profess themselves Christians."[51] Soon it was Dupleix's turn to make the same point. For more than a year, he peppered company officials at Fort St. David with complaints about what he characterized as the unlawful imprisonment of several hundred French soldiers. The British had allowed the French officers to return to Pondicherry on parole, on the promise that they would not return to the field for at least a year. But Lawrence, the commander of the British forces, was reluctant to let the common soldiers go under any terms. Dupleix repeatedly asserted that it was wildly improper for the British to make French subjects prisoners of war in times of peace.

The routine recourse to arguments about the law of nations in relation to unruly, multisided fighting is itself of interest. Even the most casual observer would have noticed that unstable loyalties and fluid subjecthood clashed with the confident and emphatic tone of protests about violations of treaty terms. With few consequences for violations reported locally or to European governments, one might wonder why the strident accusations continued. In part, officials were merely demonstrating their compliance with charges to report infractions. EIC instructions to Thomas Saunders included the warning that he would find the French at Pondicherry doing "all in their power to distress the English" and should record "exact and authentic narratives of the French proceedings" so that the EIC might present "applications for redress in case of any violations of the treaty."[52] In part, too, officials hoped to garner increased support from home. Dupleix's industrial productivity as a letter writer accompanied a certain optimism on his part that British violations might bring real consequences. When Boscawen took St. Thomé, ostensibly on behalf of Muhammad Ali Khan, Dupleix was certain that the British admiral would be severely reprimanded when French protests reached London.[53] There were also occasional specific gains to be realized through protest, as occurred when LaMettrie got his liberty and had his property restored. For French and British officers, being freed on parole rather than held indefinitely as prisoners of war was a very tangible benefit of local diplomacy.

Even while each side was lobbing complaints about illegal actions of other Europeans in the war, they were also reinforcing views that Europeans were different from local fighters precisely in their deference to the law of nations. The proxy war meant that Europeans could point directly to their Indian allies as the culprits in any breach, real or imagined, of supposedly widely recognized standards of wartime conduct. Early in the peacetime fighting, French soldiers were instrumental in planning and executing an attack that resulted in the killing of Nasir Jing, the Mughal-appointed local ruler, or nizam, of Hyderabad. French accounts insisted that his assassination was the work of the nizam's disloyal commanders. And when Dupleix wrote repeatedly to protest the treatment of French prisoners, EIC officials responded that they could be of no help since the prisoners were in the nawab's custody and only his forces were responsible for the prisoners' treatment.[54] The British gave a novel spin to the familiar argument of the barbarism of sepoys, local soldiers under British command, when the French protested events at the battle over the pagoda of Acheveram. As Clive's forces breached the walls, according to one British account, the French "flung out" a white flag to surrender. But "the Seapoys ignorant of its Meaning, push'd on the Attack, which so intimidated the Enemy, that 25 of them flung themselves into the River, of which four only were saved."[55] The British even asserted that on several occasions they had intervened to protect the French from harm. In Acheveram, if Clive "had not exerted himself in restraining the Seapoys, the French had been half cut to Pieces."[56] In another engagement, Major Lawrence claimed that his men had acted in the interest of "humanity" in saving French gunners from certain slaughter by "the Moors."[57]

Talk about local fighters' savagery on the battlefield was supplemented by comments about the unreliability of sepoys and the treachery of Asian leaders. The British and French often blamed stalled campaigns or defeats on the reluctance of local mercenaries to engage the enemy. Not surprisingly, military reversals prompted some of the sharpest negative characterizations of Indian fighters. As Chanda Saheb's army and French forces began to struggle, for example, Dupleix lashed out against his ally as unreliable and cowardly. He characterized Muhammad Ali Khan, allied with the British, in the harshest terms: "This scoundrel deserves punishment due to a traitor, for there is no crime of which he would not be guilty towards his master."[58]

Such statements remind us that contests over battlefield conduct were paired with justifications for going to war in the first place. Putting down an illegitimate rebellion became a more plausible rationale for war—one less in need of supporting evidence—when set against tirades about local armies inherently given to intrigue, infighting, and duplicity. Ideas about the aberrant nature of warfare in the East drew strength from the back-and-forth between Europeans about improper battlefield conduct. French and British officials were actively conjuring the view that only the actions of Europeans could be judged in relation to the law of nations. Legal talk about the conduct of war helped to make the case for a European framework for regional war.

Rebels in Their Own Land

In a different and distant part of the world in precisely the same years, another war, this one involving a temporary coalition of two European empires, was generating chatter about the capacity and right to regulate war. In a vast region that spilled across fluid imperial borders, interconnected Indigenous groups in the Río de la Plata backlands sustained a kinetic form of dominance through the end of the eighteenth century. The zone did not perhaps constitute a Charrúan Empire similar to the Comanche Empire in North America, but the parallel is also not far-fetched.[59] Indigenous communities occupied a vast inland region in which decisions about warfare and trade had powerful ripple effects. We miss the region's Indigenous center when we focus only on the dynamics of one or another Iberian colonial frontier, or only on Portuguese-Spanish relations.[60]

The order from the Spanish crown to evacuate seven mission towns in the Río de la Plata shocked Guaraní residents in the towns and stunned the Jesuits who presided over the communities. The Treaty of Madrid, signed by Portugal and Spain in January of 1750, made a clean swap of two territories. In exchange for surrendering a key port on the Río de la Plata, Colônia do Sacramento (Colonia del Sacramento, in Spanish), the Portuguese would acquire from the Spanish a vast swath of territory between the Uruguay and Ibicuí Rivers.[61]

The surprise expressed by the Guaraní and Jesuits to news of the Treaty of Madrid led some historians to characterize the relocation order as a mistake rooted in negotiators' ignorance about the region.[62] Spanish crown officials probably did not realize that the territory ceded to Portugal in the treaty encompassed seven thriving towns inhabited by more than 26,000 Guaraní or that the towns' residents made up roughly one-quarter of the population of the thirty mission towns.[63]

Officials in Madrid imagined, too, that there was ample land available for resettlement near mission towns on the other side of the Uruguay River or in lands south of the territory to be ceded. They did not know that other missions were already occupying the best available land near other towns or that semisedentary Indigenous groups controlled areas adjacent to the towns slated for evacuation. Spanish negotiators were undoubtedly also ignorant of the deep attachment of the Guaraní to the mission towns and lands, as well as the substantial value of the property that evacuees could not take with them: cotton and yerba maté plants, houses and churches, buildings used to process plant and animal products for trade, and free-ranging herds of cattle that provided the communities with food and with valuable hides and bone for making clothing and other goods.

Yet even if Spanish negotiators had possessed such information sooner—it was quickly provided to them by Jesuits—it is doubtful that they would have struck a different bargain. Other goals weighed heavily against the interests of the Guaraní and the Jesuits. Spaniards had long been concerned about the relentless Portuguese advance into lands claimed by the Spanish crown.[64] Portuguese settlers had been pushing steadily into territories claimed by Spain on the east side of the Uruguay River, and anxieties about Portuguese slave raiding, opposed over decades by Guaraní soldiers under Jesuit direction, were still running high. By recognizing Portuguese possession and setting a fixed boundary, the treaty offered Spain the possibility of establishing part of the Río de la Plata as permanently off-limits to the Portuguese.

The Spanish crown also regarded the port of Colônia do Sacramento as a rich catch. Rightly or wrongly, Spaniards viewed dominion over the town as the key to control of trade along the Río de la Plata. Royal instructions to the Governor of Buenos Aires asserted that the inland territories were being exchanged not just for possession of Colônia but also for Spanish "dominion and private use of the Río de la Plata."[65] Spanish forces had successfully taken Colônia from the Portuguese in 1680 and 1704–1705, only to return it later by treaty, and they had attacked but failed to capture the town in 1735–1737. The removal of Portuguese traders from the port would, in Spanish officials' estimation, reduce

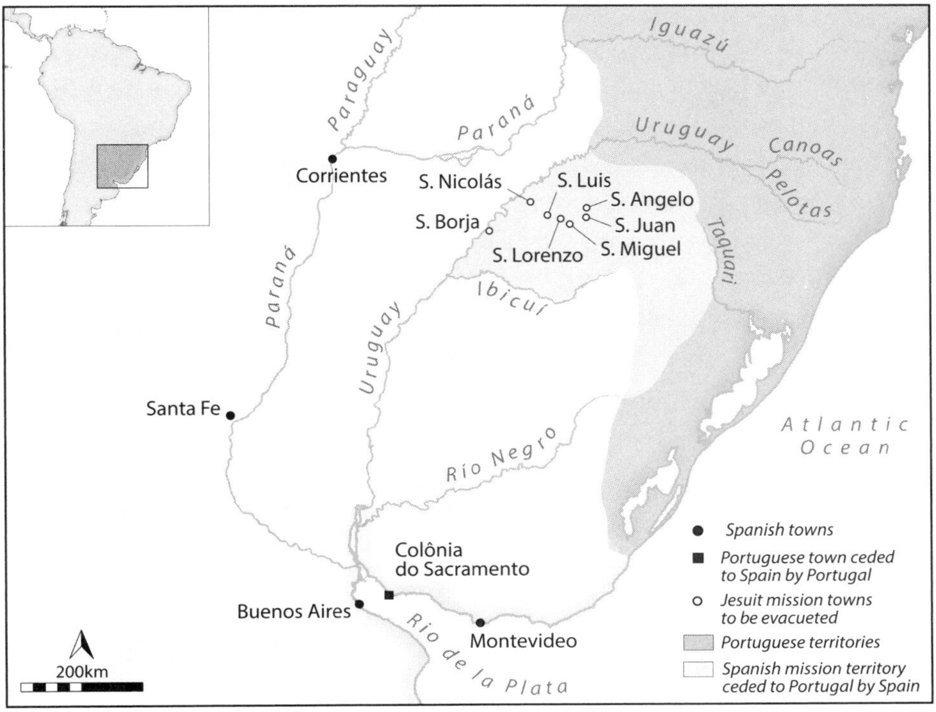

FIGURE 4.3. Map of territories in the Río de la Plata exchanged in the 1750 Treaty of Madrid.

contraband trade and open opportunities to merchants in Spanish towns along the river. Control of the port would also block Portuguese trade into the interior with semisedentary Indigenous groups, connections that threatened to merge the two prongs of Portuguese advance, one along the river and the other into Spanish lands from Brazil.

Even if the Spaniards had grasped the magnitude of suffering that the treaty would bring to mission Guaraní, by signing the treaty the crown had already pledged to enforce the terms by force. The treaty called for implementation within one year. Each crown was to appoint commissioners to travel to the region to conduct the exchange of territory, to survey the boundaries outlined in the treaty, and to enforce execution of its terms. At the treaty negotiations, after both sides had agreed on the exchange of territories, the Portuguese minister had insisted on adding a clause committing both governments to military action in case of an uprising in response to the treaty. The Jesuits had historically armed the Guaraní against Portuguese raids and blocked incursions by Portuguese rustlers, settlers, and slavers, and the Portuguese expected their opposition to the treaty. The clause pledging military repression did its work; it represented anyone who might oppose the treaty as a rebel. Jesuits in Europe quickly grasped the danger of being branded as traitors, and even as they argued that the treaty's terms were damaging to the goal of Christianizing *indios* and urgently appealed for a delay, they also ordered Jesuits in the missions to begin assisting with the Guaraní evacuation.

Fears about Jesuit rebellion drew strength from, and in turn fueled, anti-Jesuit agitation in Europe; the same fears also connected to anxieties about Indigenous rebellion on a vast scale. The Jesuit missions sat at the center of a region still largely under Indigenous control and knitted together by trade, the circulation of news, and violence. In the Chaco area to the northwest of the Guaraní mission region, Jesuits were still working to settle Guaraní-speaking people they called Chiquitos into mission towns in a zone of desultory Indigenous and settler raiding. To the east, south, and west of the mission towns lay territories controlled by other semisedentary Indigenous groups known generally as Charrúas, with subgroups variously labeled Minuanes, Boanes, and Guanaos. They traded with one another as well as with Guaraní communities and Iberian settlers, and they moved often to escape the worst ravages of European slave raiding. The Charrúas also mounted their own raids on Iberian ranches and towns, sometimes transporting livestock and goods taken in raids at one end of the region to other, distant Iberian settlements for sale.[66]

Spanish officials had initially encouraged the founding of Guaraní mission towns as a direct response to Portuguese slave raiding and other incursions, and to establish a bulwark against raids by semisedentary Indigenous groups. Beginning in the seventeenth century, small forces called *bandeiras* organized from São Paolo targeted Guaraní settlements and conducted devastating raids on mission towns in 1629, 1632, and 1636. Armed and trained under the Jesuits, Guaraní armies grew in strength and experience, and they began not only to repel raiders effectively by the second half of the seventeenth century but also to enhance Spanish military capacity across the region. Notably, Guaraní troops played a central role in the Spanish attacks on Colônia do Sacramento, and this history was not forgotten after the signing of the Treaty of Madrid. On the one hand, the Guaraní and their supporters cited their military service as evidence of the Spanish crown's pledge—and obligation—to protect them; on the other hand, the reputation of the Guaraní as proficient soldiers fed anxieties about Indigenous rebellion.

The perceived threat of Portuguese invasion had a long history, as did worries about the possibility of Portuguese alliance with Charrúas. In 1680, a Guaraní patrol led by Jesuits captured a Portuguese crew shipwrecked on the eastern bank of the Río de la Plata and took them as prisoners to Buenos Aires. According to one Jesuit report, the imprisoned Portuguese captain, Jorge Soares Macedo, admitted that he was carrying orders to form alliances with Indigenous groups he called "bohanes, martidanes and yaros."[67] The Portuguese continued to seek such alliances. In the decades after the Portuguese recovered Colônia by treaty in 1681, they approached Minuanes in the hopes of eventually unifying São Paulo and its environs with Portuguese settlements along the Río de la Plata.[68] Rumors of Portuguese interest in alliances with *infieles confederados* (confederated pagans) preoccupied Spanish officials in Montevideo and Buenos Aires, and heightened their fears of Indigenous raiding on the outskirts of river ports.

Spanish *cabildos* (town councils) reacted in predictable ways. A raid on the settlement at Yapeyú in 1701 prompted a major expedition against Minuanes. Carefully represented as a "defensive and not offensive" war, the campaign aimed "to prevent and to end the alliance" between Portuguese and Minuanes and to protect the river trade.[69] In 1722, Francisco de Brito Peixoto, captain-general of the lands around Laguna and Rio Grande, sought out Spanish intermediaries to approach Minuanes about forming an alliance with his government.

Raiding was intimately linked with captive taking. The region was not a series of frontiers but a vast, interconnected slaving complex. Raiding for slaves was not limited to the Portuguese *bandeiras* and their successors. Although enslavement of *indios* was illegal in the Spanish empire, captives taken in raids were routinely resettled in Spanish households and haciendas under vague but effective terms of bondage. Although outspoken opponents of Indigenous slavery, Jesuits also participated in the system of raiding. In the Yapeyú raid of 1701, the expedition leader reported that "more than five hundred souls" were turned over to the Jesuits "to be instructed and taught by the fathers of the Company of Jesus in the mysteries of our sacred Catholic faith."[70] We do not know their status once they went to live in mission towns. But across the region differences between servants and slaves were often imperceptible to captives.[71] Meanwhile, repeated raids to capture women and children severely damaged Charrúa and Minuane communities' reproductive capacities; according to Uruguayan anthropologist and historian Diego Bracco, slaving led directly to population collapse in these communities by the mid-nineteenth century.[72]

The lived experience of slaving affected the Guaraní's response to the order to evacuate their towns. The Guaraní logically suspected that the result of the move would be their enslavement in either Portuguese or Spanish settlements. Padre José de Barreda observed that the treaty was reviving old anxieties of the Guaraní when the Jesuits first gathered them in towns and they suspected the purpose was to "hand them over to the Portuguese or to make them slaves of the Spaniards."[73] Now the Spaniards' willingness to take up arms to remove loyal, Christian Guaraní, Barreda warned, would lead all *indios* in the region to conclude that the Spaniards would stop at nothing to oppose non-Christianized Indigenous groups. The result would be to make "all the pagan Indians of the Charrúas, Minoanes, Boanes, and Guanaos rise, and join together, turn against all these cities" in an unstoppable revolt.[74]

A cataclysmic pan-Indigenous revolt would not have seemed unlikely to anyone in the region—least of all the Guaraní. Resistance began to form as it became clear to mission Guaraní that the order to evacuate the seven mission towns had the full support of the Jesuits and that even a delay of the order was unlikely. From the start, Guaraní plans for resistance involved potential alliances with "pagan" Indigenous groups. Padre Bernardo Nusdorffer, a Jesuit from Bavaria who had lived in the region for decades and led the missions in the 1730s, wrote in 1753 that

nine "Caciques of the Pagan Guanoas and Minuanes and Charrúas entered into the Town [of San Luis] and were received by the *indios* as if
they were old friends" even though they had just a few years before been
at war.[75] The Guaraní and Charrúas, Nusdorffer wrote, then parleyed
without any of the Jesuits present, after which town leaders came to the
Jesuits "asking them to give the pagans yerba mate, tobacco, and clothes
from their storerooms." As if that private parley was not a clear enough
sign of a potential alliance for war, the Guaraní added that the Jesuits
"now do not govern us."[76]

The possibility of a Guaraní-Charrúa alliance appeared even more
likely once the Guaraní in several mission towns had resolved to oppose the forced evacuation. As they armed themselves and prepared to
fight, the Guaraní had only one place to go to evade attack and capture:
the *monte*. Technically meaning "hill" or "mountain," the word *monte*
also referred to any wooded or wilderness area without fixed settlements. The term denoted a region oppositional to the town, so that
going to the *monte* did not imply just running away but also a move from
under Spanish governance and into the wild, away from the Church—
and toward paganism. Mission Guaraní were certainly aware of the resources that their labor was producing for Jesuits and Spaniards, and
one element of retreat to the *monte* was the prospect of something akin
to a general strike. The Jesuits themselves regarded *indios* in the *monte*
as pagans or apostates, and they used this powerful association to argue
against removal. Padre Pedro Lozano warned in March of 1751 that
the most likely outcome of the order to evacuate would be the flight of
Guaraní into the "*montes* and *selvas* (jungles)," where they would be
lost to the Church—and lost as vassals to the crown. Most Guaraní
held a deep and enduring fear of being enslaved, he asserted, and their
terror would "take on new life" and drive them into the backcountry,
where they would join with the pagan *indios* who were "implacable enemies of the Spaniard."[77] In a region of chronic raiding and captive taking,
the move to the *monte* marked a potential crossing by Indigenous groups
into a dangerous status and zone.[78]

Anxieties about Indigenous raids had spiked again in recent decades.
In 1730, a series of raids by several hundred Minuanes in the region

around Montevideo produced, according to Spanish accounts, twenty deaths and emptied nearby estancias. An unstable peace was negotiated and signed in March of 1732. In 1749, Buenos Aires and Montevideo were buzzing with talk of another uptick in violence. Father Francisco Javier Miranda visited Buenos Aires that year and reported that the Spanish were "consternated and unnerved by the frequent attacks that [the *infieles*] were making in the neighborhood and almost within sight of the cities" across the region.[79] There was a familiar sense of unease, too, about the possibility that the raiding Minuanes might represent the vanguard of a Portuguese advance. In May 1749, eight months before the Treaty of Madrid was signed, some Minuanes had entered the mission town of San Miguel to inform their Christian relatives that the Portuguese "had the intention of advancing their conquests, and settling on the banks of the Río Negro."[80] The Spanish official reporting this news warned that if aided by "vagabonds"—a word probably used to signify rootless people of any ethnicity—the Portuguese "could totally destroy all the towns" of the Uruguay river region and inflict "irreversible" damage on the holdings of the Spanish crown.[81] A Spanish campaign organized in April produced new Indigenous captives and laid the groundwork for further hostilities.[82]

News of the Treaty of Madrid almost certainly played a role in intensifying Spanish-Indigenous violence close to Montevideo in 1750 and 1751. Charrúas and Minuanes were likely responding to upheaval in the mission towns and Spaniards were taking advantage of the crisis to push into Indigenous grounds. Most Indigenous interactions in the backcountry went unrecorded, and it is tricky to align patterns of raiding with the circulation of news about the treaty. Even the official record warns us off the scent. Officials in Buenos Aires received word of the treaty terms a few months after its signing, in early 1750, and as Jesuits registered their concerns and hoped for a reversal, they held off for at least a month in informing Guaraní in the missions. But it is very unlikely that news about the treaty was a well-kept secret in the Charrúan world. It was not a secret of any kind, after all, in Buenos Aires, Montevideo, and other Spanish towns.

Other evidence of the interconnectedness of frontier violence comes from the saber-rattling of Spanish town officials. The *cabildo* of Montevideo, certainly aware of tensions mounting with mission Guaraní, sought to establish the legality of strikes against Charrúas and Minuanes, In April 1751, the governor of Montevideo, José Joaquín de Viana, sent an account of recent hostilities with Minuanes that doubled as a legal tract justifying Spanish attacks on Indigenous groups and as cover for future violence. In January 1751, the report explained, *indios* had "the extreme audacity" to kill ten men, wound three others, steal between eighty and one hundred horses, and try to lead away up to five hundred cattle and oxen at a place called Calera del Rey, a mere "ten leagues from this city, and on its close outskirts." This event was followed by the capture of two Minuane "spies" who affirmed that they were spreading the word that "their people were very close to the frontiers." In early March, three more men were killed at Calera del Rey, and the Spanish raid to punish those responsible led to the killing of twenty Indigenous men "and brought to this City 82 women and children who have been distributed to the *vecinos*." Leaving no doubt that the purpose was to justify the quasi-enslavement of captives taken in Spanish attacks on Minuanes, the letter appended a document describing the history of Spanish-Minuane relations as a series of "requerimientos" in which the Minuanes signed, and then broke, peace pacts in 1731, 1746, 1749, and 1750.[83] The document builds to a chillingly matter-of-fact description of the authorization, sent by the captain-general in Buenos Aires to the Montevideo governor, "to kill any male Indian more than 10 years of age, preserving the women and children."[84]

Governor Viana was not actually asking permission to kill and capture Indigenous people. He was merely presenting justifications for campaigns and attacks and for acts of quasi-enslavement that had already taken place. No doubt Viana knew that he was operating in an atmosphere especially permissive of murderous raids. The document's path through the Spanish bureaucracy also hints at connections between mounting tensions with Guaraní and a wider campaign of violence against Indigenous communities. Viana sent the justificatory account of Spanish-Minuane violence to Buenos Aires in April 1751. Officials there appear not to have relayed it to Madrid until March of 1755, just as plans for a second campaign against the Guaraní were taking shape. The reply from Madrid came two years later. It merely stated that no grounds existed for action until the Council of the Indies received more information. The unhurried movement of Viana's report and the indifferent response in Madrid had the effect of permitting attacks on Minuanes to continue. The council's inaction turns on its head historians' usual characterization of Spanish imperial politics as structured by the quiet intransigence of local elites, as captured in the phrase "obedezco pero no cumplo" (I obey but do not comply). The Council of the Indies was defining its prerogative to decide on legitimate violence as a capacity it held without needing to exercise: "We rule but do not decide."

It is possible, too, that the council saw no need to elaborate because it had already, in connection with the Guaraní War, explicitly authorized Buenos Aires officials to make war on Charrúas and other "pagan *indios*" in order to aid in the relocation of the mission towns. A royal order to the governor of Buenos Aires in February 1753 recognized the danger that other Indigenous groups might "infest" Spanish territories where Guaraní wanted to resettle, thereby disrupting the "peaceful relocation of the seven towns." Without a trace of irony, the order encouraged the governor to seek the aid of the Jesuits to mobilize Christian *indios* as soldiers of an auxiliary force to quiet to the countryside. It explicitly ordered "total repression of the barbarian *indios*" and approved the use of "all the rigors of War [against them] as implacable enemies, or with [the force] proscribed under Law as rebels."[85]

Here, amid the voluminous correspondence between the crown and Spanish officials in Buenos Aires, we find the legal framework for a wider war being assembled. The capacious authorization for war did not require officials to distinguish between the use of force against Indigenous groups "as implacable enemies" and their punishment as rebels. In fact, the various conflicts in the region either merged these rationales or linked them in sequence. Guaraní in rebellion were threatening flight into the backcountry. Such a move would signal their shift from

the category of wayward subjects—still eligible for the king's mercy—
to the status of apostate enemies who might be captured at will and
"distributed" to settler households as quasi-slaves. With long exposure
to Christian teaching and Spanish military command, a history of com-
bating slaving raids, and their lived experience of the porous frontier
between settled and unsettled communities, Guaraní residents of mission towns undoubtedly recognized the symbolic associations and dangers of flight to the *monte*. The new twist for them was an interimperial
context in which they could no longer prove their allegiance to the
Spanish crown by serving as foot soldiers against the Portuguese. New
formations of imperial rule and interimperial alliance were crowding
out spaces for semiautonomous Indigenous peoples—and for Jesuits.

"Vassals of the Same Sovereign"

The Guaraní War assembled an interimperial framework for violence.
To begin with, the treaty created a coalition war with some unusual
features. Even during the period when Portuguese and Spanish crowns
were united, between 1580 and 1640, their jointly fought wars had been
mainly limited to interimperial contests, in particular wars against the
Dutch. Iberians under the union did not coordinate policies toward Indigenous Americans. The terms of the Treaty of Madrid were different.
It imagined the creation of a true coalition force in the field to counter
an Indigenous revolt. Because there was little precedent for such collaboration, the commissioners sent to implement the treaty received
detailed instructions about how the two sides should communicate, and
how the command structure would operate in case of war.

The instructions made each set of commissioners responsible for informing the affected populations of the need to relocate. Each side
would take stock of the movable property ("guards, *indios* in service,
food stores, armaments, and utensils") to be carried off, by mission
town inhabitants in the one case and by departing Portuguese residents
of Colônia do Sacramento in the other. Each side would also specify
how and when the evacuations would take place. Instructions about the
staging of the commissioners' meetings catalogued the material

evidence that the coalition was a true partnership, not an arrangement to subject one side to the control of the other. On arriving in the region, the commissioners should "build a house of wood, or a military tent" straddling the territories of the two crowns "as outlined in the Treaty." The interior layout of the meeting place would not be left to hazard, or to the imagination of crown agents. "There will be two entryways at opposite ends, such that the commissioner of each nation shall enter through territory belonging to his own Sovereign. A round table will be placed inside with two chairs for the principal commissioners, whose backs should face the door through which each entered." The instructions went on to specify that each principal commissioner would be allowed to bring others with him, but that the two groups had always to face each other, with the head commissioners in the middle. The parties were exhorted not to fight or argue but to join in implementing the treaty and to "conduct themselves as if they were Vassals of the same Sovereign."[86]

The instructions set out procedures in case of Indigenous insurrection. Agents of the two crowns would take turns in command of the joint forces to put down any rebellion, with the officers assuming "absolute command (only for this war, or for suspicions closely related to it)" in alternate weeks. To avoid any temptation of pulling rank, the officers in charge on the two sides would be of equal rank. The instructions even detailed procedures for the two-headed army to discipline the troops under its command. Each side's officers would deal with small offenses by factious soldiers from both camps and would enjoy full jurisdiction, with no appeal. Commanders could delegate their disciplinary authority. Commissioners would not impose the death penalty unless doing so was necessary to avoid "some grave disorder, or perturbation between the two Nations."[87] These instructions about how to perform a coalition were not closely followed, but the fact that they were conveyed at all, and in such detail, indicates the novelty of the arrangement.

When Portuguese and Spanish representatives met on the island of Martín Garcia in July 1753, they had already received a string of reports that many Guaraní in the seven mission towns were actively resisting relocation.[88] To the dismay of Jesuits still in the missions, the Jesuit visitor plenipotentiary, Padre Cristóbal Altamirano, was contributing to these reports. Newly assigned to the region, Padre Altamirano had traveled to three missions on a fact-finding visit that did not go well. A cold reception at two of the mission towns got colder at Santo Tomé, a town on the western side of the Uruguay River where Guaraní who were about to lose lands across the river were deeply sympathetic to the plight of Guaraní inhabitants of the seven towns slated for evacuation. According to one of the Jesuits who observed the visit to Santo Tomé, the Guaraní believed—partly because Altamirano did not wear the long black robes expected of the Jesuits—that "he was a Portuguese and threatened to throw him into the Uruguay."[89] Altamirano fled to the coast, and after that visit the official Jesuit position hardened.

While Jesuits in the missions were still pleading with Guaraní to comply with the order to move and avoid bloodshed, an infectious skepticism about Jesuit loyalty was spreading through coastal towns. Still more influential in hardening commissioners' views was a standoff that occurred in February 1753, outside the mission of Santa Tecla. There, the commissioners' survey team, tasked with plotting the boundary between Portuguese and Spanish territories, found their entry into the mission blocked by a group of sixty-eight armed Guaraní led by the town's *corregidor* (chief magistrate), Sepé Tiarajú. At a parley in an estancia chapel, Tiarajú made it clear that he would let the Spaniards pass—but never the Portuguese, traditional Guaraní enemies.[90]

In the context of the crown-directed coalition, it was not a winning strategy to declare the Spaniards friends and the Portuguese enemies. In Europe and in Buenos Aires, rumors were circulating that some Jesuits were actively aiding a Guaraní revolt and that Jesuit appeals to delay the towns' evacuation were little more than a ploy to buy more time for Indigenous war preparations. Mission Guaraní maintained that they were loyal subjects of the Spanish crown, and the Jesuits affirmed that the order would help implement the treaty. But declarations of loyalty were now not enough to protect against accusations of rebellion. It did not help that beneath affirmations of their obedience, both Jesuit and Guaraní letter writers argued in different ways that the order to evacuate the seven towns was in fact bad law.

The initial Jesuit response came in the form of a letter from Padre Nusdorffer delivered to the Spanish commissioner, the Marqués de Valdelirios, on his arrival in Buenos Aires. Nusdorffer's tract follows a strand of sixteenth-century scholastic thought that defined moral possibility as an essential condition of law. The view held that for a law to be legitimate, it first had to be possible.[91] Nusdorffer outlined five reasons that the ordered evacuation of the mission towns was impossible to accomplish. It was impossible given "the shortness of time . . . what has to be transported . . . those who have to execute [the order] . . . the distance of the destination . . . [and] the mode in which it will have to be done."[92] Although asking only for a delay in the treaty's implementation, Nusdorffer's reasoning presented a fundamental challenge to the treaty. If its execution was impossible, the evacuation order itself was legally flawed.

Other Jesuits took a slightly different approach, but they delivered the same basic message. Their letters recited the history of Guaraní service to the crown as evidence of a firm pact of reciprocal obligation. Writing in March of 1751, Padre Pedro Lozano noted that Guaraní soldiers had formed the bulwark of Spanish military defenses all along the frontier without their "ever wanting to pull down wages."[93] Composing "the principal forces not only against foreign enemies of the Crown of Castile but also against disobedient or rebellious domestic vassals" in Paraguay, the Guaraní had not hesitated in responding to every call for service.[94] Here Jesuits were drawing on another well-developed scholastic tradition in characterizing such service as evidence of a pact between crown and subjects. Lozano warned that the order to evacuate mission towns would signify, to the Guaraní, that the monarch had broken this pact: the Guaraní "will say that after our great Monarch promised to keep them always present with regard to everything having to do with their consolation, relief, and preservation, he has not fulfilled his word . . . because he is giving them into the hands of enemies who have always solicited their destruction and extermination."[95] For their part, the Guaraní had upheld their side of the bargain by being always constant in their "fidelity and service."[96]

This line of argument by Jesuits carried risks. Perhaps aware that it cast aspersions on royal conduct, Lozano buried the argument pages into a long letter, after detailed descriptions of the enmity of the Portuguese and the service of the Guaraní. The new provincial, Padre José de Barreda, was less cautious. He baldly stated that Philip V had promised to protect the Guaraní "in their lands, and defend them from their enemies." The promise, Barreda observed, had made it possible to persuade the Guaraní to settle in towns in the first place. Further, it made the Guaraní claim to their lands unbreakable because it was based in "the natural right of their possession, for a span of one hundred and thirty years, confirmed by repeated letters by Our Sovereigns."[97]

Had they imagined what was coming—the Jesuit order's expulsion from both empires followed by its dissolution by the pope—the missionaries might have chosen merely to plead for mercy for the suffering Guaraní. The Jesuits' penchant for neoscholastic arguments about the rights of subjects to resist or ignore illegitimate laws was not just ineffective; it carried an implicit challenge to the authority of the two crowns. An educated audience would have understood that the Jesuits' position bestowed on the Guaraní a quality that the crowns were now determined to withhold from them—their subjecthood. In referring to the Guaraní's possession of the land, Barreda was investing them with status and standing equal to those of Spaniards and Portuguese, not just through their possession of natural rights but also in their participation in the political order as crown subjects. Lozano was equating the Guaraní with Spaniards in emphasizing their right to protection by the crown. On the surface, Nusdorffer's view was the mildest because it merely asked for a delay in resettlement and explained the reasons. But underneath lay a powerful condemnation of the moral vacuity of the treaty, a condition that invested in the Guaraní the right to evade laws flowing from it.

The Jesuits were of course careful to frame their objections as reasoned appeals for justice. They must have encouraged the mission Guaraní to do the same in their own letters criticizing the treaty. The *corregidor* Mighel Guaiho of San Juan Bautista began by declaring the order to leave the towns to be a hoax perpetrated by the Portuguese. The Guaraní could "not believe that this may be the will of our good, Holy King, or we do not treat it as such."[98] Incredulity had the rhetorical advantage of celebrating the king's benevolence, but it also called into question the motives and judgment of crown officials.

At least one other Guaraní petitioner went further and characterized the possession of Guaraní lands as unbreakable. Nicolás Ñeengirú, *corregidor* of Concepción and later a leader of the armed rebellion, wrote to the governor of Buenos Aires on 20 July 1723—probably without knowing that only five days before the Portuguese and Spaniards at Martín Garcia had declared the mission Guaraní to be rebels. Ñeengirú first stated that God had given the land to the Guaraní people. He mentioned Father Roque Gonzalez, the first Jesuit in the region and someone featured in ceremonies of reverence to ancestors' bones. The reference points to the Guaraní's spiritual attachment to the land.[99] But Ñeengirú also rested his case more on more prosaic proofs: "Only our hands have worked . . . and prepared this land," he wrote. "Neither the Portuguese nor the Spaniards have done such things as build a magnificent church, a nice town, ranches for our cattle, yerba mate and cotton plantations, farms; what was achieved came about from our hard work." And he ended by asking, "Well, how is it that you wrongly want to take our possessions from the fruit of our own labor?"[100]

For Ñeengirú, the Guaraní could not be rebels because they had their own political legitimacy. Although he avoided making a claim to total autonomy from the crown—conforming to the Guaraní preference for the status quo of Spanish protection—Ñeengirú was asserting that the Guaraní could not lawfully be separated from "the fruit of [their] own labor." Their claim to the land did not depend on any other authority, including that of the Jesuits and the Spanish crown. Ñeengirú was lumping together the Spaniards and the Portuguese as people who had no comparable relation to the land and therefore no greater claim to it.

For Ñeengirú and other Guaraní, these arguments did not conflict with expressions of allegiance to the Spanish king. But whereas Guaraní loyalty and Spanish protection were rooted in reciprocal obligations, with the sovereign's authority persisting over the Guaraní only so long as the king fulfilled his side of the bargain, the argument that the Guaraní held stronger to the land than any European represented a significant challenge to Iberian authority. Not only was the treaty bad law, Ñeengirú was implying, it was no law at all.

In drawing rooms and libraries, such arguments might have appeared harmless enough, the stuff of Jesuit pedantry and Guaraní spiritual attachments. But war, and the context of an unsettled region of chronic raiding, made the claims dangerous. According to Iberian commissioners and their court sponsors, the mission Guaraní (and the Jesuits supposedly aiding in their resistance) were rebelling against the authority of *both* crowns in refusing to evacuate their towns. At the same time, by asserting autonomous rights to the land, they were locating themselves outside the ambit of Spanish protection and rule. This shift was not only, as the Jesuits and some Guaraní suggested, the result of a breakdown—or even a misguided repudiation—of reciprocal obligations of sovereign and subjects. The position hinted at a larger argument that the European-imposed order was itself illegitimate.

However ineffective, the Guaraní rapprochement with Charrúas and Minuanes strengthened the perception that the Guaraní were challenging the European-imposed order. Their recourse to the *monte* might potentially (and quickly) erase decades of Catholic teaching and prompt a return to paganism.[101] At the same time, the coalition of Portuguese and Spaniards pitted the Guaraní against not just their immediate superiors and the wishes of their king. They were effectively challenging the exclusive right of Christian kings to engage in pacts and set the terms of war and peace.

There are hints that some Jesuits saw the dangers implied by their rhetoric. But they also sought, in a different way, to question the legitimacy of the treaty by declaring the Portuguese to be enemies, treaty or no treaty. Lozano recited the history of Portuguese aggression, and he highlighted the Portuguese penchant for violence outside a state of war: "*In time of peace,*" he wrote, "and still being vassals of the King of Spain, [the Portuguese] attacked the Guaraní Nation, taking more than 300,000 Indians from it. . . . *In time of peace* between the two Crowns, they dared in 1679 to enter the Río de la Plata to found Colonia del Sacramento. *In time of peace* in 1696, they tried to surprise the City of Santa Cruz de la Sierra, to get closer to Potosí. *In time of peace* around

1721, they began to found the settlement of Jesus in the mines of Cuyabá near the Paraguay River. . . . *In time of peace* in 1723, they came to found Montevideo . . . *and still in a time of peace* they attempted anything they could against these Provinces."[102] Drawing attention to the long history of peacetime aggression was intended to throw into question the Portuguese capacity to make and adhere to treaties. In this regard, Lozano was using a rhetorical device similar to the one Portuguese and Spanish officials relied on to conflate mission Guaraní with Charrúas and Minuanes. Like the Indigenous inhabitants of the *monte*, the perfidious Portuguese were inveterate peacetime raiders. They might sign treaties, but they remained agents of perpetual war.

The campaign against the Guaraní soon revealed the weakness of the coalition. An early phase of fighting in 1753 featured reverses and some bungling by separate Spanish and Portuguese forces. The armies suffered from logistical missteps, indifferent conscripts, and insufficient provisioning in hostile territories, and they were not prepared to take on the motivated, if ill-equipped, Guaraní forces. The strangeness of the coalition provided each army with ready-made excuses for lackluster outings. The Portuguese commander noted that he was constrained from pressing farther into Spanish territory because he was fighting only as leader of an "auxiliary force" and barred from acting as an invader. The Spanish commander blamed the poverty and disorderliness of conscripts who melted away in waves of desertion at Yapeyú, on the doorstep of the mission towns in revolt.[103]

The reverses of the first campaign gave way to a deepening resolve to triumph, and to a year of joint planning in 1755, followed by a coordinated assault on the rebellious missions in 1756. At the battle at Caaibaté in February, a short truce collapsed when the army reported that Guaraní soldiers were perfecting their defenses rather than preparing to surrender. In the onslaught that followed, more than 1,500 Guaraní were killed and an unrecorded number taken prisoner. After that defeat, armed Guaraní conducted ambushes and raids as the coalition army advanced to occupy all seven towns. Still pressured by the Portuguese to hand over the towns, the Spaniards organized a yearlong operation to round up thousands of Guaraní dispersed in the countryside and gather them for the move across the river. The misery of the march comes through even in self-congratulatory reports by the Spanish official in charge, who bragged about "the good treatment" experienced by Guaraní who came in from the *monte*. At San Angel mission, where Guaraní residents gathered to celebrate the Feast of the Assumption on 15 August 1757, the Spanish commander placed sixty soldiers at the exits of the church and enclosed the celebrants in a large patio. It is easy to imagine their terror, though the commander reported that he tried to calm fears that "they would all be put to the sword." He gave the residents four days to gather "their poor effects, and the cattle that they could" and to join a ragged caravan making the dangerous crossing to the other side of the Uruguay River.[104]

By the time the evacuation was complete, Spanish officials were beginning to doubt that the Portuguese intended ever to abandon Colônia. With further hostilities looming, the Spanish crown annulled the Treaty of Madrid in 1761. A year later, the coalition was dead, and the Portuguese and Spanish were on opposite sides of the Seven Years' War. As interimperial fighting again engulfed the region, Spanish forces encircled Colônia do Sacramento. Once again, they called for Guaraní soldiers to assist in the siege—an old habit.

Yet something fundamental had changed in the region. The brief coalition war had established a kinship between Spaniards and Portuguese in opposition to Indigenous polities and a Jesuit "republic." The consolidation of European power had been forged by the treaty. The alignment of imperial interests had also formed as Montevideo and Buenos Aires elites took advantage of the crisis to broaden the assault against Indigenous communities across the region and to weaken the Jesuit hold on the coveted interior. Sponsors of violence drew on familiar arguments of extinguishing rebellion and making defensive wars, subtly amplifying the dangers posed by an unseen and unrecorded Indigenous confederation. The actions of the coalition forces, meanwhile, suggested a future in which European settlers would encircle and encompass Indigenous territories. An interpolity order was becoming an interimperial regime.

A Secret Republic?

As occurred on the Coromandel Coast, debates about law in the Guaraní War altered the standing of participants to regulate war. The effects reverberated in Europe, through sprawling controversies about the Jesuit order. In direct commentary on the Guaraní War, the most powerful minister of the Portuguese government, Sebastião José de Carvalho e Melo, the future Marquês de Pombal, led the attack on the Jesuits in a tract published anonymously in 1757. He probably coauthored the pamphlet and certainly sponsored and actively disseminated it.[105] Much of the evidence cited to denigrate the Jesuits and support the accusation that they had secretly founded an independent republic in the Río de la Plata focused on their connections to the unruly comportment of Guaraní warriors.

A central point of critique rested on Jesuit responsibility for Indigenous atrocities. The pamphlet retold the story of the first phase of the war, when Guaraní had advanced on the Portuguese fort at Rio Pardo, an event that led to the capture by the Portuguese of fifty Indigenous prisoners. The tract cited reports by Portuguese commanders that the prisoners, when asked to explain their "motives for the cruelties they had practiced" in battle against Portuguese soldiers, declared that "their Holy Fathers had assured them that many badly wounded Portuguese would recover, and that the most secure thing was to cut off their heads."[106] The pamphlet also described an incident before the battle at Caaibaté in 1756, when a scouting party of sixteen Spanish soldiers crossed paths with a group of Guaraní who waved a white flag and offered the men food and drink. The party turned on the Spaniards and "cruelly killed them, stripping them after they were dead of all they carried."[107] The pamphlet did not blame the Jesuits directly for Guaraní treachery, but it implied that the treacherous use of a European sign of peace—the white flag—showed that the Jesuits had taught the Guaraní the conventions of European warfare and how to subvert them.

The tract made even plainer Pombal's view that the Jesuits were responsible for Guaraní brutality. The Guaraní practice of "stripping the countryside of all the necessities for the subsistence of the Portuguese troops" betrayed an outsider's influence, the pamphlet suggested, since the Guaraní's "ignorance" made them incapable of coming up with such strategies on their own.[108] The Portuguese governor-general was quoted on evidence that the Jesuits were teaching the Guaraní "military architecture" so they could build fortifications.[109] The Guaraní were represented as utterly subjected to the Jesuits, who treated them "like slaves" and kept them in "the most extraordinary ignorance."[110]

It was bad enough, the tract elaborated, that the Jesuits had encouraged rebellion. That fact alone made them guilty of lèse-majesté, or treason. But the Jesuits had gone much further. Besides teaching the Guaraní about artillery, gunpowder, bullets, military formations, and fortifications—all "the same sort of practices in the wars of Europe"—the Jesuits were guilty of founding their own "powerful Republic" and creating "a war promoted and sustained by the same Padres *against two monarchs*."[111] In contrast to evidence that the Guaraní were making clear distinctions between the Portuguese and the Spaniards, the pamphlet accused the Jesuits of teaching the Guaraní to believe "that all white secular men were people without law and without religion."

Pombal and his allies accused the Jesuits of encouraging a race war. They had cultivated in the Guaraní "an implacable hatred of secular whites" as enemies who had to be hunted and killed "without quarter."[112] Indigenous cruelty flowed directly from a slavish subordination to Jesuits as "sovereign despots" who were teaching that "there was no power superior to that of the Padres." The Jesuits were turning the Guaraní not just against the Spanish crown, in other words, but against all the crowns of Europe.[113] In the process, members of the Jesuit order were placing it in a position equal to that of European governments.

Such arguments fueled an anti-Jesuit storm in Europe. In 1758, Pombal accused the order of masterminding an attempt on the Portuguese king's life, an event that began a wave of Jesuit repression. Less than a year later, Pombal was successful in getting the crown to expel the Jesuits from Portugal and its empire. Widely translated, his anti-Jesuit tract found a particularly receptive audience among Parisian Jansenists and Gallicans, groups with overlapping membership seeking secular government dominance over the authority of the pope. Anti-Jesuit Portuguese writings helped to stimulate in France "a pamphlet war that the Jesuits could not win" and inspired efforts in Spain to blame the order for the Esquilace riots in 1766.[114] Jesuit foes succeeded more than many had reason to hope. France suppressed the order in 1764, the Spanish crown expelled Jesuits from all its realms in 1767, and in 1773 the papacy ordered the complete dissolution of the order.

The most serious accusation against Jesuits was that they placed loyalty to the order above political allegiances. As in Pombal's tract, critiques outside Portugal focused on the Jesuits' imagined attempt to erect "a state within and subversive of every other state."[115] It is clear that anti-Jesuit sentiment was deeply intertwined with opposition to the order's commercial success and sensitive to the perception that they had amassed huge fortunes at the expense of both other merchant communities and vulnerable subordinates. But even closer to the heart of the anti-Jesuit movement stood a growing opposition to authorities that claimed autonomy from European governments. As in the Río de la Plata, where officials imagined Jesuit and Guaraní disloyalty as intertwined, such autonomy appeared dangerously contagious. Jesuits sowed disorder, in this view, because empires teemed with local political communities asserting their independent right to rule.

Imperial Violence and the Law of Nations

Rather than straining to show a causal link between small wars beyond Europe and evolving European ideas about the law of nations, we gain insight from placing the phenomena in the same frame. The themes of conduct in war and definitions of statehood were intertwined in small wars far from Europe in the middle of the eighteenth century—*before* the publication of Emer de Vattel's influential *Le Droit des Gens* (*The Law of Nations*) in 1758.[116] Although he was not commenting directly on the Jesuit problem, Vattel was self-consciously opposing a Catholic, neoscholastic approach to the natural law foundations of the law of nations. Within just a few decades, *The Law of Nations* was in the libraries of the most prominent statesmen of Europe and influential elites in settler colonies.[117]

It is tempting to portray Vattel's work as marking a clear turning point toward positive international law based on the agreements of sovereign nation-states. But if we read Vattel against the history of imperial small wars before the publication and dissemination of his work, his approach appears both less original and less Eurocentric in its implications. Pombal found a link between European commitments to state authority and a world under the spell of empires growing in power and acting together. We can make the same connection, for different purposes.

The ties between imperial violence and changes to the law of nations become clearer if, as Ian Hunter has suggested, we abandon the notion that the early modern law of nations was "a body of doctrine with philosophical foundations."[118] Instead, we can think of it as "a sprawling discursive genre" made up of patchy elements of doctrine; diverse strands of theological, legal, and political argumentation; and improvised narratives about the origins and nature of human sociability.[119] For Vattel, the process of turning this swirl of disordered political thought into a framework for international order occurred in the space between two philosophically inconsistent positions. The first was rooted in a version of scholastic natural law theories that regarded all human action as ordered in relation to universalist notions of justice. The second pointed to the self-interested action of sovereign states as generative of law. Between these two seemingly inconsistent propositions, Vattel identified a "discursive space" for law arising from states' interpretations of the legal foundations of their actions.[120] Vattel imagined those interpretations as reflecting an intricate Protestant scaffolding of state authority, as well as the faint but distinctive imprint of the imagination of universalism. As Hunter puts it, states acted "as if" their self-interested actions were guided, however faintly, by natural law principles. They did so by characterizing the "balance of power" among states as a condition both favorable to the security of states and supportive of the common good.[121]

The framework had important implications for law and war. In *The Law of Nations*, Vattel described just war, in keeping with a natural law tradition, as foundational to the idea that only one party to a war could have a just cause. But Vattel quickly suspended this argument and proposed that more than one nation could have a just cause since each one could decide the justice of war for itself. He then embraced this indeterminacy as an opening to view states' diplomatic practice as constitutive of law. The effect occurred through states' attention to, and judgments about, mid-scale conventions about the rights and conduct of war. For Vattel, states did not apply the laws of war, nor did they apply the law of nations in making peace treaties. They pursued self-interest and engaged in a "practice of judgment" about an array of flexible conventions of limited scope, without disturbing their underlying commitment to the orderly harmonization of competing interests. Here, as Hunter summarizes, "the function of the rules is only to set the broad and fluid parameters within which judgment or right may vary according to circumstance."[122]

Participants in imperial wars, whether small or large, were making precisely these kinds of interpretative assessments of the right to make war and about the conduct of war. Their distance from centers of power made imperial agents directly responsible for judgments about the lawfulness of violence in specific circumstances. Imperial officials took up this task with enthusiasm, a clear sign that they regarded it as central to their official duties. They addressed justifications and protests both to local agents of other empires and to metropolitan superiors, confirming that they imagined themselves to be participating directly in a consequential legal politics within an ensemble of European empire-states. Tracking ubiquitous law talk in empires serves as a corrective for the usual, later story of a balance of power composed in Europe and then transported to the extra-European world.[123]

Vattel's interest in the balance of power remains relevant to our story, though. For Vattel, the balance of power did not represent merely an equilibrium of states. It instead reflected a loose consociation of states committed to interpolity order and prepared to punish transgressors of peace and violators of shared principles of the conduct of war.[124] Like rogue polities, European sovereign states might disturb the peace and require correction. To justify an alliance against Louis XIV, Vattel held up the example of the French king as a "notorious warmonger" fixated on expanding Bourbon power.[125] Only war against France could rectify this errant program. Vattel discussed how similar ordering mechanisms might work outside Europe in a few cases. The most important related to his condemnation of Mediterranean violence by the Barbary States and his call for their punishment. Vattel insisted that these states should be punished precisely *because* they belonged to the family of nations and should be brought into conformity with European laws of war.[126] Yet at the same time, he labeled North African states "barbaric" and opposed to the security and standards of comportment of "civilized" states. Vattel insisted that "all nations have a right to enter into a league" to punish rogue states.[127] The idea of a consociation of states for the defense of order would cast a wide shadow.

Had Vattel elaborated further, it would have helped his readers answer the vexing question of whether he was imagining the European law of nations as universal. In some ways, though, a focus on this question gets in the way of our ability to bring into view connections, indirect or direct, between empires and European writing on the law of nations.[128] One clear link involved the question of how to regard political communities that did not show signs of the commitment to national virtues that Vattel associated with territorialized Protestant states. He regarded Indigenous people in the Americas as prime examples of peoples of "unsettled habitation."[129] Interestingly, Vattel extended similar criteria in condemning ecclesiastics and Catholic orders for their pretensions of autonomy. He did not mention Jesuits, but he might have done so in complaining that ecclesiastics had "even attempted to withdraw themselves entirely, and in every respect, from all subjection to the political authority." Such strategies represented "a mortal stab to society."[130]

Although Catholic institutions and nomadic political communities were excluded from statehood for different reasons, their equivalence in that regard remained. The groups shared the inability to pursue "legitimate and formal warfare" with pirates, bandits, and anyone who resorted to violence "without lawful authority, or without apparent cause, as likewise without the usual formalities, and solely with a view to plunder."[131] The similarity to the Iberian sleight of hand in associating Jesuits with Guaraní and Guaraní with non-Christian Indigenous communities is difficult to miss. So is the functional equivalence of Catholic orders, Indigenous Americans, and pirates when it came to the ability to prosecute legitimate war.[132] The explicit equivalence of such political communities is less important than the implicit message in Vattel's writing that they were unified by their opposition to state authority and their pursuit of unauthorized violence.

This formulation still begged the question of who would decide on violations of order. Here state practice again came into play. Vattel regarded peace treaties as existing in that same fluid space between natural law obligations and nations' pursuit of self-interest. This construction turned peace into a political arrangement that states signed onto because it aligned with their interests.[133] An agreement forged through the pursuit of self-interest could, then, be abandoned when conditions changed and presented a threat to a nation's self-interest. Vattel frowned on the tendency "to introduce obscure or ambiguous clauses into a treaty of peace" to fabricate excuses to return to war. But he also regarded every treaty as containing ambiguity, and therefore no treaty was inviolable.[134] Indeed, treaties' inherent ambiguity meant that the decision to return to war fell squarely within the "practice of judgment" of states. As if this room for maneuver was not enough, Vattel added that states could also legitimately return to war if they were asserting that a new wrong had been committed. All that was required, according to Vattel, was for nations to present arguments and evidence with "some colour of reason."[135]

These elements of Vattel's approach help us to relate the European legal imagination to imperial legal politics in small wars in the eighteenth century—but only if we avoid the temptation to trace applications or influences and instead consider that European imperial agents and European legal writers were arriving, in different locales, at similar solutions to related problems. Vattel was describing Europe as a "political system that was a subset of the larger society of states."[136] Other regions composed of multiple political communities were being imagined as political systems with a similar relation to the law of nations—a relation best captured in the legal imperative for military action to secure order.

In the Río de la Plata and on the Coromandel Coast, arguments about self-defense and the right to repress rebellions came easily to hand to justify violence. Both rationales conveniently pointed toward greater, systemic threats to order. In the Río de la Plata, an actual coalition represented European interests, whereas on the Coromandel Coast the conflict pitted two groups of European agents against each other. But even in the absence of a coalition, diplomatic back-and-forth constructed a European frame of reference for judging the conduct of war and the legitimacy of local rule. There was little that was abstract or theoretical in the grounds for exclusion of non-European polities from these exchanges. Their own legal actions and statements were drowned out by the din of imperial agents' repetitive chatter about law. If civilizational standards served as a cudgel with which European agents struck opponents, the hammer got heavier as the blows landed.

Local polities were far from silent victims. Like Europeans, they represented themselves as autonomous political actors by engaging in diplomacy and war. Guaraní leaders nurtured their enmity to Portugal and asserted their right to possess territory in letters to the Spanish crown. Charrúas and Minuanes engaged in raids and counterraids to protect their inland empire, and they formed and tested alliances in all directions. On the Coromandel Coast, local leaders positioned the British and French as *their* proxies, and it was *their* diplomacy with Mysore and Marathas that steered the course of the war. It is not an exaggeration to say that thickening European exchanges about the laws of war flowed in part from anxieties about relative European imperial weakness in these regions. Oddly, the muffled debates about proper battlefield conduct in far places sounded to some like a quiet announcement of European state capacity.

Politically plural regions beyond Europe encompassed assertive political communities and posed a challenge to European visions of dominance within the global order. Imperial small wars allowed Europeans to imagine the law of nations as the product of states in action anywhere in the world. The conflicts raised urgent questions about who had standing to regulate war. They pushed Europeans to insist on the exclusion of political communities and entities from statehood. The category encompassed religious orders and Indigenous polities; eventually, it would include trading companies. Far from Europe and in multisided small wars, the contours of a new global order of armed peace was taking shape. It would be regulated by European states acting together or in competition and enforced by violence on patrol.

Chapter 5

Saving Subjects, Finding Enemies

In March 1830, the British sloop *Comet*, under the command of Alexander Sandilands, anchored off the Cocos-Keeling Islands, a group of twenty-seven small coral reef islands in the vast expanse of the eastern Indian Ocean. Sandilands was conducting a wide-ranging patrol of the Pacific to report on "the Progress of the Inhabitants in Civilization and Christianity [and] their intercourse with other places."[1] His report to Rear-Admiral Owen of the East India Station began with routine topics like the hazards of the anchorage and the minor promise of the islands as a refreshment station for passing ships. Then Sandilands's narrative took an unusual turn. He described two rough settlements on the islands. In one small compound, a British subject named John Clunies Ross ruled a group comprising "his wife, five children, and a servant maid, eleven Englishmen, one Portuguese cook and a Javanese boy." In another, Ross's former employer, Alexander Hare, presided over some fifty-five adults who were "Natives of the Eastern Islands" and several dozen children. The children were sequestered in makeshift prisons where they were being held for what Sandilands called "prostitution"—by which he meant their future sexual exploitation by Hare.[2]

Sandilands urged Admiral Owen to send a naval force to put an end to Hare's deplorable "system." Instead, Owen reprimanded Sandilands for exposing Hare and Ross to the dangers of insurrection. A navy captain's first duty, Owen explained, was to protect British subjects. Whatever their faults—and even their crimes—Hare and Ross were British subjects far from home. The navy was required to protect them.[3]

Owen knew that his position was consistent with Sandilands's instructions. Like other navy ships dispatched on similar missions with vague objectives, the *Comet* had been sent on patrol in order to protect the persons and the interests of British subjects anywhere in the world. Sandilands's voyage was typical of circuits of maritime patrolling in the period. Most naval itineraries had prearranged stops, but captains carried only vague instructions about what they and their crews should do when they arrived at each site. Charged with sheltering subjects and their interests from harm, commanders were also supposed to refrain from actions that might lead to war. Yet commanders carried broad authorization to use violence when they judged it necessary. Faced with the shocking discovery of Hare's sexual violence, Sandilands hesitated before intervening directly only because Hare was a British subject and his victims were not.

In the increasingly militarized empires of the nineteenth century, it was commonplace for commanders like Sandilands to make spontaneous decisions about the use of force. They routinely took actions that international lawyers would now label "measures short of war." We know about the logic and the results of their actions because officials often followed them with written justifications. It was an old imperial practice to follow small episodes of violence with justificatory reports. And as previous chapters have shown, Europeans had long given armed men far from home permission to use violence under limited circumstances. But conditions in the long nineteenth century were making the practices both more systemic and more consequential.

The scale and scope of military patrolling had grown substantially. European—and, increasingly, U.S.—navies dispatched ships to distant stretches of sea and to coastal regions where empires asserted contested and tenuous claims and recognized overlapping spheres of influence. The counterpart to European naval patrols was the growing reliance on specialized army forces for territorial patrolling in empires. Examples include multiethnic armies in South Asia and specialized cavalry units in North America, Russia, and Latin America. Armies and militias pushed at the porous borders of politically crowded regions, often inserting themselves in complexes of raiding or acting to enforce settler designs

on land and local markets. Commanders cited the need to protect merchants, sojourners, and settlers, and they sometimes urged metropolitan
governments to back their violence with more strenuous demonstrations
of force.

I call the resulting pattern of violence a global regime of armed peace.
The regime was characterized by widespread, chronic violence that
clashed with common characterizations of an era of rising and unpre-
cedented peace. By ratcheting up anxieties about individual and collective danger to Europeans in colonial settings, protection emergencies
prompted violent interventions and assembled a unilateral right to engage in limited war. A widening arc of permissible small violence was
embedded in interimperial regional and global power.

Interventions in the regime of armed peace did not always stay small.
In settler colonies, the regime featured not moderation but extermination. The broad authorization for limited war framed the possibility of
defining whole communities as natural enemies who could be attacked
anywhere at any time to protect imperial subjects. The reclassification
of Indigenous groups as enemies removed them from imperial protection and mooted the necessity of detailed justifications of violence. In
Europe, meanwhile, protection talk expanded to include not just the
security of subjects but also the defense of vaguely defined imperial
interests. More than defensive reactions to protection emergencies,
measures short of war in empires acquired the character of legitimate
and necessary support for regional and global order.

This chapter examines violence on the threshold of war and peace and
practices that established its lawfulness in sprawling, militarized empires
of the nineteenth-century world. I examine small-scale violence in the
operations of the British Navy in the Pacific region and analyze the legal
routines of mounted militias in one part of the Spanish empire. In these
and other places, protection emergencies prompted broader campaigns
of violence. Sequences of "limited" intervention repeatedly opened the
door to atrocity. Redefined as enemies, some Indigenous subjects became vulnerable to attack anywhere—at least until perceived dangers to
European subjects receded. A future-conditional peace was firmly and
increasingly associated with utopian visions of white civilization. The

chapter then considers the parallels between the logic of violence on patrol and commentary by utilitarian and liberal writers on war in empires. In practice and in theory, imperial violence was conjuring, in Nick Harkaway's phrase, a world of "hyper-violent peace."[4]

Protection Emergencies

One of the century's best-known protection emergencies served as a catalyst to war. In 1839, detained British merchants refused to hand over their cargoes of opium to Chinese officials in the waters off Canton. Charles Elliot, the chief superintendent of British trade in China, instructed the merchants to surrender the opium so he could deliver it to Chinese officials. His critics would later argue that by seizing and turning over the opium Elliot had committed the British government to indemnifying the traders and had set the course for war.

Justifying violence by referencing dangers to subjects, Elliot defended his actions by stating that he had merely been opposing Chinese "aggressive measures against British life, liberty, and property."[5] Debates in London before the outbreak of the First Opium War kept the focus on the urgent need to protect British subjects and their property in China. Member of Parliament Joseph Hume declared that the rationale for war was brought into existence "the moment British subjects . . . were placed in prison."[6] The blockade and bombardment by Royal Navy ships in Chinese ports that followed were consistent with patterns of smaller-scale, less celebrated actions in the period to protect British subjects.[7]

The global extension of British influence and power in the nineteenth century depended on the ascendance of the Royal Navy. After the end of the Napoleonic Wars, the British Navy found itself patrolling a constitutionally diverse empire with fluid borders.[8] Peace had delivered new colonies, some of which—examples include Ceylon, the Cape Colony, and Malta—were strategically positioned to serve as bases or fueling stations for navy ships or as regional command centers. The East India Company (EIC) had its own navy, which it utilized to patrol and police sea lanes and harbors across the Indian Ocean and in the Persian Gulf. In the Atlantic, an uneasy rapprochement with U.S. and French navies in the North Atlantic contrasted with the growing influence of the British Navy in the South Atlantic, where British patrols to intercept slave trading and indirect involvement in conflicts surrounding South American independence imprinted British political and economic influence. Around the globe, the number of men employed by the Royal Navy was at an all-time high, as was the number of mutinies and other protests against naval discipline and shipboard conditions. New technologies, in particular the speed and maneuverability of steamships, were magnifying the power of the Royal Navy, which could respond faster to calls for a show of force and could surpass sailing ships in navigating riverine passageways and becalmed harbors.

Navy personnel and ships were first responders to calls for the protection of British subjects. Those calls became increasingly frequent in the mid-nineteenth century as British merchants reached farther into distant markets and regularly sought government support for their ventures. Throughout the colonies, and beyond, mid-level officials and consuls raised alarms about threats to individual British subjects and urged the selective but frequent use of British force. Both merchants and officials decried the seizure of trading vessels and called on the navy for protection of British shipping as well as retaliation against sea raiders. Protection emergencies swept the empire in the 1840s. Some of these crises, like the altercation over opium in Canton's harbor, became catalysts for war. Most generated sharp and brief engagements recorded by commanders and then quickly forgotten.

Between formal declarations of war and diplomatic maneuvering lay a range of responses to protection emergencies: blockade, bombardment, patrols, and raids by landing parties. In West Africa, British navy captains patrolling to contain the slave trade conducted sharp, brief attacks on coastal trading stations.[9] In Southeast Asia, naval ships bombarded Dayak settlements on the Borneo coast in 1843 and 1844, and again in 1847, causing several thousand civilian casualties.[10] In the century's most famous protection emergency in 1850, British Foreign Secretary Lord Palmerston ordered British Navy ships to blockade Athens until the Greek government compensated David Pacifico for damage and loss in anti-Semitic riots. Pacifico was a Gibraltar-born merchant who had worked for the Portuguese government but was appealing for help to the British government as a subject.[11] Clusters of other actions to protect British subjects and interests involved captains who stood to benefit directly from intercepting slavers or killing and wounding pirates.

The familiar label of "gunboat diplomacy" for such actions hides the legal logic and character of these phenomena. It is not enough to observe a systemic move toward interventionism and an increasingly robust, and overtly economic, imperialism in the nineteenth century. Acceptable use of limited force in roving imperial armies and navies did more than advance British imperialism. They assembled a long-lasting global regime of armed peace predicated on a European right to unilateral intervention, up to vaguely defined limits, and impunity for acts of peacetime violence.[12]

In the British Navy, justifications for violent intervention traveled along conventional pathways of the empire's information order. Captains wrote reports that they hoped would eventually find their way, endorsements appended, to London government officials. Various kinds of information jostled for space in the pages of captains' reports. The documents followed a rough template in which information about sea approaches, anchorages, and other geophysical conditions prefaced broad-ranging commentary on political matters, from evaluations of the sovereign status of local rulers to speculation on the interests and actions of rival empires. Moral judgments filtered into passages assessing levels of "civilization," and evaluations of resources available for naval ships blended with opinions about the potential of various sites to serve British commercial interests. Captains also recounted the details of specific engagements and expeditions on land, interspersing dry recitations of events with explanations of decisions taken on the spot. The vividness of the descriptions of dangers to British subjects is striking. So is the sophistication with which commanders appealed to hot-button political issues at home, such as abolition and the cause of free trade.

Many reports emphasized not just immediate dangers but also the more far-reaching goal of projecting British *interests*. Commanders knew that the government could not be relied upon to unquestioningly support bellicose acts short of war, even when the object was to protect British subjects. Anti-imperial sentiments, after all, crossed the political spectrum in Europe.[13] In Britain, reformers, buoyed by free trade advocates, were loudly bemoaning the costs of maintaining the empire. The Colonial Office lawyer James Stephen warned that there were limits to the logic of protection: "If some 50 or 60 of the Queen's subjects . . . settle themselves as a distant Community in a settlement some 100s of miles . . . from any other British Colony, they have no fair right to expect the advantages of the Institutions . . . of other parts of the British dominions."[14] The idea that the empire was a sinkhole for resources reinforced calls for measured responses to colonial crises. Short and inexpensive engagements were politically more palatable than prolonged and costly wars.

This background gave shape to a system in which imperial agents were authorized to make judgments about violence with the understanding that their decisions might be reviewed later by officials in Europe. In most cases, navy captains sailed with instructions that were intentionally vague and included orders to protect imperial subjects and interests. Assessing threats and how best to respond to them required captains to conduct legal inquiries, judge individual and community culpability, and assess political dangers of both violence and inaction. They were even charged with answering complex questions about political capacity, for example about whether local rulers were truly sovereign and whether they were worthy treaty partners.[15]

In considering such questions, captains brought their own interests into the mix as men of political intrigue who manipulated incentives for professional advancement and gain. Many in the period considered themselves reformers and abolitionists.[16] They had to survey political arrangements from the seas, with the benefit of generally brief landings—a peculiar vantage point from which to discern the nature of political and legal authority on land. Familiar with symbolic proofs of possession, captains offered their actions as support for inchoate claims against those of imperial rivals. They relied on what they knew, or could quickly learn, about risks or harm to vulnerable subjects and the actions of local polities and other empires. Captains' talk of protection supplemented their work in bolstering claims of possession in contested regions. They labored to show superiors that they were working to block the advance of rival empires, seeking to establish imperial influence without imposing costly rule, and using force selectively in the service of protection. Their actions sometimes prompted wider wars. Much more often, they produced series of unilateral and unregulated interventions.

Captains as Judges

When Captain H. A. Morshead arrived aboard HMS *Dido* in the Samoan Islands (then called the Navigator Islands by the British), he learned that the previous Royal Navy captain to stop at the islands had "left a case for me to adjust." The matter involved John Stowers, a British subject, who had complained that he had received "no protection whatever" and that locals had raided his home and carried away $500 in livestock and other property. Captain Morshead "convened the Chiefs" and asked them to provide statements about the reason for the attack on Stowers. Morshead wanted to know if the violence was justified— some payback for a previous injury, perhaps. The chiefs' statements, he concluded, were "very natural but frivolous and inadmissible as a cause of outrage." Yet the captain also pronounced as credible the chiefs' claim that Stowers had harmed them when he had "made a gun carriage for their enemies and taught them how to use it."[17]

At the end of what we can only call an informal trial, Captain Morshead ruled that the chiefs should pay $300 to Stowers. The sum would return the $500 value of the stolen property, minus Morshead's estimate of fair compensation for the damage caused by the gun carriage business. Before continuing his patrol of the South Pacific, a circuit begun in Honolulu that would lead the *Dido* to Tahiti, Pitcairn, Valparaiso, and Saint Helena before returning home, the captain left instructions with George Pritchard, the British consul, to make sure that the chiefs made good on their payment. Morshead quietly bragged, in the way that captains often did in their reports, about the wisdom of his judgment, assuring his superiors that he had "no doubt [the chiefs] will be punctual" in making payment.[18]

This small episode on a long Pacific naval cruise highlights the legal underpinnings of violence on patrol in the nineteenth-century British Empire.[19] Morshead was a captain, but he was also an imperial legal agent. He assessed a plea for protection by a British subject, conducted an ad hoc investigation, made a finding about whether an attack by islanders constituted a lawful punishment in their eyes, measured the harm of a weapons sale, and devised and arranged for enforcement of a penalty. In this case, the result was an order for monetary compensation, not reprisal. But the same legal processes in other cases produced decisions by captains and commanders to use force. Their quiet legal role to direct small, violent interventions cast imperial power across the Pacific region.

The pattern emerges clearly on the Northwest coast of North America, a crowded region of First Nation peoples and European traders where a handful of European settlements were the focus of increasingly sharp European imperial rivalry. The tentacles of Russian fur trading from the north extended into a broad area still claimed by the Spanish, but now infrequently visited by Spanish ships. Captain Cook's 1778 voyage to Nootka Sound, and his stop at what would later be called Vancouver Island, had revealed to the British the potential profits from trans-Pacific trading in sea otter pelts. Coastal Indigenous groups, including the Nuu-chah-nulth, Makah, Salish, Kwakwaka'wakw, and Haida peoples, were responding to the growing trade with Europeans and Americans by organizing and extending the fur trade.

Possession and protection figured prominently in early British naval actions on the coast. After the Spanish intercepted British ships and blocked British attempts to found establishments in Nootka Sound, the British and Spanish governments signed the first Nootka Convention in 1790. Negotiations revolved around claims of possession: the Spanish based their claims on a series of markers erected by the Bodega-Hezeta expedition of 1775, and the British pointed to the construction of several buildings by a trader named John Meares, who claimed initially to have purchased the land from an Indigenous group. The British government sent Captain George Vancouver to oversee implementation of the convention on his voyage to the Pacific. His negotiations with the Spanish commissioner Juan Francisco de la Bodega y Quadra produced little light. Vancouver realized that the Meares establishment was only a "small hut" that the trader had "abandoned when he left the place"—a slim thread on which to base arguments for British possession.[20] Vancouver also recognized his limited power to negotiate; his instructions did not outline the measures he should take to confirm British claims. He decided to interpret broadly his charge of "facilitating the commercial advantages of Great Britain in this part of the world" and to install a British subject in a permanent station on the coast. The conversations of the two naval commanders, Vancouver and Bodega y Quadra, formed the basis for the second Nootka Convention, signed in 1794. It awarded the Spaniards control over the coastline south of Neah Bay and designated all points north, including Nootka Sound, as areas of free navigation and trade.[21]

British Navy ships remained the principal representatives of British power in the region in the nineteenth century. The methods of the armed peace began, ironically, in the context of open war. The War of 1812 roiled tensions between British and American traders at the mouth of the Columbia River, prompting both groups to predict debilitating attacks from the sea on bundle-of-sticks fortifications. When a wave of U.S. captures of British whalers and merchant ships prompted the British Admiralty to dispatch a small squadron to the region in 1813, it carried instructions to protect British subjects. Captain James Hillyar, leader of the squadron, opened his secret instructions on leaving Rio de Janeiro for Cape Horn: "The principal object of the Service on which you are employed is to protect and render every assistance in your power to the British Traders from Canada." Even in wartime, the order to protect came first, before the command "to destroy . . . any settlements which the Americans may have formed." As was typical, the instructions were short on specifics. Hillyar and the other captains would have to decide what constituted appropriate and lawful violence on the other side of the world.[22]

It was not Hillyar but another captain, William Black, who arrived first in this wave of naval intervention on the Northwest coast in 1813. Black showed some flair for improvising. He decided to take formal

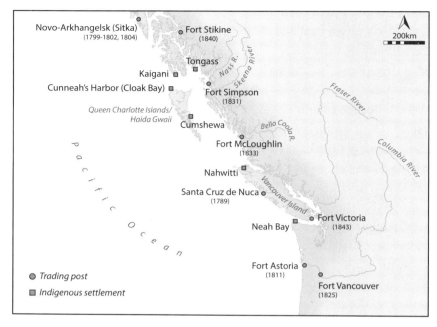

FIGURE 5.1. Map of Pacific Coast of North America in the early nineteenth century.

possession on behalf of the British government of tiny Fort Astoria and rename it Fort George—even though the British traders told him they had already purchased the fort from Americans fleeing in fear of a British naval attack. It seems likely that Black was claiming possession to enhance the chances of profiting, together with his crew, from the capture of the fort as a prize of war. But despite his creative application of the laws of war for one purpose, Black stuck to a narrower interpretation when it came to distributing profits from his actions. He told British traders that he could not sell them a captured ship for their use unless it had been condemned by the nearest admiralty court—conveniently, for his purposes, located two oceans away, at the Cape Colony.[23]

It was not just commonplace but required for captains to act as imperial legal agents. Captain Black's penchant for legal interpretation was shared by other captains and commanders dispatched to the wider region. As the focal point of imperial tensions shifted to other parts of the

Pacific, British captains responded to protection emergencies and took up vague commercial supporting roles. In 1836, Captain Edward Russell used the threat of force to push the king of Hawaii into enacting laws to protect British subjects and their property. In 1843, Captain George Paulet of HMS *Carysfort* went so far as to declare—without authorization—that Hawaii was a British protectorate; London officials first approved, then disavowed, the act.[24] In Southeast Asia, navy ships bombarded Dayak settlements on the Borneo coast in 1843 and 1844, and again in 1847, causing thousands of civilian casualties that lined the pockets of captains collecting head payments for injuring and killing pirates. A legal inquiry into whether the Dayaks were in fact pirates ended as it began, in a mass of legal uncertainty.[25]

These repeated encounters were assembling a system of quiet legal authority to make limited war. The Admiralty continued to dispatch ships with vague instructions, sometimes written by the captains themselves, to protect imperial subjects and commerce, and to adjust itineraries and decide on the use of force as needed. Traders and officials wrote repeatedly to London to call for more frequent patrols. In 1845, the former resident of New Zealand, James Burley, wrote to exhort the Earl of Aberdeen to send warships to "all the islands of the Pacific & open a friendly communication with their inhabitants." Burley explained that "friendly intercourse" was impossible without a show of force. The navy had to affirm its commitment "to punish such outrages as have frequently occurred & the wish to protect both the Islanders & His Subjects from a recurrence of these." That meant affirming captains' and commanders' authority to hear complaints by locals who would presumably, with the option of pleading their case in a quasi-legal proceeding, be less inclined to burn ships and murder their crews. Eventually, the legal responsibilities of the navy might be transferred, Burley explained, to British residents assigned to all the key groups of islands.[26]

Where they had already been appointed, consuls exhorted London officials to make it clear to navy captains that they did have very wide discretion to use violence. In 1845, George Pritchard, consul to the Samoan Islands, complained that he had been stationed there for five months without being able to "rent or purchase an inch of ground" for a house or consulate. Locals clearly thought that making land available would pave the road to colonization. "They believe," Pritchard wrote, that "the first Ship is to send Missionaries then a consul, and next to take possession." Two years later, Pritchard was complaining that Captain Patrick Blake, by refusing to punish islanders, had encouraged them to think they could "injure British persons with impunity."[27]

The Admiralty at first constructed the armed peace in an ad hoc fashion. It was little more than a collection of many moving parts. Eventually, officials formally took up the question of the scope for navy captains' discretion in ordering violence. Admiral Seymour's response to the consul Prichard patiently outlined Captain Blake's judicial role. He affirmed that a captain always carried authorization "to use his judgment" in applying force whenever a wrong was "committed against his Majesty's Subjects" and no superior was on hand to issue orders. Seymour observed that Captain Blake had acted as a wise judge when he found in several of the cases "brought before him" insufficient proof of wrongdoing by islanders. His caution preserved his right in other cases to inflict "severe punishment" on perpetrators or their villages.[28]

After referring the question of captains' discretion up to the highest echelons of the Foreign Office, officials confirmed that these legal practices were in fact imperial policy. Here was how they described jurisdiction exercised from the deck of a ship: "[W]hen any British Ship of War visits each Island and the Captain finds that any British subjects settled therein have sustained wrongs; the Captain should be authorized to demand & exact redress from the acting and responsible author." If a captain found that a British subject was responsible for injuries to locals, he "should endeavor to persuade the British Subject to make adequate reparations." If the British subject refused to comply, the captain had the option to authorize local leaders to assume jurisdiction; that is, "in the exercise of their own authority," locals could expel the offending British subject. Even then, the captain retained a responsibility to protect and was instructed to "receive [the offender] on board his Ship, and carry him away from the Island"—now effectively acting as enforcer of local justice. Officials warned that when British subjects were involved in a dispute with a subject of another foreign power, captains should "not interfere, unless with the consent of both Parties, as arbiter of their differences." And if a dispute had nothing to do with British subjects, the captain should "abstain from interference, unless appealed to by both Parties."[29]

These statements were intended merely to recognize practices already common across the region. But the fact that they were common, and occasionally committed to print, did not make them into any sort of code. The whole system of violence on patrol depended on the authorization to act first and regale the Admiralty with legal reasons later.

The workings of the regime are clearly visible on the Pacific coast of North America. After the 1846 settlement corralled the British north of the forty-ninth parallel, the navy's attention veered from unruly Americans to dangerous Indigenous communities.[30] The militarization of coastal waters helped to create the conditions for small violence to flourish.[31] In a series of conflicts with Indigenous polities, captains remained the main narrators of events and the principal agents responsible for choosing between diplomacy and violence. The navy was effectively in charge of mapping Indigenous political authority in the region, but rather than pronouncing on broader questions about Indigenous sovereignty, captains experimented in asserting British jurisdiction in response to Indigenous attacks on British subjects.[32]

In one of a string of protection emergencies involving Indigenous violence against Britons, a Nahwitti band in 1850 killed three British sailors who were deserters from a merchant ship. Captain George Wellesley in the Daedalus traveled to the place of the killing to arrest the Indigenous men responsible. After a skirmish, the crew contented itself with burning empty houses. The rear-admiral of the Pacific station, Fairfax Moresby, wanted to punish the whole Nahwitti band unless they surrendered the men responsible for the murder. The group at first refused to hand over the men and fled into the interior as the British landing party destroyed their camp and killed several Nahwitti men who remained. A few days later, when some Nahwitti returned to deliver the corpses of those they claimed were the murderers, Moresby celebrated British restraint and the neatness of reprisal by proxy.

The admiral then sent Captain Augustus Leopold Kuper on the frigate Thetis to reassert Britain's possession of the Queen Charlotte Islands.

Captain Kuper found that the threat of American incursions was over-blown and the promise of gold mining on the islands was "overrated."[33] Instead of opposing Americans, he followed the trail of another protection crisis after a company shepherd was murdered at a sheep station near Victoria. The British again demanded the surrender of the two suspects, but this time nothing happened. HMS *Thetis* then landed "130 Officers, seamen and Marines" and notified locals of the plan "to treat them as enemies unless they submitted to the demands of justice."[34] Eventually, a group came forward to surrender one of the suspects, and another was captured. Once again, the navy improvised a trial. A jury "composed of the officers present" found the men guilty and sentenced them to be hanged, a punishment carried out before an audience of "the whole tribe." The navy took credit for resolving the crisis without firing a shot.[35]

London officials wondered whether the navy might be going too far in its exercise of legal authority. Moresby's actions drew the attention of officials in London, and the incident added to other cases from across the Pacific where captains' judicial power raised questions. In 1850, the Foreign Office asked the Law Officers of the crown to provide an opinion as to "the extent to which Officers Commanding H.M. Ships of War may exact redress from Natives of the Pacific Islands, in cases where the wrongs done by them to British Subjects extend to loss of life by unprovoked and deplorable murder."[36] The language seemed designed to elicit affirmation of captains' discretion. The opinion that came back was more restrictive than the Foreign Office might have anticipated. The law officers recognized the difficulty of fixing "the proper line of conduct to be pursued by the Commanders of British Ships of War under the circumstances stated." But, they continued, some standards of evidence had to be met. Commanders, they advised, had to "actually witness the unprovoked commission of murder or any atrocious crime against British Subjects" for them to be justified in "demanding redress & the punishment of offenders." If there were crimes alleged but not witnessed against British subjects, navy commanders should show "the utmost caution & forbearance before resorting to any exercise of force whatever."[37]

Even while urging restraint, the memorandum recognized wide latitude for British commanders enacting reprisal. It conferred on them the capacity to decide whether acts were "unprovoked" or "atrocious." And while providing guidelines about evidence, it left captains and commanders in charge of interviewing witnesses and deciding when necessity trumped the need for caution. It affirmed, in other words, their responsibilities and authority as legal officers. The guidelines about restraint did not have much effect. Navy captains continued to liberally authorize attacks as retaliation for Indigenous aggression and "crimes." Responses to protection emergencies composed a regional regime of legitimate, limited force and extended it across an oceanic sphere of influence.

We glimpse the regime's continuities decades later, on the other side of the Pacific, in the Solomon Islands, where British Navy ships in the 1870s and 1880s were lashing out at islanders for their attacks on labor recruiters, who sometimes simply snatched their victims. Some attacks by islanders on visiting ships were clearly retaliatory in nature—payback for previous violence by whites—while others might have been opportunistic raids to grab trade goods. A series of reports about "outrages" against crews led the Admiralty to dispatch HMS *Emerald* to the Solomon Islands in 1881. Captain W. H. Maxwell's orders were to discover who was responsible for the murder of a lieutenant and five men aboard the schooner *Sandfly*. Maxwell was instructed to find the perpetrators and "follow them up wherever they may go" and give them "the severe punishment they so well deserve."[38] Maxwell interviewed local chiefs to assign responsibility for the *Sandfly* attack and several other attacks on schooner crews. Without much attention to the quality of the information he was receiving, the captain identified the villages reportedly home to attackers, then landed parties of plunder and destruction. Since news of the presence of a warship in the area traveled quickly, Maxwell's troops found village after village empty. At Raita, the village supposedly responsible for the *Sandfly* attack, the landing party of four officers and sixty seamen and marines got "busy with the work of destruction." They cut down or pulled up crops and trees and set fire to all the dwellings. They repeated the scorched-earth tactics at a string of other nearby villages.

Captain Maxwell was not blind to the flaws of his method of reprisal. He thought that the attack on the *Sandfly* had been unprovoked, but he also got hints of violence by labor recruiters. One chief told Maxwell that "the labour schooners had taken the law into their own hands, had landed their men, attacked the village, burnt it, cut down the cocoa-nut trees, and killed several natives." Maxwell was not sure the report was credible. He suspected that islanders were using the British to engage their own local enemies. After a chief accompanying one of the landing parties tomahawked a "poor old woman," Maxwell resolved not to use islanders to help carry out punishments. Finally, he tired of the performances of inquiry and reprisal. He suggested to the Admiralty that "the constant presence of one or two efficient gunboats" and sustained diplomatic relations with a few chiefs might be a better recipe for order.

The system of limited violence was difficult to calibrate. Five years later another schooner, *Young Dick*, was attacked and nearly all its crew and a government agent were killed. Reflecting on how to respond, Rear-Admiral George Tryon again raised doubts about the usual system of reprisal. Catching those responsible for the attack was only a very remote possibility, and further "work of destruction" might backfire and create "a state of indiscriminate war of natives against whites." Tryon even suggested that recruiters "voluntarily withdrew themselves from the protection of laws of their own country" when they seized islanders and prompted violence in response. Even if they were worthy of protection, he recognized, conditions in the islands might make it impossible for the trade to be "practically supervised on the spot."[39]

Debates were already raging about how to hold recruiters responsible for their violence against islanders. In 1871, John Coath, captain of the schooner *Jason*, was charged and tried in Queensland for kidnapping nine Pacific Islanders. Coath's defense at the trial involved an intriguing argument about jurisdiction. Because Coath's victims lived beyond the jurisdiction of British courts, the defense asserted, he could not be found guilty of a crime against them. In fact, Coath's lawyer claimed, the captives became free as soon as they were brought aboard the *Jason*. If he had carried them to Fiji or another non-British territory, he might have been guilty of kidnapping them, according to this logic; in transporting them to Queensland, he was preserving their liberty. This audacious argument did not stick, and Coath was found guilty. The next year, Parliament's Kidnapping Act extended the jurisdiction of the

Queensland Supreme Court over British subjects in Pacific territories not under another European power. Ostensibly designed to strengthen controls on settler violence, the act actually helped to normalize practices of quasi-forced labor recruitment by bringing the practice formally under imperial purview.[40]

Imperial violence in the Western Pacific resembled practices of violence on patrol across the region. But new contexts also altered the meaning of protection—and the measure and nature of force applied. The most immediate catalyst of reprisals by naval ships remained protection emergencies in the form of attacks on British traders and quasi-slavers. Violence on patrol was supposed to be quick and brutal enough to send a message. But navy officers were unsatisfied with the repeating attacks on empty villages. They sought a better system, suggesting the placement of armed vessels off the coast and the closer regulation of British captains and crews. Tweaks to the regime of armed peace did not, however, change the basic process of assembling ad hoc inquiries and making case-by-case decisions about violence.

Friends and Enemies

Histories of nineteenth-century imperial violence often treat naval and land campaigns separately. They also tend to focus on actions within a single empire, an approach that associates imperial violence with projects of imperial and national state formation. But protection emergencies unfolded in structurally similar ways on land and sea, and trends toward political consolidation do not fully explain the dynamics of violence. Even as empires expanded their jurisdiction in pluripolitical regions and opposed Indigenous autonomy, serial acts of violence did more than incorporate unruly territories and subjects. They made Indigenous polities subject to being variously assigned by Europeans to the status of subjects, rebels, or enemies.

We can glimpse the way bundled protection emergencies resolved into war in the Río de la Plata in the early nineteenth century. The region was home to Guaraní recently released from Jesuit missions, as well as seminomadic groups labeled "pagans" by Spaniards and

Portuguese, and it was bounded by ranching concerns and crisscrossed by itinerant traders and smugglers. Years of encroachment by Portuguese and Spanish settlers and slavers had splintered Indigenous groups and encompassed them in networks of trade and labor. Charrúas and Minuanes were among those actively trading with settlers and in some cases operating as clients or proxies of the Portuguese as they sought to extend their influence. At the turn of the nineteenth century, the region's political economy centered on a lucrative contraband trade in hides, only partially channeled into official circuits. Spanish and Portuguese elites were experimenting with ways to project power into the countryside in order to privatize wild herds and establish title to land.

Like many other regions, the Río de la Plata was a site of militarization and new forms of patrolling. Militias on horseback were organized in major towns. We get a sense of the goals and politics of patrolling by examining efforts to step up rural policing in the hinterlands of Montevideo. In the 1770s and 1780s, the Montevideo town council began to appeal to Madrid for a show of military force in the countryside through the creation of *partidas*—sorties of specialized military outfits into the interior. The viceroy complied, and in 1796 he created a force of *blandengues* in Montevideo modeled on a similar corps founded in 1752 in Buenos Aires. Viceroy Áviles explained in Buenos Aires in 1800 that the main goals were "to contain the raids of the *charrúas* and *minuanes* . . . and to bring into civil and Christian society that other class of vagrants, even more pernicious, who are dispersed throughout the countryside."[41]

In advocating the creation of *blandengue* forces, Spanish officials routinely characterized the countryside as the disorderly domain of rustlers, smugglers, thieves, and *indios*—a region of chronic conflict in desperate need of order. Increasingly, Charrúas and Minuanes were singled out for "pacification." *Blandengue* captains were themselves partly responsible for this shift in rhetoric. Many of the men in the new force were recruited, through an act of amnesty, from among groups of fugitives subsisting on occasional work or smuggling and closely identified with the itinerant poor of the countryside. José Gervasio Artigas, who would become the leader of a backcountry revolution in the Banda Oriental, was a *blandengue* captain and a former smuggler.

The first forays of *blandengues* against Indigenous communities intensified violence in the region by producing an uptick in Indigenous attacks on estancias. Some of these attacks were undoubtedly reprisals for *blandengue* raids in which Indigenous women and children were taken as captives and sold or assigned as quasi-slaves to estancias and urban households. In 1799, the viceroy insisted on mounting two attempts to negotiate for peace with Indigenous groups, with one expedition led by the *blandengue* official Juan Ventura Ifrán.

The diary of Ifrán's patrol, written in 1799, conveys the sheer tedium of backcountry patrolling.[42] The force of about fifty *blandengues* was bogged down by heavy winter rains and had difficulty even locating Indigenous bands with whom to parley. It was only after two months of travel that Ifrán finally encountered some camps of the "Minuana nation." He was able to convince about twenty-two Minuanes to accept the "protection" of his forces and accompany the troops to a settlement—though later the quasi-captives would desert the expedition. Ifrán's group then located a larger band of Minuanes. Attempts to convince the cacique of the group, Masalana, to follow Ifrán to a settlement did not go well. Masalana declared that he would rather "die in the countryside," and he withdrew with his followers across the Uruguay River to avoid further interactions.

The militarization of the region could not be reduced to the logic of European-Indigenous tensions. Christianized Native people operated across these groups and at crucial moments drove negotiations. Christians in Masalana's group urged the cacique not to trust Ifrán's forces because they had no ties to "true Christians." The diary also shows how the failure of one set of negotiations could set up violence in the next encounter. Soon after Masalana withdrew, Ifrán's party came across another Indigenous encampment. This time Ifrán ordered his men to sneak up on the settlement at night. He claimed that he instructed one of the Christian Charrúas accompanying the *blandengues* to shout out an offer of peace at dawn, but in fact his forces were already in position to attack and it was no surprise when a skirmish broke out. Ifrán's men killed five Minuanes. The rest fled, leaving a sizable herd of horses—probably the intended target of Ifrán's group all along; the soldiers immediately took possession of them.

Skirmishes of this sort were recurring across the region. For *blanden-gues*, such engagements resulted directly from a standing authorization for violence. They also prompted specific narratives of acting in self-defense, either in direct response to Indigenous attacks or in delayed response to raids close in time or place. Ifrán was conforming to this expectation when he carefully noted that the Minuanes surrounded by his men had opened fire first.

As with the British in Pacific North America, violence was also accompanied by occasional attempts by military forces to use makeshift legal proceedings to assert authority. While Ifrán was still on his peace mission, Captain Jorge Pacheco was laying the groundwork for a wider war by taking testimony from ranchers about Indigenous attacks, an activity he combined with quasi-prosecutorial investigation. In general, Pacheco struck a tone of judicial moderation in describing his exercise of restraint in using force. On one occasion, he wrote to the viceroy that he had come across a small band of "infieles" in an area of numerous attacks, but that he had kept in mind the viceroy's "pious exhortations . . . to regard with horror the loss of human life" and had resisted the use of arms, although "it would have been an easy thing to exterminate [the *indios*]."[43]

Men on patrol rarely lost sight of their place within the imperial legal order. In another incident, Pacheco gathered testimony and referred it to Buenos Aires for action. A group of Pacheco's men on patrol apprehended Lucas Barrera, described as a "mulato," and Juan Manuel, identified as a "pagan Indian." The young men had recently returned after several months living in an Indigenous community. It was the second capture for Juan Manuel, who had been seized as a participant in a raid by settlers a year before and "given" in service by Captain Artigas to a local rancher before running away with Barrera. To live with "pagan Indians" and return were hardly crimes. But while the two young men were away, an Indigenous raid on a nearby estancia had resulted in the death of a rancher and the capture of his wife. Pacheco suspected that the two men had been among the raiders, and he began to take testimony from potential witnesses. No one could place the men at the raid, though one reported they had made "indecent proposals" to a woman at a neighboring estancia and asked about other women in the area. If he had chosen to punish the men, Pacheco would have had ample legal cover. Instead, he sent them to Buenos Aires, with a letter explaining that he "should not involve himself in passing judgment," both because he had too much else to do and because the captives were so young. Pacheco hoped that in the city the young men might learn a trade and become "useful" to the state.[44]

The implication that it was his choice whether or not to pass judgment is revealing. Pacheco was tying the decision to captives' potential for peaceful integration and the level of threat they posed. It was not enough to determine who was ostensibly Christian, and who was pagan. As in Ifrán's diary, the details of the case showed the perceived dangers of hispanized Indigenous men acting as enemies. Even after Pacheco sent the young captives to the city, he continued to pursue the case. When his forces recaptured the widow of the slain rancher, Pacheco personally took her deposition. She did not recall seeing a *mulato* or an *indio cristiano* among the raiders—other than the raiders' leader. When the widow's statement reached Buenos Aires, the two youths were freed.[45]

Violence on patrol continued. Only a month after taking the first set of depositions in the case, Pacheco left on his own to patrol the area north of the Río Negro. His diary openly refers to *indios* as "enemies" and recounts a series of attacks on them by his men. After one skirmish, Pacheco and his troops "counted in the field 37 men and 2 women dead, including the Cacique Juan Blanco of the Charrúas and a cacique of the Minuanes Zará." Pacheco found one captive woman and two boys, and in turn took captives of his own: seven youths, thirteen women, and eleven children. He also seized, and described in more detail, the capture of 327 horses. In another engagement a few days later, all the armed Indigenous fighters were killed and another group of fifty-two captives were taken.[46]

These examples reveal a logic of frontier violence that prioritized the defense of settlers but also pulled and stretched the notion of protection. In one dimension, the framework encountered limits. "Pagan Indians" were technically vassals of the crown, but as threats to estancias multiplied and narratives of their supposed rejection of peaceful incorporation circulated, they could not themselves be objects of protection. In another dimension, the protection of settlers expanded into a vague defense of order—an armed peace designed to prevent future attacks that made room for repeated violence and captive taking.

It was a neat trick to represent forces seeking to find and attack Indigenous communities as being on a defensive mission. The same twist in logic transformed the seizure of herds and captives into protective measures. A crucial part of violence on patrol was to treat each skirmish as an isolated event narrated by *blandengue* officers operating as petty legal officials. They took depositions and made decisions on the spot about when violence was justified. The procedures inserted *blandengue* violence into a broader program described as pacification. Pacheco affirmed this move when he announced to the viceroy that his latest patrol had rid a wide swath of territory "of the cruel devastations that it was daily experiencing."[47]

No one was yet referring to this action as an all-out war to defeat or exterminate Charrúas and Minuanes. Native peoples were to be incorporated in the imperial order through punishment as well as through captivity defined as an act of mercy. At the limit of such actions was the supposition that Indigenous communities might have to be destroyed in order to be saved. Protection emergencies that began with anxieties about the dangers posed to estancia owners and town dwellers of roaming Charrúas and Minuanes resolved into implicit acceptance of their redefinition as enemies.

Decades after the Ifrán and Pacheco patrols with their justifications for serial attacks on Charrúas and Minuanes, violence against Indigenous people in the Río de la Plata turned into quasi-war. In 1831, troops under the command of the newly formed República Oriental del Uruguay invited Charrúas for talks at a location later dubbed Salsipuedes (Get-Out-If-You-Can). A surprise attack became a massacre. Dozens of captives were taken to Montevideo, where later an enterprising Frenchman received authorization to take four of the prisoners (three men, including a cacique, and one woman) to Paris. Sénaqué, Vaimaca Pirú, Tacuabé, and Micaela Guyunusa were exhibited as "savages" and "prisoners" of "the Indian tribe Charrúas, recently exterminated."[48] In Uruguay, the massacre marked the end of Charrúas and Minuanes as recognized political communities. The transition from violence on patrol to a campaign of extermination was swift, facilitated by the delegation of authority to identify and eliminate threats to security and order.

Enemies and Extermination

The path from serial protection emergencies to all-out war on enemy-subjects belonged to a wider pattern. Historians sometimes obscure parallels by treating cases of settler-Indigenous violence in isolation and by portraying European brutality as simply lawless. Yet we can deplore imperial violence and its effects while still capturing the way law helped to turn limited interventions into the prelude to atrocity.

To bring into sharper focus how this transition worked, consider another example, the mounting violence against Aborigines in Tasmania in the 1820s. Small-scale, intermittent violence was endemic in the colony after its seizure by the British in 1803. Interactions between Aboriginal Tasmanians and the bushrangers and convicts who moved beyond Hobart featured at least fifty violent incidents between 1813 and 1823. As in New South Wales, many Aborigine attacks on white settlers were responses to provocations, especially the movement of settlers or their livestock into areas of scarce and coveted resources alongside increasingly frequent seizures by white men of Aboriginal women and children. In 1810, Aborigines at Coal River slaughtered cattle after white raiders abducted Aboriginal children; Oyster Bay Tasmanians also became warlike after a raid for children on their community.[49]

A classic protection emergency in 1823 propelled interpolity violence to a new phase. A group of Oyster Bay Aborigines killed two stock keepers, prompting a hunt for the perpetrators and leading to the capture, summary trial, conviction, and execution of four Oyster Bay men. In response to this episode and others, the colonial government stumbled toward a policy of authorizing indiscriminate attacks on Aborigines while ostensibly marking some limits. A series of government statements defined the conditions under which Aboriginal Tasmanians could be treated as enemies. A government notice of November 1826 loosely based on a directive from the imperial government in London specified that Aborigines engaged in violence against settlers should not be punished as criminals but instead opposed "as if they proceeded from subjects of any accredited State."[50] That meant settlers could shoot first and ask questions later—though it was not clear what proof, if any, would be required to confirm Aborigines' hostile intentions.[51]

In 1828, the government expanded the category of "enemies" to include Blacks found in settled districts without passes. Government instructions still warned settlers to undertake violence only in self-defense and not to act without the approval of a magistrate, a military officer, or someone else with delegated power, although there was little enforcement of such limits. Also in 1828, the government's declaration of martial law expanded definitions of permissible violence. Aborigines should be encouraged to "retire" to unsettled parts of the island, while in theory those who accepted resettlement should be left alone.[52] This logic automatically redefined Aborigines in the path of white settlement as enemies who had provoked attack by failing to withdraw. A "frenzy of land handouts," meanwhile, was rapidly expanding the area of settlement and creating the conditions for open warfare.[53]

Settler violence was decentralized, ad hoc, and deadly in its effects. Locals formed pursuit parties to devote a day or two to chasing groups of Aborigines after attacks. Roving parties undertook more sustained patrols, some under military command and others authorized by magistrates. Vigilante groups also came together to "hunt" Aborigines. Participants in raiding parties were mostly poor, and many were conscripts: soldiers and convict field police in militia groups; assigned convicts angling for reduced sentences in civilian parties and servants, shopkeepers, and convicts in vigilante gangs. The actions of these bands gave the lie to claims that white violence was being undertaken in self-defense. The parties operated at night to try and spot Aboriginal campfires to find settlements, and their attacks featured indiscriminate killing, followed by open reports of kill rates of men, women, and children. Disciplinary measures against leaders of patrols for excessive violence were vanishingly rare.[54]

Strikingly, some observers at the time characterized the violence against Tasmanians as a campaign of "extermination" that was simultaneously a

FIGURE 5.2. Governor George Arthur's Proclamation to the Aborigines of Tasmania, ca. 1828–1830. Original in Mitchell Library, State Library of New South Wales.

peacemaking project because it represented a necessary alternative to an uncontrolled "war of private persons."[55] This representation of atrocity as necessary to the prevention of atrocity found support in two other interpretations of the violence. One view, expressed succinctly in the Aborigines Committee report of 1830, labeled Aboriginal violence as "wanton and savage."[56] The characterization ignored evidence that violence by Tasmanians often followed attacks on their women and incursions on their territory. A parallel approach was to blame white ruffians—a motley group of former convicts, soldiers, and impoverished settlers—for brutality against Tasmanians in the face of government attempts to encourage restraint.[57] Accepted as accurate, these accounts contrasted an unruly "war of private persons" with rebellion or a state of public war.

Since Tasmanians were not the same as either criminal subjects or soldiers of a separate polity, there was no settled legal framework for the violence. Rather than prompting new political or legal language, the situation permitted officials to move adroitly, often without explanation, between characterizing Tasmanians as rebels or enemies. The slippage and the lack of a third possibility proved convenient. When colonial officials ignored repeated requests to meet Tasmanian leaders in Hobart to negotiate the terms of a peace, they were treating the defeated men simultaneously as prisoners of war and as subjects under government protection. Their status remained uncertain at the point that several hundred Tasmanians were sent to an impoverished exile in the Bass Strait Islands between 1830 and 1835.[58]

Here and elsewhere, small wars served as more than the necessary prelude to the closure of frontiers and the consolidation of state power.[59] There was real and important legal work involved in transforming protection emergencies, with their ad hoc methods of justifying violence, into quiet wars in which rationales for violence moved readily from intra-imperial to interpolitical registers. Attacks against Indigenous groups relied on shifting definitions of them as recalcitrant subjects and hardened enemies. Seemingly isolated actions to punish or discipline groups accused of anti-settler violence developed quickly into quiet (or not-so-quiet) wars of extermination.

The origins of these campaigns in protection emergencies gave the violence, however brutal, the character of legitimate defensive actions and limited conflicts. The wars against Native peoples in the Western territories of the nineteenth-century United States, the serial frontier wars of Southern Africa, the continual violence between settler and Aboriginal communities in New South Wales and Tasmania, the violence of expansion into Indigenous lands by South American republics, the relentless push by Russians into Central Asia, and French advances into Northern Africa and Indochina—these and other serial small wars featured justifications by Europeans originating in the protection of imperial subjects and, increasingly, of imperial interests and of something much less tangible: regional order.

Protecting Imperial Interests

Protection emergencies engendered violence in part because of increasingly expansive ideas about what precisely needed protection. The goal of saving subjects was easily understood, and visceral reactions to violence against European sojourners and settlers drove many interventions. But subjects were not always at risk, and insecurities of property also figured prominently in protection emergencies. So did more diffuse geopolitical considerations that grew from efforts to defend imperial interests and translated into a still broader agenda of promoting regional order.[60]

In Britain, the move from calls for the protection of subjects to advocacy for protecting imperial interests tracked debates about free trade. Historians assessing the relation between liberalism and empire have asked how it was that advocacy of free trade aligned with support for imperialism, and its attendant violence. One way of reconciling these positions is to bundle them under the heading of the "imperialism of free trade," a phrase and perspective advanced by John Gallagher and Ronald Robinson in a now-classic article.[61] Gallagher and Robinson were challenging the view that the middle decades of the nineteenth century represented a phase of anti-imperialism contrasting with the high imperialism of the last quarter of the nineteenth century. Instead, they argued, political action in support of commercial interests spanned both phases. Military actions were a tool to force markets open—with the goal of creating a global regime of free trade. This account lined up with a broader narrative about how an era of free trade later was eclipsed by the rise of protectionism, as tariffs were imposed or raised on key commodities.

A focus on protection emergencies as foundational to imperial violence suggests a different interpretation of the links between free trade and imperialism. Utilitarian writers and their liberal followers took up the problem of reconciling the dream of world peace with the reality of European global power. Jeremy Bentham exhorted European governments to pursue peace by giving up their colonies.[62] Holding "distant dependencies," he wrote, would always "increase the chances of war." Empires multiplied conflicts in places where control was insecure, where remoteness made settled rule perpetually elusive, and where the use of force was essential to order. European powers could save money and reduce corruption by eliminating all that and shrinking their military presence in colonies. Bentham even urged Britain not "to guarantee foreign constitutions" since such obligations could pull the country into wars. The only way to create the conditions for peace was through "1. The reduction and fixation of the force of the several nations that compose the European system; [and] 2. The emancipation of the distant dependencies of each state."[63]

Conquest and the retention of colonies, in this view, operated against collective interests. Yet Bentham also recognized that here was no clear or reliable mechanism for deciding on what conditions equated to national or imperial interests. Sovereigns and their ministers would always claim to be acting on behalf of "the nation," he pointed out. Even more troubling was the tendency to confuse the interests of empire-states with those of the ruling few. Even the most seemingly objective search for the nation's interests would lead to frustration; in the absence of authoritative voices on the subject one had to rely on newspapers and their bellicose and crude pronouncements. One could not simply identify some clear and limited set of interests and, then, extrapolate them to nations. In the transition from individual to collective scales, "interests" lost their rootedness in morality and law, according to Bentham. "Injustice, oppression, fraud, lying," if undertaken in the pursuit of individual interests, might be regarded as "crimes" or "vices," but when they appeared in connection with national interests, Bentham wrote, the same actions were "sublimated into virtues."[64]

Bentham's peculiar answer to this problem—the indeterminacy of interests—was to represent European dominance as fundamental to global security. While arguing that Britain should maintain a bare-bones navy, one merely "sufficient to defend its commerce against pirates," Bentham also recognized that the effectiveness of such a radically diminished force would depend on widespread consensus about the superiority of British military might.[65] More generally, when Bentham stated that perpetual peace would benefit "the common welfare of all civilised nations," he immediately added that he was referring "more particularly" to the common welfare of Great Britain and France.[66] Beyond and above elusive specific interests of colonists, empires, or ruling elites, Bentham posited the existence of a common welfare defined by European interests in security and produced mainly through the alignment of Britain and France.

Free traders in London at midcentury would move beyond Bentham to use the concept of "interests" to reconcile free trade advocacy with support for imperial ventures. The link is surprising since free trade advocates, not unlike Bentham, also began from a position of a strong critique of imperialism. Richard Cobden, the Manchester leader of the free trade movement in Britain, consistently opposed colonial expenditures and criticized imperial interventions, aligning with Bentham's anti-imperialism. Yet many free traders embraced Edward Gibbon Wakefield's vision of "systematic colonization," and the ranks of colonial reformers and London free traders overlapped more than at the margins. Wakefield championed schemes to promote colonization through direct sponsorship of emigration, having absorbed from Malthus the idea of a labor surplus in Britain. To this perspective he added the notion of a land surplus in the colonies. Wakefield and his followers imagined creating a perfect land-labor balance in the colonies by sponsoring settlers who would make agricultural capitalism possible.

Wakefield's vision intersected with dreams of a British empire of trade. Not just the settler colonies but also other regions of the world would come to form a vast market for British goods. In his "Letter from Sydney," which was written not in Sydney but in London's Newgate Prison (where Wakefield was serving time for abducting a fifteen-year-old girl), Wakefield envisioned the colony in Australia as growing through the immigration of a labor force not just from Britain but from all around the Pacific and Asia. He predicted that the result would be that British traders could "enjoy free trade with millions of fellow subjects of Chinese origin, and *through them* . . . with hundreds of millions of customers" in China.[67] The vision was one of a tiered empire of trade, with an inner circle of colonial settler societies forming something like a trade federation, with their influence expanded through the incorporation of non-Britons as subjects, and with British commercial reach beyond settler colonies into places where Britain had no direct control.

Many political figures who endorsed Wakefield's vision and his specific colonization schemes self-consciously sought to reconcile this position with support for free trade. Robert Torrens, the free trade advocate and political economist usually given credit for the theory of comparative advantage, came out in favor of regulating colonial trade to encourage commerce between the metropole and colonies—so long as no party was prevented from buying cheaper goods. Torrens brought in ideas about British security in order to explain how colonization schemes and free trade policies were compatible. In his view, settler colonies would not only create markets for British goods but would also secure British interests globally through spreading, as he put it, "the British name, the British laws, the British influence throughout all climes of the world."[68]

Another approach to reconciling free trade and systematic colonization was offered by William Molesworth. As a member of Parliament, Molesworth was outspoken in his criticism of the Colonial Office for its mismanagement of crown colonies. He asserted that the Colonial Office had placed the colonies in "a state of disorganization and danger" and criticized the government's wasteful global military expenditures. But Molesworth also asserted that colonies were of "the greatest advantage to a commercial country like this." Like Wakefield and Torrens, Molesworth imagined that free British settlers would buy British, a notion that he tied to a racial vision of Anglo-American global influence. At the same time, he suggested that making property in land accessible to all British subjects in the colonies, whether white or not, would nurture market expansion.[69]

Molesworth then went further. He accused the most orthodox free traders of misunderstanding the global order. Some people, he noted—and here he meant orthodox free traders—supposed that colonies held no advantages over foreign states when it came to trade and that the rise of free trade would neutralize the benefits of empire. "This doctrine," Molesworth warned, "rests on the assumption that the world abounds in 'independent states,' able and willing to purchase British goods." It also assumed, he added, "that the sooner we convert [the colonies] into 'independent states,' the better for them and for us."[70] For Molesworth, there was nothing a priori about the alignment of independent states with British commercial interests.

For men like Torrens and Molesworth, the empire organized and constituted a diffuse regulatory order *and* a security zone conducive to British commerce. Free trade, paradoxically, depended on force, and force was different from war. Limited force was required to ensure security for individual Britons and their interests across the globe. One colonial reformer and ally of Bentham, James Mackintosh, made this connection clearly when he tied the idea of national interest to the logic of protection emergencies. He wrote that it was a "great national interest as well as duty to watch over the international rights of every Briton." Then, echoing Molesworth's musings on how to achieve that effect, he argued that the best way to establish security for British subjects was to insist on protection from "every government."[71]

This formulation turned patrolling by the Royal Navy into an enforcement measure to ensure that other states would not endanger the interests of British subjects. The global peace envisioned was of a peculiar kind, in other words. Peace would result from the alignment of states committed to guaranteeing the movement of subjects, goods, and capital across political borders. Order was essential, and any move by other polities to threaten it represented an attack on imperial interests, and vice versa. The equation defined almost any kind of imperial violence as disciplinary and lawful.

Over the course of the nineteenth century, the idea of a global regime protecting Western interests pervaded visions of peace based on commercial expansion, democratic alliances, and visions of global dominance by white civilization.[72] The corollary of the idea that empires generated war was the increasingly prevalent view that commerce was not only promoting peace but, as John Stuart Mill put it, was also "rendering war obsolete."[73] Emerging "dreamworlds" of Anglo-American hegemony featured race as "the conceptual foundation for utopian fantasies of peace."[74] Advocates held tight to a pretense of Western innocence. In their eyes, the dream of a peaceful, white-dominated world had nothing to do with warmongering; it was a call to political order and alignment under the projection (or threat) of limited force.

Such positions provide essential context for understanding protection emergencies and their ties to imperial history.[75] The ideological underpinnings of nineteenth-century global empire extended well beyond the imperialism of free trade and a tenuous universalism. The legal routines of European armies and navies on patrol helped to assemble the new global regime. Protection emergencies staged more expansive, consequential commitments to order. Limited violence in far places had to save imperial subjects, protect property and investments, and project security across pluripolitical regions—a tall order and one that captured the imagination of a diverse array of imperial critics and supporters. The violence was not supposed to equate to war, and it in fact headlined pronouncements about the coming of global peace.

On Limited War

It seemed like a settled doctrine by the eighteenth century that only sovereigns had the right to engage in war. They could lawfully do so not only when pursuing a just cause but whenever they could present compelling reasons for war as essential to a nation's welfare. Emer de Vattel, Christian Wolff, and other writers argued that the requirement to publicly declare reasons for war would operate as a check on raging violence by exposing reasons to the gaze of the international community and separating legitimate reasons for going to war from mere pretexts.[76] One result was a movement to publish war manifestos that outlined the reasons for going to war.[77] Another was a shift away from considerations of the right to make war and toward the regulation of conduct in war. The project of devising Enlightenment-inspired rules to limit the destructiveness of war became the focus of nineteenth-century developments in the laws of war. Frances Lieber's 1863 code, written during the U.S. Civil War, set out the pillars of this movement, including the separation of combatants and civilians and the nonviolent treatment of prisoners of war.[78]

Insistence on declaring reasons for war (*jus ad bellum*) and claims of authority to regulate conduct in war (*jus in bello*) are the usual categories traced in a progressive campaign to contain and control the destructive effects of war. Historians have relied on these touchstones in describing nineteenth-century practices to substitute measures short of war—including acts of intervention, reprisal, and emergency—for open and declared war.[79] Distinctions between acts of intervention, reprisal, and emergency remained very blurred, and they all involved violence by a stronger polity against weaker political communities.[80] Whereas regular warfare following a declaration of war permitted each side to unleash full-scale violence against an enemy, with only the need to conform to standards of *jus in bello*, the violence of intervention, reprisal, and emergency was peacetime violence that had a close kinship with disciplinary action. T. J. Lawrence wrote in the *Principles of International Law* that this kind of violence comprised mainly "measures of police against weak and recalcitrant powers." And Clausewitz called the result "tame and half-hearted" war, a kind of "armed neutrality" involving a perpetual threat of further violence as a way of forcing negotiations and keeping the focus on maneuvers to attain "some small advantage."[81]

A focus on protection emergencies allows us to understand this "disciplinary" variant of limited war as a regime that emerged globally, and in important ways, through the replication of small wars in the service of imperial power. This is not to deny the phenomenon's parallel European origins. European reformers claimed a strong commitment to peace and held up constitutionalism, confederation, and the balance of power in Europe as templates of global order without major wars.

They identified the practice of imperial armies and navies reacting to protection emergencies with measured violence as a reflection of a civilized Europe devoted to peace. A closer look at protection emergencies has shown that their legal logic opened paths from limited intervention to violent land grabs, raiding for captives, exile of Indigenous communities, labor trafficking on a vast scale, and even campaigns of extermination. What's more, the exercise of limited force came in prolonged waves. Legal practices of intervention, reprisal, and emergency treated individual episodes of violence as discrete disciplinary measures, even as they summed to something often indistinguishable from all-out war. Decades of peace in Europe paralleled an extended era of violence in empires, but the logic of disciplinary violence was everywhere and the regime of armed peace was fully global.[82]

Protection emergencies created a legally permissive environment for imperial small wars. Calls to protect subjects led to the delegation of decision-making to commanders in the field about when and where to resort to violence. Classifying new groups as enemies and referencing the dangers to "civilized" society allowed settlers to claim the same authority. Imperial governments represented violence on patrol as a form of peacemaking. In the same way that Bentham championed decolonization while presuming continued British naval dominance, imperial reformers regarded serial small wars as preconditions for regional and global order.

Protection emergencies were an old phenomenon generating new effects. In early modern Europe, the duty to protect co-religionists had justified cross-border interventions. To some degree, imperatives of confessional protection had laid the groundwork for a widening circle of inclusion about those who should be protected.[83] But there is more to the story of the history of protection than the gradual expansion of the objects of protection to include all humanity.[84] Destructive imperial wars resulted from calls to save subjects, and interventions composed a global regime of sharp violence in small, repeating bits—a state of less-than-war and not-yet-peace. Global armed peace was neither a precursor to humanitarian intervention nor a mere guarantor of the movement of capital and labor. It was a flexible framework that fused imperial power with violence outside a state of war.

Conclusion

Specters of Imperial Violence

Empires of the late nineteenth and twentieth centuries were bloody affairs. From the seizure and division of continents to the expansion of systems of dehumanizing coerced labor, the record cannot be reconciled with visions of a more just and rational international order. As empires amassed and clung to power, they met with a dizzying array of anti-imperial movements and revolts. The response was the systematization of repression, juxtaposed oddly with studied ignorance in European public spheres about the scale and scope of colonial violence.[1]

Rather than labeling these decades a long phase of "decolonization," as if the end of empires was predictable and resulted from a plan, we find in them evidence of continuities of patterns of serial, small warfare in previous centuries. The frequency and unpredictable escalation of imperial conflicts inspired an increased use of the label "small wars." Its ready application seemed to imply that the conflicts were historically new. But the novelty lay not in the dynamics of these conflicts but in the way they were being discussed. Decolonization brought a proliferation of new binaries: revolt and repression, insurgency and counterinsurgency, guerrilla and conventional warfare, and state and non-state violence.

To tell the story of war in these decades would require another book. I instead point in this conclusion to the most salient continuities between law and violence in the age of empires and the international order of the twentieth and twenty-first centuries. In doing so, I will draw on findings from earlier chapters and assess what they tell us about the spatial and temporal dimensions of limited war. Last, I will gauge what histories of imperial violence can tell us about the hidden dangers of new small wars.

Empire-States

In March 2017, a U.S. Predator drone hovered for long minutes over the Syrian town of Karama. An operator typed a message to intelligence analysts working in another location to report that all civilians had fled the town and only enemies remained. A new bit of information followed quickly: a tip from ground forces that one of the buildings was likely a training center for ISIS fighters. The intelligence team swiftly authorized the release of the drone's most powerful bomb. Surprised operators took screenshots in the next few minutes as dozens of severely injured people stumbled out of the burning building. By the team's estimates, the blast had killed or severely injured several dozen people. Most of the victims appeared to be civilians, and many were women and children.[2]

The strike force logged the attack as a defensive measure. The label was routinely applied in the work of Talon Anvil, the secret U.S. cell responsible for this attack and other drone strikes against the Islamic State in Syria between 2014 and 2019. Under a system of controls ostensibly designed to limit civilian deaths, each drone bomb or missile launch required review and authorization. At first, multilayered approvals for offensive operations made it difficult to order attacks while drones were still in position. Then, beginning in late 2016, the U.S. government made a pair of key adjustments. First, decisions about the use of force were pushed to lower-level personnel, who would have easier and faster access to intelligence reports and could watch the targets in real time. Second, definitions of self-defense were expanded to make it possible to get quick approval to launch attacks on targets far from the front lines.[3]

A few years later, in late February 2022, Russian forces prepared to invade Ukraine. The United States reported intercepting intelligence that to produce a pretext for the invasion, the Russians were planning to stage an attack on Russian speakers in eastern Ukraine. In the end, the Russians invaded without even the pretense of provocation. Russian president Vladimir Putin appeared on Russian state television on February 24 to recite a laundry list of rationales for the invasion. Putin insisted that the Ukraine invasion was not a war but a "special military operation." As it had years before, in the lead-up to the Russian annexation of Crimea, protection figured prominently as a justification for a war that was not a war. "The purpose of this operation," Putin declared, "is to protect people who, for eight years now, have been facing humiliation and genocide perpetrated by the Kyiv regime." In the following weeks, as the fighting in Ukraine intensified, the Russian call for protection ripened into an argument that the invasion had been necessary—not just to prevent imagined violence toward ethnic Russians but also to disrupt fictitious plans for an unprovoked biological attack by Ukraine and the West on Russia.[4]

Legal arguments and practices in both cases carried clear echoes of the imperial past. In the United States, legal routines surrounding drone strikes in the Trump administration possessed striking similarities to the practices in nineteenth-century imperial military forces on patrol. Pushing decisions about the lawfulness of strikes down the chain of command and stretching already elastic definitions of self-defense marked continuities. In Putin's defense of the Ukraine invasion, imperial law talk was on bright display. The announced aim of protecting Russian minorities recalled the logic of protection emergencies across the nineteenth-century world. As in the past, talk about protection set up the possibility of a quick transition from actions to defend would-be subjects abroad to calls for the protection of Russian interests and regional order. Even the paranoid-sounding accusations about Western plans to usher in a wave of killing of ethnic Russians harked back to justifications of imperial wars as a means to forestall more destructive violence.

Such continuities challenge aspects of a story of progressive regulation of warfare that hinges on a set of turning points. One emphasizes the importance of the Lieber Code in 1863, a first attempt at codification of standards of conduct in war, and an effort that prefaced the Hague Convention in 1907 and the adoption of the Geneva Conventions of 1949.[5] Another represents the Kellogg-Briand Pact of 1928 as the culmination of attempts to outlaw war and create the conditions for perpetual peace.[6] Still a third narrative centers on efforts, beginning in the late twentieth century and led by the United States, to make war humane.[7] These accounts point to significant trends, and they recognize that moves toward greater regulation of war often produced unintended, even tragic, consequences. International standards of conduct in war left plenty of room for horrific violence under the cover of law. The Kellogg-Briand Pact did not encompass regulation of measures short of war, and it was, in any case, soon followed by a cataclysmic world war. Efforts by the United States to make war more humane under international law ushered in conflicts in which the United States openly, and even systematically, bent or flouted those same standards.[8]

These accounts do not contradict my findings about the way empires rendered small-scale violence lawful and permissible. Yet the emphasis on turning points in the regulation of war shifts our attention away from continuities in global violence.[9] A simple contrast between a phase of imperial wars supposedly unconstrained by law and a later phase of regulated, modern warfare is misleading. Whereas later small wars might seem to operate in the interstices of international order, some legal rationales and practices of war in fact cut across colonial and postcolonial worlds. Like earlier centuries of imperial conquest, decolonization was structured around serial conflicts often not classed as war. And postcolonial small wars did not mark a return to the lawlessness of colonial wars precisely because imperial warfare was never operating outside the law.[10]

Continuities

Defenders of the lawfulness of imperial violence pop up in odd places. Metropolitan legal writers churned out arguments for limited war as just war. Writers like Francisco Suárez and Hugo Grotius colored private violence as legitimate parts of public war. Participants in imperial small wars came up with their own justifications, sometimes drawing on what they think they knew about legal doctrines, sometimes improvising, as English officials did in Jamaica to devise support for a colonial right to make war.

Chatter about law and war echoed up and down imperial chains of command and extended far beyond official and scholarly circles. Consider the examples of Spanish conquistadors and English soldiers describing the legal character of violence against Indigenous Americans, or the methodical way British naval officers recorded decisions to strike against Indigenous communities in reprisal. This law talk was not all empty rhetoric. Often the same people calling for the use of force to protect subjects, imperial interests, and regional order were also loudly decrying injustices and the moral and political dangers of untempered violence in empires. People in distant territories played on ambiguities of subjecthood and rebellion as they gave their own reasons for pursuing violence short of war.

The disordered production of justifications for "small" violence did not stop at the end of the nineteenth century. As the opening examples of this chapter suggest, the scramble to come up with reasons for aggression continued to have a distinctly imperial feel. Violence in far places was and still is packaged in tiny, legally manageable pieces—with justifications presented in each case using modular elements, some conveniently stretched to dubious limits but still serviceable.

The content of rationales for the use of force in earlier centuries persisted within familiar, decentered processes. Capacious definitions of self-defense cut across starkly different periods and places. We saw that the fear of imminent attack was enough to justify preemptive raids in early empires. As Portuguese garrisons in the Indian Ocean or English enclaves in the Caribbean acquired the character of political communities, their leaders could point to the imperatives of defending communities of households. The approach drove an interest in reconciling private raiding and public war. Much later, nineteenth-century imperial officials were still explaining violence in terms of protection. They issued standing authorization for small strikes to protect subjects and creatively spun new arguments about the need to protect imperial interests and regional order. Familiar to us still, elastic discourses of self-defense and seemingly indestructible impulses for reprisal were packaged and repackaged across centuries.

The dream of keeping small wars small also persisted. No matter how terrible its immediate results, limited violence seemed preferable to open war and unconstrained fighting. The idea of limited war haunted accounts of imperial violence. Even horrific campaigns of dispossession and extermination, like the killing and forced exile of Aboriginal Tasmanians in the early nineteenth century, were described as temporary and necessary to order. Among the flaws in this logic was the regularity with which routine acts of limited violence like raids or brief interventions led directly to atrocities. Yet limited war retained its associations with peacemaking and the prevention of extreme violence.

These patterns forged a global order in which small wars not only flourished but also carried the potential for greater conflagrations. Participants engaged in small conflicts were like actors on a stage with a hole in the middle. Everyone knew where the danger lay, and that knowledge influenced movement and speech without eliminating the fear of falling. The passage to full-scale war was not through gradual escalation. The bigger danger, everyone knew, was in following the logical sequences of limited war right up to the edge of the abyss of cataclysmic violence. In the global regime of plunder, serial truces and their inevitable breakdown turned massacres into lawful responses to the failure of others to make and keep the peace. Later, as in the wars against Indigenous nations in North America, chronic, small-scale violence set the stage for massacres without the need for new legal arguments. Slight inflections of discourse could redefine protected subjects as criminals who deserved punishment, as rebels who could be lawfully executed, or as enemies who merited annihilation.

Across centuries, we find armies of commentators, whether participants or bystanders, law trained or illiterate, describing limited violence as a structural, even expected, condition of interpolity relations. Statements about the legal foundations for violence were opportunistic and disjointed, and they sometimes bordered on incoherence. But they served their purpose. Repetition made legal approaches as common as the actions they described. The "forever wars" of the twenty-first century belong, in this sense, to a much longer pattern of promoting wars as limited commitments. With so many similar episodes and arguments repeating, we have reason to ask about sources of instability and change.

Instabilities

Participants reached for binary categories in describing imperial violence. The possibility of quick changes in status from vassal to rebel or from rebel to enemy (and back again) grounded even the most chaotic and destructive campaigns of conquest and imperial warfare.[11] A studied looseness of legal definitions also proved useful. It extended the aura of law into remote corners of conflict and commentary. The call to produce on-the-spot rationales for violence turned colonial officials, military commanders, and Indigenous leaders into adroit quasi-lawyers. Captives, soldiers, and Indigenous combatants joined in, and they also alternated between portraying themselves or others as subjects in revolt and as fighters engaged in war across political lines.

The impoverished vocabulary for violence at the threshold of war and peace had consequences beyond mere confusion. At one level, differences between rebels and enemies were unimportant since both could be lawfully attacked and treated to extreme violence, from torture and execution to dispossession and slaughter. Most societies did not deny subjects a theoretical right to rebel, but an abstract right could not guarantee protection for subjects accused of disloyalty. The advantages of indeterminacy were lost on no one. As occurred in Spanish conquest in the Americas, Europeans sometimes declared whole communities to be vassals while reminding audiences that vassals might, by inclination or sudden lapse of judgment, turn back into enemies or become rebels deserving the harshest punishment. The power to choose labels for warring opponents worked to cast authority over fragmented political landscapes and preserve invaders' claims to be acting as peacemakers.

Behind the rebel-enemy pairing lay the distinction between membership in or exclusion from political communities. Here, too, the potential to flit rapidly between characterizing groups as insiders and branding them as outsiders offered a convenient answer to difficult questions about the boundaries of war and peace. Rebels were insiders who could lawfully be disciplined as criminal subjects or traitors. Enemies were outsiders who could be subjected to extreme forms of violence without explanation.[12] Questions of the limits on violence were relevant in each case. Labeling Indigenous people as enemies retained the possibility of redefining them later as insiders by an act of grace that exalted the authority of distant rulers. And even the most dangerous enemies were *potential* insiders. The mere possibility that they would be incorporated as subjects in empires warned against endorsing unlimited violence against them. In Tasmania, the combination of systematic killing of Aborigines with a policy of conciliation shows how the idea of fluid political membership placed war and protection in the same frame.[13]

Marking changes in political membership was hardly straightforward. The counterpart to the question of who belonged inside and who lay outside the bounds of empires was the puzzle of who had authority over whom. Even the most hierarchical empires and the most command-minded sovereigns encouraged political communities and local elites to preserve elements of autonomy. Societies ensnared in empires regularly positioned themselves to perform roles associated with both insider and outsider status. It is useful to think of the result as a world in which all individuals and groups were moving among states of belonging.[14] Always positioning themselves in relation to multiple legal authorities, historical actors rendered political authority in spectral forms—because states, too, were being born and dying or hovering between formation and decline.[15] In flitting between categories of insider and outsider, combatants were beating their wings hard enough to create the illusion of stasis—an imagined in-between condition of semi-enmity, partial rebellion, temporary captivity, or quasi-subservience. Purposeful indistinction in status corresponded to emanations of violence between war and peace.

The possibilities of movement in relation to states of belonging, together with the challenges of sustaining an in-between status, confronted European imperial agents as well as people opposing their power. Building on ubiquitous practices in which it was possible to pact for peace and recognize superior military authority without ceding sovereignty, political communities often sought advantage in their designation as subjects. Like Granadans over centuries in relation to Catholic monarchs, they paid tribute and called themselves vassals in order to carve out space and time for autonomy. A state of political indistinction reserved the right to rebel or return to open warfare. Such strategies were hardly opaque to imperial agents. Indeed, a striking degree of mutual intelligibility helped to bring Europeans and Indigenous polities into the same legal and political framework.

This history places the sharpening contrast, so often noted, between Europeans as civilized and "others" as savages in a new light. As European correspondence regarding the mid-eighteenth-century wars in the Río de la Plata and on the Coromandel Coast shows, references to the savagery of non-European conduct in war operated as a foil for a discourse about Europeans as arbiters of standards of war and statehood. But the trend also responded to intensifying engagement with Indigenous political communities as allies and proxies. In fact, it was often the relative *weakness* of European forces that urged imperial agents to reach for the label of savagery and to assert authority over conduct in war. One result was that people already in thickly entangled relationships with Europeans often bore the brunt of imperial violence. Insider status might have been coveted, but it was also dangerous. Those who looked or acted more like insiders than outsiders and those who maneuvered as diplomatic equals came to be labeled as enemies or rebels more readily than people who kept their distance. Charrúas and Minuanes in the Río de la Plata presided over a kinetic, pluripolitical region by moving out of the way of Spanish and Portuguese settlers; they appeared to pose a greater danger to settlements when rumors surfaced of their potential alliance with the Christianized Guaraní. Close neighbors, recent converts, former allies, and rivals for authority became, in moments of crisis, prime targets of unfettered violence.

The many instabilities of ways of justifying and regulating violence warn against taking historical European claims to global dominance at face value. Conquest and rule prompted virtuoso performances of legal authority on many sides. Opposition to imperial authority was deeply destabilizing precisely because it invoked well-known alternatives to arguments about the justice of war and the status of political communities. Imperial violence followed patterns, to be sure, and they contained the possibility, even the statistical near certainty, of deep injustice. But even legal patterns are not the same as rules. Law operated as a framework for conflicts that stretched, challenged, and at times made a mockery of boundaries between war and peace.

A Time and Place for War

The phenomenon of "hyper-violent peace" altered political landscapes.[16] The spatial effects of serial small wars played out in multiple dimensions. Imperial violence created opportunities for political consolidation, as when sponsorship of raids enhanced royal power over warlords or when borderlands violence eroded or destroyed the independence of Indigenous political communities. But the same violence might nurture political fragmentation. Colonial elites and company officials seized authority over war, even asserting at times a local right to make war, as occurred in garrison empires of the sixteenth and seventeenth centuries. They did so to enhance their own power within a layered imperial field of influence.

When Europeans claimed the authority to regulate war in pluripolitical regions, their tenuous and incomplete control in most of the world left them promoting unstable power in a jumbled order of old and new states. Describing collections of states as the proper context of regulatory regimes made sense of pluripolitical regions. But the process also required a working definition of states—a vexed question. Concepts like "quasi-sovereignty" and "protection" could capture ambiguities of statehood in a world of empires.[17] Intermittent violence could serve the same purpose.

Small wars scrambled political control over land and sea space. This is not the same as saying that the conflicts conjured a "middle ground" where limits on violence had to be negotiated. In fact, many of the usual ways of characterizing interactions between Europeans and Indigenous peoples fall against the history of imperial small wars. The view that Europeans and Indigenous peoples stumbled toward legal compromise in places where neither held a monopoly of violence is useful only up to a point.[18] Mutual intelligibility was far more prevalent than misunderstanding, and it also made imperial rule incomplete and dependent on shifting political alignments. Even after fighting paused, and even after supposed victory, pluralism and indeterminacy of rule persisted.[19] The conflicts highlighted in this book in politically crowded regions of the Atlantic, Indian Ocean, and Pacific worlds illustrate how continual, low-level, and very real violence left people guessing about their positions in relation to multiple political authorities.

The spatial effects of raids, truces, the making and disbanding of alliances, and the authorization of attacks of retaliation or punishment—these processes unsettled imperial orders. Empires jostled with micropolities and within their own unstable and layered systems of authority. As Europeans sought plunder and trade overseas, companies and sojourners depended on intermittent violence to make new political communities. In debates about how to turn garrisons into colonies, officials sought to stabilize links between raiding and settlement to give settlements the right of self-defense.[20] The ripple effects reached the intimate spaces of households—entities at the threshold of private and public space charged with holding and disciplining captives and coerced labor. Violence-laced networks of alliance, meanwhile, carried both the promise of security and the potential for small conflicts to ripen into war. However violent and disruptive, conquest was presented as an act of simplifying a bewilderingly complex political landscape.

Space and geography fused empires, law, and war. Across garrison empires embedded in regimes of plunder, it was necessary to designate places where booty could be converted to property. Just as colonies could acquire the character of pieces of the realm, other spaces, from ships to roving armies, carried imperial authority. As Europeans erected gallows, built fortresses, sponsored raids, and multiplied households, they sketched a landscape connecting war to colonial institutions. Such spaces of law were essential in conveying captives across political lines—a process that itself created lines—and assigning them to labor in public works or private households. Legal authority in all its delegated forms, from household and garrison governments to command over roving armies and navies, could be used to support a local right to make war, engage proxies, collude with other empires, and order violence as punishment.

The spatial effects of limited violence extended across whole regions. Imperial small wars nurtured political fragmentation *and* imperial consolidation. As Europeans claimed the authority to regulate war in pluripolitical regions, their incomplete, weak control in most of the world led them to promote the idea of their privileged position of authority over loose ensembles of states as regulatory regimes. Local elites and colonial or company officials claimed the authority to command diverse communities and advance their own fortunes while enhancing the legitimacy of imperial governments. Painfully aware of the political pluralism of vast regions outside spheres of imperial control, they continued to deploy techniques of making alliances and conducting proxy wars while also experimenting with imperial coalitions to multiply the threat and impact of violence against small polities and corporate holdouts. A kinetic form of warmaking promised a way to put and keep imperial opponents in their place—by threatening them with captivity or pushing them to newly partitioned territories or places of exile. As empires militarized and extended their reach, they increasingly portrayed cross-polity interventions as acts of policing, preparing the way for the familiar horrors of nineteenth- and twentieth-century mass "disciplining" of political opponents in empires through torture, incarceration, and more small wars.

Timing was also in play. The permanent threat of war hovered over continual outbreaks of violence. Truces measured phases of temporary peace in years and contained the seeds of an inevitable—and lawful—return to war. Imperial agents constructed a local right to war by asserting the character of imperial outposts as pieces of empire and semiautonomous political communities. They cited imperial directives to make war when it served their interests, and they exaggerated their immunity from peace treaties to perpetuate profitable plunder. Short spurts of violence in the shadow of empires could serve broad imperial interests, too, by separating the responsibility for war from governments. On-again, off-again violence defined imperial influence.

Two other aspects of timing deserve mention. One is the specter of perpetual war. In early modern conquests, the background condition of a steady state of war transformed serial truces into mechanisms for a return to fighting. The regime of armed peace that debuted in the nineteenth century depended on the perpetual threat of limited strikes. Not unlike the global power behind programs of targeted killing or cross-border incursions in the twenty-first century, empire-states constructed, and thrived on, an atmosphere of unspecified dread. The "forever wars" of the postimperial world are in this sense nothing new.[21]

Another temporal effect to highlight is the sequencing of events. Emergencies, real or imagined, structured imperial violence, but so did expectation and routine. Plotted steps toward punishment and reprisal gave responses to emergency their shape and rhythm, as when interventions followed protection emergencies in nineteenth-century empires. Such steps did not require the suspension of law at all. They relied, in fact, on logical and accepted progressions from a perceived violation of peace to a violent reaction, from pact making to plunder, and from negotiation to slaughter.

These spatial and temporal frameworks of small wars explain why and how, in the context of empires, Europeans consistently claimed peace as the intended object of their violence. The formula reeked of tragic irony. But it also reflected an irresistible connection between justifications for violence and a future imagined—but unreachable— stability in which violence would no longer be necessary. The fiction of that future did not make representations of imperial violence as a prelude to peace any less alluring.

Limited War and Global History

European writers attempted in unsystematic ways to clarify the legal foundations of limited war. Francisco Suárez and other scholastic writers enumerated conditions under which private violence might be absorbed into authorized public war. Alberico Gentili, Hugo Grotius, and other writers analyzed the law of truce making and plunder, and they traced how just war doctrines stretched to encompass spontaneous acts to resume war. Emer de Vattel defined a narrow path for political communities other than powerful empire-states to join an ensemble of states regulating war. The implied universalism of this approach coexisted with its reinforcement of exclusive European authority over standards of conduct in war. On his way to imagining the codification of international law, Jeremy Bentham upheld the necessity of colonial violence for the protection of property and other imperial interests standing in for the common good.

These and other attempts to grapple with the problems of limited war composed one dimension of the legal framework of imperial violence. The speech and writings of participants in imperial small wars made up another. A stunningly diverse array of historical actors concocted legal arguments in defense of imperial violence. Indigenous leaders of rebellions as well as mid- and low-level European commanders gave small wars legitimacy. Their arguments were more than ex post facto justifications. The narratives helped to structure broad, recurring patterns of violence. One example is the transition from garrison empires built on the combination of maritime raiding and captivity to a massive, imperially protected Atlantic complex of plantation slavery. Another is the Europeanization of the laws of war by European company officials and military commanders charged with making decisions about conduct in war and the standing of local political communities. Even before imperial armies and navies on patrol produced a regime of armed peace by determining when, and against whom, to use force, empires consistently delegated the power to authorize violence. Legal theories about imperial force and its limits took shape in actions far from Europe. European interlocutors across the world offered their own legal interpretations of violence by and against empires.

This perspective warns us against searching for non-European contributions to international law only by scanning elite pronouncements using European concepts. Political communities everywhere were fully engaged for a long time in debating the justice of violence. Europeans' approach to the law of conquest closely matched ways of war already in play across the early modern world. Practices of plunder—including captive taking—spanned centuries and regions. The case for European authority over the laws of war developed not just within Europe but also far from Europe, in the context of imperial small wars and interventions. We can rewrite histories of international law to include these varied influences and sites. Commentary on limited war by European writers is only one starting place and only one strand of a multifaceted, truly global process.[22]

Europeans held tightly to the myth that small wars in far places were containable. The claim became its own argument for why a condition of perpetual violence in empires was acceptable. Late nineteenth- and twentieth-century wars reflected these long historical tendencies. The French insistence that the Algerian War was not a full-scale war followed the pattern.[23] So did European consternation as two imperial wars at the end of the nineteenth century, the Crimean War and the South African War (Second Boer War), dragged on and took a higher toll than politicians at home had bargained for. British wars of decolonization—at the time, just imperial wars since decolonization was hardly a given— inspired the same claim about containment.[24] Still later, the legal framework for U.S. war in Indochina merged arguments that the war was not imperial with the view that it might be kept small. Even as international lawyers insisted that the Vietnam War fell within the category of international conflict, the U.S. government's repeated message to the public was that it would be a brief, limited intervention on behalf of an ally and on the model of imperial intervention, not war.[25]

Besides causing significant suffering, imperial small wars had other big effects. Patterns of violence in empires between 1400 and 1900 helped to compose and alter global regimes. Early empires benefited from, and cultivated, a regime of raiding and captive taking, with regional variants, in which European law and practices mirrored those of other polities. In the long nineteenth century, imperial agents and their sponsors began to assert authority over the regulation of war, and they propelled a regime of armed peace that reserved for European powers the right to conduct reprisals and intervene across borders. Imagined limits on war within these successive global regimes created space for varieties of violence at the threshold between war and peace.

As we have seen, the logic of limited war opened routes to extreme violence. The slaughter of civilians and the enslavement of war captives that followed belonged to a familiar choreography of conquest. Arguments about protection produced rationales for short strikes and devastating waves of violence. This history might help inform our understandings of later atrocities.[26] In the examples I offered earlier in this chapter—-U.S. campaigns of targeted killing and the Russian invasion of Ukraine—deaths of civilians were explained using older languages and logic. By revealing imperial modalities and discourses in past centuries, we can learn to spot them in the present.

Yet, history also suggests that no measure of containment of war will likely work to keep small wars small. The conflicts reproduce themselves precisely because they follow a familiar sequence of actions. The hybridity of war and peace makes it easier to start small wars and to keep them going. The conflicts tend to occur in series, generating long waves of violence. And they bring with them the awful promise of atrocity. The only sure way to prevent war crimes as an effect of small wars, it seems, is to not start them at all.

Nonviolence on a massive scale has been urged before, of course, even sometimes to some good effect. It is no panacea. The permissive space for small wars is endemic to a global order of unequal power. And there will always be arguments that small wars are necessary to oppose tyranny or aggression, or to prevent bigger wars. The history I have told at least exposes the myth that law worked to contain violence. It structured violence and presented historical actors with possible worlds of acceptable mixes of small and cataclysmic violence.

What is clear is that for centuries the world has worked with an impoverished vocabulary to describe violence at the threshold of war and peace. The project of imagining limited war as a lesser evil also has a long history, as do death and disaster on frightening scales in the context of so-called limited war. As in the protest chants against the Vietnam War that I still remember, history tells us to say no to war, at any scale.

ACKNOWLEDGMENTS

Although I wrote much of this book during various stages of the pandemic's great confinement, the work was never solitary. Writing global history requires a willingness to ask repeatedly for help and advice from other scholars. I benefited time and again from their generosity, and from the provocative questions they raised. Even or especially when speaking from behind masks or appearing in pixelated squares on my computer screen, they were essential to the project.

Public lectures and seminars were occasions for much of the help I received. At the Toynbee Prize lecture in 2019, I launched some preliminary findings about small wars in global history. An invitation to deliver the George Macaulay Trevelyan lectures at the University of Cambridge gave me a chance to test the book's central arguments before an erudite, engaged audience. I benefited from opportunities to present pieces of the book-in-progress at the American Society for Legal History and at Duke University, Tsinghua University, New York University, Stanford University, the Freie University of Berlin, the University of New South Wales, Monash University, Queen's University (Canada), and Queen's University (Northern Ireland), among others. At Yale, students and faculty in the History Department and at the Law School shared suggestions, corrections, and encouragement. I am grateful, too, for the opportunity to work on the book at the Institute for Advanced Study and for support from the Guggenheim Foundation and the American Academy in Berlin, where I was the Anna-Maria Kellen fellow in spring 2022.

Painfully aware that I will fail in my efforts to remember everyone who helped, I give warm thanks to Carmen Alveal, Deborah Amos, Sunil Amrith, David Armitage, Bain Attwood, Ângela Barreto Xavier, José María Beneyto, Daniel Benjamin, Annabel Brett, Holly Brewer, Ari

Bryen, Pedro Cardim, Christopher Clark, Adam Clulow, Joy Connolly, Elizabeth Cross, Ignacio de la Rasilla, Jorge Díaz Ceballos, Shaunnagh Dorsett, Lawrence Douglas, Hussein Fancy, Lisa Ford, Sarah Barringer Gordon, Daniel Hershenzon, Lenny Hodges, Daniel Hulsebosch, Ian Hunter, Cleo Kearns, Amalia Kessler, Benedict Kingsbury, Martti Koskenniemi, Tess Lewis, Vladislava Lilic, John J. Martin, Timo McGregor, Renaud Morieux, Samuel Moyn, Jeppe Mulich, Cristina Nogueira da Silva, Charles Parker, David S. Parker, Alexandre Pelegrino, Katherine Pelletier, Mark Peterson, Jennifer Pitts, Bhavani Raman, John Rambow, Jake Richards, Gabriel Rocha, Thomas Santa Maria, Stuart Schwartz, Doris Sher, John Shovlin, Sujit Sivasundaram, Philip Stern, Benjamin Straumann, Francesca Trivellato, Nancy van Deusen, Inge van Hulle, Natasha Wheatley, James Whitman, and John Witt.

Research and writing would have been a lonely affair, and much less fun, without Eduardo Garcia's company, calls and visits by our daughters, Victoria and Gaby, and pub lunches with Sandy Solomon and Peter Lake. Family members cheered me on even when I interrupted meals with grim facts about small wars and put them to work as a focus group evaluating alternative titles.

In the middle of my time working on the book, my mother, Charlotte Russ Benton, died in her sleep at the age of ninety-seven. Until the end, she had the moxie and sharp intelligence that had propelled her from a small Midwestern town to the University of Chicago, and beyond. She would have carried this book to dinner with her friends and cornered strangers in elevators to read them blurbs and reviews. I dedicate the book to the memory of her irrepressible intellectual curiosity and her unconditional love.

NOTES

Abbreviations

AGI	Archivo General de Indias
AGN	Archivo General de la Nación (Uruguay)
BL	The British Library
CSP	Calendar of State Papers, Colonial
IOR	India Office Records
TNA	The National Archives of Britain

Chapter 1: From Small Wars to Atrocity in Empires

1. The governor of the Cape Colony, Henry Pottinger, ordered the livestock returned, the prisoners released, the lieutenant colonel responsible for the raid transferred, and the shopkeeper who started it branded as a troublemaker. Pottinger was not known for his gentle treatment of Xhosa; he saw the unauthorized attack an affront to his efforts to sort "friendly" and enemy Xhosas and to stabilize the frontier by pushing enemy groups beyond what were then the outer limits of the colony. Henry Pottinger to George Berkeley, 20 April 1847, Basil le Cordeur and Christopher Saunders, *The War of the Axe, 1847: Correspondence between the governor of the Cape Colony, Sir Henry Pottinger, and the commander of the British forces at the Cape, Sir George Berkeley, and others* (Johannesburg: Brenthurst Press, 1981).

2. The description of Xhosa violence is quoted in Basil le Cordeur and Christopher Saunders, "Introduction," Le Cordeur and Saunders, eds. *The War of the Axe*, 15. On the lead-up to the Zulu wars, see Alan Lester, Kate Boehme, and Peter Mitchell, *Ruling the World: Freedom, Civilisation and Liberalism in the Nineteenth-Century British Empire* (New York: Cambridge University Press, 2021), 317–323.

3. On European-African wars in southern Africa, see John Laband, *The Land Wars: The Dispossession of the Khoisan and the AmaXhosa in the Cape Colony* (Cape Town: Penguin, 2020). For an example of a work on governmentality on frontiers, see Benjamin D. Hopkins, *Ruling the Savage Periphery: Frontier Governance and the Making of the Modern State* (Cambridge, MA: Harvard University Press, 2020). On the exclusion from or queuing by non-Western polities to enter the international legal community, see Gerrit W. Gong, *The Standard of "Civilization" in International Society* (New York: Oxford University Press, 1984); see also Samuel Moyn, *Humane: How the United States Abandoned Peace and Reinvented War* (New York: Farrar, Straus and Giroux, 2021), for a view of colonial wars as operating outside the laws of war (96, 102, 109).

4. Hannah Arendt, *On Violence* (New York: Harcourt, 1969), 3.

5. Exemplary overviews of the history of law and war in political thought are Pablo Kalmanovitz, *The Laws of War in International Thought* (New York: Oxford University Press, 2020); Jens Bartelson, *War in International Thought* (New York: Cambridge University Press, 2017); Stephen C. Neff, *War and the Law of Nations: A General History* (New York: Cambridge University Press, 2008). See also Christopher Greenwood, "The Concept of War in Modern International Law," *International and Comparative Law Quarterly* 36 (1987): 283–306; and Elizabeth Wilmshurst, ed., *International Law and the Classification of Conflicts* (Oxford: Oxford University Press, 2012). On political thought and civil war, see David Armitage, *Civil Wars: A History in Ideas* (New York: Vintage, 2018). For claims about shifts in the laws of war in the twentieth century, see Oona A. Hathaway and Scott J. Shapiro, *The Internationalists: How a Radical Plan to Outlaw War Remade the World* (New York: Simon & Schuster, 2017); David Kennedy, *Of War and Law* (Princeton, NJ: Princeton University Press, 2006); and Moyn, *Humane*.

6. My argument about small wars and atrocity shares some elements with Samuel Moyn's account in *Humane* of how U.S. efforts to humanize war in the twentieth century backfired. But whereas Moyn contrasts regulated, modern warfare with supposedly lawless colonial wars, I point to continuities of global legal regimes across the early modern and modern worlds. I also locate the theory of limited war in both legal writings and in practices of warfare that were legally legible across very different societies and regions.

7. On law and pitched battles, see James Q. Whitman, *The Verdict of Battle: The Law of Victory and the Making of Modern War* (Cambridge, MA: Harvard University Press, 2012). A recent history of violence in the twentieth-century British Empire that verges on polemic is Caroline Elkins, *Legacy of Violence: A History of the British Empire* (New York: Knopf, 2022); for a critique, see Lauren Benton, "Evil Empires? The Long Shadow of British Colonialism," *Foreign Affairs* 101, no. 4 (2022): 190–196. Dierk Walter discusses the dearth of attention to imperial wars in his book on the subject; his approach continues to emphasize asymmetric force and contrasting cultures of violence. *Colonial Violence: European Empires and the Use of Force* (London: Hurst & Company, 2017), 5, 9–10.

8. On King Philip's War, which was known by other names by contemporaries, as a turning point in colonial North America, see Jenny Hale Pulsipher, *Subjects unto the Same King: Indians, English, and the Contest for Authority in Colonial New England* (Philadelphia: University of Pennsylvania, 2006); Daniel K. Richter, *Facing East from Indian Country: A Native History of Early America* (Cambridge, MA: Harvard University Press, 2003), chapter 3; and Lisa Brooks, *Our Beloved Kin: A New History of King Philip's War* (New Haven, CT: Yale University Press, 2018). On social and cultural currents in Atlantic wars, see Geoffrey Plank, *Atlantic Wars: From the Fifteenth Century to the Age of Revolution* (New York: Oxford University Press, 2020); and Elena Schneider, *The Occupation of Havana: War, Trade, and Slavery in the Atlantic World* (Chapel Hill: University of North Carolina Press, 2018). Discussions of violence in Atlantic slavery are in Trevor Burnard, "Atlantic Slave Systems and Violence," in *A Global History of Early Modern Violence*, eds. Erica Charters, Marie Houllemare, and Peter H. Wilson (Manchester, UK: Manchester University Press, 2021), 201–217; Brett Rushforth, *Bonds of Alliance: Indigenous and Atlantic Slaveries in New France* (Chapel Hill: University of North Carolina Press, 2013); and Vincent Brown, *Tacky's Revolt: The Story of an Atlantic Slave War* (Cambridge, MA: Belknap Press, 2020).

On waves of revolutionary violence, see Sujit Sivasundaram, *Waves Across the South: A New History of Revolution and Empire* (Chicago: University of Chicago Press, 2021); on counterrevolution across empire, see Lauren Benton and Lisa Ford, *Rage for Order: The British Empire and the Origins of International Law, 1800–1850* (Cambridge, MA: Harvard University Press, 2016).

9. Mary L. Dudziak, *War Time: An Idea, Its History, Its Consequences* (New York: Oxford University Press, 2013).

10. Carl von Clausewitz, *On War* (New York: Penguin, 1999 [1832]).

11. Clausewitz's lectures on small wars have only recently been translated into English. See James W. Davis, "Introduction to Clausewitz on Small War," in Christopher Daase and James W. Davis, *Clausewitz on Small War* (New York: Oxford University Press, 2016), 1–18, 1; and Sibylle Scheipers, *On Small War: Carl von Clausewitz and People's War* (New York: Oxford University Press, 2018).

12. The mining of history for this purpose is exemplified by Max Boot, *The Savage Wars of Peace: Small Wars and the Rise of American Power* (New York: Basic Books, 2014 [2002]).

13. Examples of a vast literature include Ivan Arreguín-Toft, *How the Weak Win Wars: A Theory of Asymmetric Conflict* (New York: Cambridge University Press, 2005); and Rod Thornton, *Asymmetric Warfare: Threat and Response in the 21st Century* (Malden, MA: Polity Press, 2007).

14. He placed special emphasis on tactics in small wars, and he went so far as to state that "the entirety of Small Wars belongs to tactics." Carl von Clausewitz, "My Lectures on Small War, held at the War College in 1810 and 1811," in Daase and Davis, *Clausewitz on Small War*, 1–18, 22, 23. Clausewitz regarded "tactics" as subordinate to "strategy." On small wars and popular uprisings, see Carl von Clausewitz, "The Arming of the People," in Daase and Davis, *Clausewitz on Small War*, 221–226, 221.

15. James W. Davis, "Introduction to Clausewitz on Small War," in Christopher Daase and James W. Davis, *Clausewitz on Small War* (New York: Oxford University Press, 2016), 1–18, 17.

16. C. E. Callwell, *Small Wars: Their Principles and Practice* (Omaha: University of Nebraska Press, 1996 [1896]), 7, 11.

17. Callwell repeatedly alludes to the "moral effect" of European military operations against non-European forces (for example, *Small Wars*, 76, 109, 110, 157, 158). Caroline Elkins discusses Callwell's representation of the "moral effect" of European violence against "uncivilized" peoples and shows that the phrase was picked up and repeated by numerous British officials and commentators (*Legacy of Violence*, 200, 598).

18. Carl Schmitt, *The Nomos of the Earth in the International Law of the Jus Publicum Europaeum* (New York: Telos, 2003), 49, 52, 86, 92.

19. For Schmitt, the New World was a world of lawlessness—a "state of exception" that paralleled the English construction of martial law as "analogous to the idea of a designated zone of free and empty space." Schmitt, *The Nomos of the Earth*, 98.

20. Carl Schmitt, *Theory of the Partisan: Intermediate Commentary on the Concept of the Political* (New York: Telos Press, 2007); Daniel Clayton, "Partisan Space," in *Spatiality, Sovereignty and Carl Schmitt*, ed. Stephen Legg (New York: Routledge, 2011), 211–219; Jan-Werner Müller, *A Dangerous Mind: Carl Schmitt in Post-War European Thought* (New Haven, CT: Yale University Press, 2003), 133–155.

21. On this point in relation to piracy, see Lauren Benton, "Legal Spaces of Empire: Piracy and the Origins of Ocean Regionalism," in *Comparative Studies in Society and History*, 47, no. 4 (2005): 700–724.

22. In a somewhat similar vein, Charles Tilly argued for the recognition of war in dynamic relation to a broader set of forms of violence. Charles Tilly, *The Politics of Collective Violence* (New York: Cambridge University Press, 2003), chapters 1–2. Dylan Craig suggests the term "interstitial war" to label post-1945 violence that occurred "within gaps between states' imperial reach and their juridical borders," an approach that also moves beyond tactics or justifications in characterizing small wars while highlighting violence at the inside-outside threshold of sovereign power. Dylan Craig, *Sovereignty, War, and the Global State* (Cham, Switzerland: Palgrave Macmillan, 2020), chapter 1, 20.

23. For an attempt at a typology of objectives and justifications of imperial wars, see Walter, *Colonial Violence*, chapter 2.

24. For an overview, see Lothar Brock and Hendrik Simon, eds., *The Justification of War and International Order: From Past to Present* (New York: Oxford University Press, 2021).

25. Martti Koskenniemi draws the context tightly. He adapts the term *bricolage* from Lévi-Strauss to describe the way European legal writers drew on materials from their subregional European legal systems and their "domestic legal training" as they characterized the juridical order beyond Europe. See Martti Koskenniemi, *To the Uttermost Parts of the Earth: Legal Imagination and International Power, 1300–1870* (Cambridge, UK: Cambridge University Press, 2021) 2, 9. Contextual analyses of political and legal thought can be illuminating, and to a certain extent are necessary. On their strengths and limitations in the history of international law, see Lauren Benton, "Beyond Anachronism: Histories of International Law and Global Legal Politics," in *Journal of the History of International Law* 21 (2019): 7–40.

26. *Calcoen: A Dutch Narrative of the Second Voyage of Vasco da Gama in Calicut* (printed in Antwerp ca. 1504, translated and printed in London, 1874).

27. Of course, political agents did not have perfect knowledge of interlocutors' expectations, and misinterpretations of protocol could lead to trouble. On protocol, see Sanjay Subrahmanyam, *The Career and Legend of Vasco da Gama* (New York: Cambridge University Press, 1997), chapter 3; J. V. Melo, "In Search of a Shared Language: The Goan Diplomatic Protocol," *Journal of Early Modern History* 20, no. 4 (2016): 390–407; Stefan Halikowski-Smith, "'The Friendship of Kings Was in the Ambassadors': Portuguese Diplomatic Embassies in Asia and Africa during the Sixteenth and Seventeenth Centuries." *Portuguese Studies*, vol. 22, no. 1, 2006: 101–134; and, more generally, Lauren Benton and Adam Clulow, "Legal Encounters and the Origins of Global Law," in *Cambridge History of the World*, vol. 6, ed. Jerry Bentley, Sanjay Subrahmanyam, and Merry Wiesner-Hanks (New York: Cambridge University Press, 2015), part II, 80–100.

28. On "creative misunderstandings" as the medium of the "middle ground" of cultural compromise in places where no one held a monopoly of violence, see Richard White, *The Middle Ground: Indians, Empires, and Republics in the Great Lakes Region, 1650–1815* (New York: Cambridge University Press, 2010), xiii. Walter also emphasizes contrasts of "cultures of violence" and the "incomprehensibility of drawn-out warfare" to Europeans (*Colonial Violence*, chapter 3, 49). On incommensurability and encounters, see Sanjay Subrahmanyam, *Courtly Encounters: Translating Courtliness and Violence in Early Modern Eurasia* (Cambridge, MA: Harvard University Press, 2012).

29. Inga Clendinnen, *Aztecs: An Interpretation* (New York: Cambridge University Press, 1991), 3; Inga Clendinnen, "'Fierce and Unnatural Cruelty': Cortés and the Conquest of Mexico," *Representations* 33, no. 1 (1991): 65–100, 81. The term "Spaniards" is anachronistic in this context since Spain did not yet exist as a nation and soldiers often identified themselves according to their region of birth, but I use it here and elsewhere in the book as a convenient and conventional term.

30. Clendinnen, "Fierce and Unnatural Cruelty," 71.

31. For a careful, invaluable account of the lead-up to violence, including the offer and rejection of tribute, see Camilla Townsend, *Fifth Sun: A New History of the Aztecs* (New York: Oxford University Press, 2021), 88, 104.

32. Clendinnen, "Fierce and Unnatural Cruelty," 93. Cortés recognized this disability. A key part of his strategy to ingratiate himself with the crown, while he was effectively in rebellion against the governor of Cuba, was to found the city of Vera Cruz and become head of its *cabildo* (municipal council).

33. Clendinnen develops the theme of mutual misunderstanding as the backdrop to violence in a book-length reflection on Governor Phillips's spearing by an Indigenous Australian in the early days of the Botany Bay settlement. See Inga Clendinnen, *Dancing with Strangers: Europeans and Australians at First Contact* (New York: Cambridge University Press, 2005). On mutual intelligibility and global legal orders, see Lauren Benton, "In Defense of Ignorance: Frameworks for Legal Politics in the Atlantic World," in Brian Owensby and Richard Ross, *Justice in a New World: Negotiating Legal Intelligibility in British, Iberian, and Indigenous America* (New York University Press, 2018), 273–290; and Lauren Benton, *Law and Colonial Cultures: Legal Regimes in World History* (New York: Cambridge University Press, 2002); compare Marshall Sahlins, *Islands in History* (Chicago: University of Chicago Press, 1987).

34. On interpolity law, see Benton and Clulow, "Legal Encounters and the Origins of Global Law."

35. This effort builds on recent research into the legal strategies of Indigenous groups, enslaved people, convicts, freed Blacks, and others. For example, see Bianca Premo and Yanna Yannakakis, "A Court of Sticks and Branches: Indian Jurisdiction in Colonial Southern Mexico and Beyond," *American Historical Review* 124, no. 1 (2019): 28–55; Michelle A. McKinley, *Fractional Freedoms: Slavery, Intimacy, and Legal Mobilization in Colonial Lima* (New York: Cambridge University Press, 2018); Alejandro de la Fuente and Ariela Gross, *Becoming Free, Becoming Black: Race, Freedom, and Law in Cuba, Virginia, and Louisiana* (New York: Cambridge University Press 2020); Rebecca J. Scott and Jean M. Hébard, *Freedom Papers: An Atlantic Odyssey in the Age of Emancipation* (Cambridge, MA: Harvard University Press, 2014); Kimberly Welch, *Black Litigants in the Antebellum American South* (Chapel Hill: University of North Carolina Press, 2018); and Martha S. Jones, *Birthright Citizens: A History of Race and Rights in Antebellum America* (New York: Cambridge University Press, 2018).

36. For example, Arnulf Becker Lorca, *Mestizo International Law: A Global Intellectual History, 1842–1933* (New York: Cambridge University Press, 2014); and see Liliana Obregón, "Peripheral Histories of International Law," *Annual Review of Law and Social Science* 15, no. 1 (2019): 437–451. A parallel strand of the literature on widening participation in international law tracks the growing participation of U.S. and Latin American jurists in nineteenth- and

twentieth-century international law; for example, Juan Pablo Scarfi, *The Hidden History of International Law in the Americas: Empire and Legal Networks* (New York: Oxford University Press, 2017); Benjamin Allen Coates, *Legalist Empire: International Law and American Foreign Relations in the Early Twentieth Century* (New York: Oxford University Press, 2016). On self-determination, see Adom Getachew, *Worldmaking after Empire: The Rise and Fall of Self-Determination* (Princeton, NJ: Princeton University Press, 2020).

37. The best account remains Frederick Russell, *The Just War in the Middle Ages* (New York: Cambridge University Press, 1975).

38. In general, too, as the standard history goes, Grotius was making a novel move in emphasizing the moral requirement that combatants observe prevailing norms in the conduct of war. See Pablo Kalmanovitz, *The Laws of War in International Thought* (New York: Oxford University Press, 2020); Jens Bartelson, *War in International Thought* (New York: Cambridge University Press, 2018).

39. John Fabian Witt, *Lincoln's Code: The Laws of War in American History* (New York: Free Press, 2012), 18.

40. Witt, *Lincoln's Code*, 20.

41. Susan Pedersen, *The Guardians: The League of Nations and the Crisis of Empire* (New York: Oxford University Press, 2017); Mark Mazower, *No Enchanted Palace: The End of Empire and the Ideological Origins of the United Nations* (Princeton, NJ: Princeton University Press, 209); Moyn, *Humane.*

42. Jonathan Barnes, "The Just War," in *The Cambridge History of Later Medieval Philosophy: From the Rediscovery of Aristotle to the Disintegration of Scholasticism, 1100–1600*, ed. Norman Kretzmann, Anthony Kenny, and Jan Pinborg (Cambridge, UK: Cambridge University Press, 1982), 771–784; Russell, *The Just War in the Middle Ages.* Debating what constituted an injury, writers asserted that concrete acts like unlawful taking of property clearly qualified, but so did actions presumed to be an affront to vaguely defined standards of justice. See, for example, Russell, *The Just War in the Middle Ages*, 65, on Gratian. For the political theologian Francisco de Vitoria, Indigenous Americans' violation of the natural right to trade and travel served as a legitimate underpinning for Spanish title; for Grotius, private parties could lawfully punish violations of natural law. See Anthony Pagden, "Conquest and the Just War: The 'School of Salamanca' and the 'Affair of the Indies,'" in *Empire and Modern Political Thought*, ed. Sankar Muthu (New York: Cambridge University Press, 2012), 30–60; Richard Tuck, "Introduction," in Hugo Grotius, *The Rights of War and Peace*, 3 vols., ed. Richard Tuck (Indianapolis: Liberty Fund, 2005), ix–xxxiv, especially xx, xxvii; and see Benjamin Straumann, "The Right to Punish as a Just Cause of War in Hugo Grotius' Natural Law," *Studies in the History of Ethics* 2 (2006): 1–20. Offensive behavior might also present a challenge to the legal order of "the whole world which is in a sense a commonwealth," as Vitoria put it (Pagden quoting Vitoria, in "Conquest and the Just War," 43). Pagden points out that Vitoria appeared to cast the *ius gentium* as something broader than the Roman law governing Rome's relations with non-Roman peoples and to represent it as a secondary natural law that applied to all men and was recognized by all polities.

43. Annabel Brett, "The Space of Politics and the Space of War in Hugo Grotius's *De iure belli ac pacis*," *Global Intellectual History* 1, no. 1 (2016), 33–60; and see chapter 3 in this volume.

44. Arnulf Becker Lorca, *Mestizo International Law: A Global Intellectual History, 1842–1933* (New York: Cambridge University Press, 2014).

45. On the persistence of micropolities in the international order, see Lauren Benton and Adam Clulow, "Protection Shopping among Empires: Suspended Sovereignty in the Cocos-Keeling Islands," *Past & Present* 257, no. 1 (2022): 209–247; on the persistence of empires, see Jane Burbank and Fred Cooper, *Empires in World History: Power and the Politics of Difference* (Princeton, NJ: Princeton University Press, 2011), chapters 13 and 14. For a valuable critical overview of the history of theories of war in international relations, see Jens Bartelson, "War and the Turn to History in International Relations," in *Routledge Handbook of Historical International Relations,* ed. Benjamin de Carvalho, Julia Costa Lopez, and Halvard Leira (New York: Routledge, 2021), 127–137.

46. On debates about the status of pirates, see Lauren Benton, *A Search for Sovereignty: Law and Geography in European Empires, 1400–1900* (New York: Cambridge University Press, 2010), chapter 3. James Q. Whitman offers a brilliant analysis of the Roman doctrine of postliminium, or the restoration of rights and property to freed captives, in a work in progress on the legal history of property. See also Clifford Ando, *Law, Language, and Empire in the Roman Tradition* (Philadelphia: University of Pennsylvania Press, 2011), 14–15, 73.

47. The nature of time between war and peace has been taken up from a different angle by Murad Idris, who seeks to trace, instead of a theory of limited war, various strands of a theory of limited (or less-idealized) peace. See Murad Idris, *War for Peace: Genealogies of a Violent Ideal in Western and Islamic Thought* (Oxford: Oxford University Press, 2019), 319. In his history of colonial violence, Walter notes the difficulties of distinguishing between war and peace in empires, but he tends to characterize attempts to define the legal framework of imperial wars as crass legalism or semantic games. Walter, *Colonial Violence*, 78–79.

48. Impoverished Europeans were also ensnared. See Clare Anderson, *Convicts: A Global History* (New York: Cambridge University Press, 2022).

49. Dudziak, *War Time.*

Chapter 2: Conquest by Raid and Massacre

1. The Spanish text of the requerimiento is in Bartolomé de las Casas, *Historia de las Indias*, ed. Agustín Millares Carlo, 3 vols. (Mexico City: Fondo de cultura económica, 1951), 3: 26–27. Translation, National Humanities Center, https://nationalhumanitiescenter.org/pds/amerbegin/contact/text7/requirement.pdf (accessed 1 October 2018).

2. Las Casas, *Historia de las Indias*, 3: 56, 28–31. The strangeness of the legal language of the requerimiento has attracted a great deal of commentary by scholars across fields. For example, the Latin American historian D. A. Brading called the statement "a cynical piece of legal gibberish" (D. A. Brading, *The First America: The Spanish Monarchy, Creole Patriots and the Liberal State 1492–1867* [New York: Cambridge University Press, 1991], 81), and the prominent literary scholar Stephen Greenblatt described it as a "strange blend of ritual, cynicism, legal fiction, and perverse idealism" (Stephen Greenblatt, *Marvelous Possessions: The Wonder of the New World* [Chicago: University of Chicago Press, 2008], 98). Many legal historians begin their discussion with such quotes from other scholars; see, for example, Stephen Neff, *Justice among Nations: A*

History of International Law (Cambridge, MA: Harvard University Press, 2014), 113; others are more careful, such as Tamar Herzog, *A Short History of European Law: The Last Two and a Half Millennia* (New York: Cambridge University Press, 2018), 156. For a good overview of the treatment of the requerimiento as a "legal absurdity," see Paja Faudree, "Reading the *Requerimiento* Performatively: Speech Acts and the Conquest of the New World," *Colonial Latin American Review* 24, no. 4 (2015): 456–478, especially 457–458.

3. Patricia Seed, *Ceremonies of Possession in Europe's Conquest of the New World, 1492–1640* (Cambridge, UK: Cambridge University Press, 1993), chapter 3.

4. Russell, *The Just War in the Middle Ages*, chapter 2.

5. The familiarity worked on many levels. Conquistadors like Hernán Cortés were acutely aware that reading the requerimiento and performing other rituals offered some small protection from accusations that they were usurping crown authority by making war without authorization. The crown, rivals, and the papacy were key audiences for the reading. See Luigi Nuzzo, *El Lenguaje Jurídico de la Conquista: Estrategias de control en las Indias Españolas* (Ciudad de México: Editorial Tirant lo Blanch, 2021), 64–66; and James Muldoon, *Popes, Lawyers, and Infidels: The Church and the Non-Christian World, 1250–1550* (Philadelphia: University of Pennsylvania Press, 1979), 142. The requerimiento also had more widespread currency in late medieval Castile. Besides being used in sieges and royal petitions, it featured in civic disputes. Yanay Israeli shows that its key ritual element was "the display, reading, and production of documents," and it functioned to present adversaries with demands before "judicial escalation" of disputes. Yanay Israeli, "The *Requerimiento* in the Old World: Making Demands and Keeping Records in the Legal Culture of Late Medieval Castile," *Law and History Review* 40, no. 1 (2022): 37–62, 43, 60.

6. Letter from Oriola's mayor to Jaume III in Maria Teresa Ferrer i Mallol, *La Frontera amb l'Islam en el segle XIV: cristians i sarraïns al País Valencià* (Barcelona: Consell Superiord'Investigacions Científiques, 1988), 63.

7. Adrian Keith Goldsworthy, *Pax Romana: War, Peace and Conquest in the Roman World* (London: Weidenfeld & Nicolson, 2016) 382, and see 54–56.

8. Adrian Keith Goldsworthy, *Roman Warfare* (New York: Basic Books, 2019), 14–16.

9. Goldsworthy, *Roman Warfare*, 75, 81.

10. Goldsworthy, *Roman Warfare*, 84.

11. During this period, the majority of Roman troops were stationed in frontier regions. Adrian Goldsworthy, *Pax Romana*, 381; Arthur Eckstein, *Mediterranean Anarchy, Interstate War, and the Rise of Rome* (Berkeley: University of California, 2007). Later accounts of fetial rituals, priestly actions announcing the commencement of war, implicitly addressed the relation between raiding and war. Populations about to come under attack theoretically had the opportunity to surrender, usually in exchange for protection against violence to their lives and property. But the emphasis was on commencing, not preventing, war. Clifford Ando, *Law, Language, and Empire in the Roman Tradition* (Philadelphia: University of Pennsylvania Press, 2011), 51–52. At the same time, fetial rituals pointed to the limits of war by emphasizing the way private or disaggregated violence could be brought under the cover of war and Romans could assert authority over the intensity of responses to provocation. Goldsworthy, *Roman Warfare*, 15–16.

12. Philip De Souza, "Rome's Contribution to the Development of Piracy," *Memoirs of the American Academy in Rome: Supplementary Volumes* 6 (2008): 71–96.

13. Milka Levy Rubin, "The Surrender Agreements: Origins and Authenticity," in *The Umayyad World*, ed. Andrew Marsham (New York: Routledge, 2021), 200. On plundering after surrender, see William V. Harris, *War and Imperialism in Republican Rome, 327–70 B.C.* (Oxford: Clarendon Press, 1979), 75.

14. A valuable overview of earlier narratives of the Arab conquests, including the migration thesis, is in the introduction to Fred Donner, *The Early Islamic Conquests* (Princeton, NJ: Princeton University Press, 1981). The characterization of the conquests as an expansionist project envisioned and led by Middle Eastern Arabs finds repetition in popular histories. Hugh Kennedy, for example, describes his popular account as "a tale of how a small number . . . of determined and highly motivated men were able to cover vast distances, through rugged and inhospitable lands, to conquer major empires and kingdoms and to rule their lands," and describes the speed of these events as "amazing." Hugh Kennedy, *The Great Arab Conquests: How the Spread of Islam Changed the World We Live In* (Philadelphia: Da Capo Press, 2008), 1, 3.

15. Viewed in this light, Arabs appear as the "most successful of the peripheral peoples" on the edges of imperial spheres of influence or inhabiting zones of interimperial tension. Robert G. Hoyland, *In God's Path: The Arab Conquests and the Creation of an Islamic Empire* (New York: Oxford University Press, 2015), 11.

16. See Levy Rubin, "The Surrender Agreements," and Aseel Najib, "Common Wealth: Land Taxation in Early Islam," Ph.D. Dissertation, Columbia University, 2023, chapter 5.

17. Hoyland, *In God's Path*, 39, 44, 47, 67.

18. Hoyland, *In God's Path*, 93.

19. Formal agreements of this type included the Roman/Byzantine *deditio in fidem*, which involved surrender in connection with a pledge by the invader to act in good faith in implementing the conditions with a measure of justice and mercy. The arrangement was formalized in a treaty or pact. Gerhard Wirth, "Rome and Its Germanic Partners in the Fourth Century," in *Kingdoms of the Empire: The Integration of Barbarians in Late Antiquity*, ed. Walter Pohl (New York: Brill, 1997), 13–56.

20. In another famous episode, the Mongols attacked Russia in reprisal for the murder of ambassadors. J. McIver Weatherford, *Genghis Kahn and the Making of the Modern World* (New York: Crown, 2004), 146, 179, 186.

21. Inga Clendinnen, "'Fierce and Unnatural Cruelty': Cortés and the Conquest of Mexico," *Representations* 33 (1991): 65–100. And see the discussion of this claim in the introduction, earlier.

22. Neil L. Whitehead, "Tribes Make States and States Make Tribes: Warfare and the Creation of Colonial Tribes and States in Northeastern South America," in *War in the Tribal Zone: Expanding States and Indigenous Warfare*, ed. R. Brian Ferguson and Neil L. Whitehead (Santa Fe, NM: School of American Research Press, 1992), 127–150, 142.

23. The best-known example is Napoleon A. Chagnon, *Yąnomamö: The Fierce People* (New York: Holt, Rinehart and Winston, 1983). For a discussion of this tendency, see Brian Sandberg, "Ravages and Depredations: Raiding War and Globalization in the Early Modern World," in *A Global History of Early Modern Violence*, ed. Erica Charters, Marie Houllemare, and Peter H. Wilson (Manchester, UK: Manchester University Press, 2021), 88–122, 88. John Jeffries Martin observes that Michel de Montaigne, echoing New World voyage chronicles, characterized

violence, including cannibalism, among Tupís as a function of their dedication to revenge and feuding rather than war ("Cannibalism as a Feuding Ritual in Early Modern Europe," *Acta Histriae* 25 [2017]: 1, 97–108).

24. Charles de Rochefort, *Histoire naturelle et morale des Iles Antilles de l'Amerique . . . Avec un vocabulaire Caraibe* (Rotterdam: Arnould Leers), 1658; quoted in Whitehead, "Tribes Make States," 143.

25. See chapter 3 on Portuguese raiding in Africa and the Indian Ocean. On the similarities of European and African (and other early modern) raiding, see Brian Sandberg, "Ravages and Depredations," 92. On European slave trading and intensified raiding in seventeenth-century West Africa, see Paul Lovejoy, *Transformations in Slavery: A History of Slavery in Africa* (New York: Cambridge University Press, 2011), chapters 3–4. European settlement stimulated raiding in North America in multiple ways, in particular through the cascading effects of increased demand for captives among Indigenous communities. Thomas Abler, "Beavers and Muskets: Iroquois Military Fortunes in the Face of European Colonization," in Ferguson and Whitehead, eds., *War in the Tribal Zone*, 151–174, 159; and Brett Rushforth, *Bonds of Alliance: Indigenous and Atlantic Slaveries in New France* (Chapel Hill: University of North Carolina Press, 2012), 196.

26. Brian Sandberg, *War and Conflict in the Early Modern World: 1500–1700* (Malden, MA: Polity Press, 2016), chapter 7.

27. Sandberg, "Ravages and Depredations," 92.

28. The phrase is from D. J. Mattingly, "War and Peace in Roman North Africa: Observations and Models of State-Tribe Interaction," in Ferguson and Whitehead, eds., *War in the Tribal Zone*, 31–60, 53.

29. This aspect of truces and the violence that followed truce breaking recalled European practices of feuds, vendettas, and duels—varieties of "small" violence in which participants invoked honor and stoked accusations of betrayal and insult. On the way vendettas could shade into warfare, see Edward Muir, *Mad Blood Stirring: Vendetta in Renaissance Italy* (Baltimore, MD: Johns Hopkins University Press, 1993, 1998). On justifications for massacres, see Stephen D. Bowd, *Renaissance Mass Murder: Civilians and Soldiers during the Italian Wars* (New York: Oxford University Press, 2018), especially chapter 4; Alison Games, *Inventing the English Massacre: Amboyna in History and Memory* (New York: Oxford University Press, 2020); and Adam Clulow, *Amboina, 1623: Fear and Conspiracy on the Edge of Empire* (New York: Columbia University Press, 2019).

30. For a fascinating study of political alliance across religious and political lines, see Hussein Fancy, *The Mercenary Mediterranean: Sovereignty, Religion, and Violence in the Medieval Crown of Aragon* (Chicago: University of Chicago Press, 2016); on shared practices of negotiation and diplomacy, see John E. Wansbrough, *Lingua Franca in the Mediterranean* (Richmond, Surrey, UK: Curzon Press, 1996).

31. Livestock raids could produce significant windfalls. Forces from Cordoba in 1191 conducted an attack on Christian-held Silva and took 3,000 prisoners and 15,000 head of cattle. James Brodman, *Ransoming Captives in Crusader Spain: The Order of the Merced on the Christian-Islamic Frontier* (Philadelphia: University of Pennsylvania Press, 1986), chapter 1, 3. On the cultural significance of livestock raiding, see Javier Irigoyen-Garcia, *The Spanish Arcadia: Sheep Herding, Pastoral Discourse, and Ethnicity in Early Modern Spain* (Toronto: University of Toronto Press, 2014), 86–87.

32. Derek Lomax, *The Reconquest of Spain* (New York: Longman, 1978), 47–50; R. A. Fletcher, "Reconquest and Crusade in Spain c. 1050–1150," in José-Juan López-Portillo, *Spain, Portugal and the Atlantic Frontier of Medieval Europe* (Burlington, UK: Ashgate, 2013), 69–85, 73; and Eduardo Manzano Moreno, *Historia de España: Época medieval* (Madrid: Critica Marcial-pons, 2010).

33. On the sale and purchase of protection more generally, see Lauren Benton and Adam Clulow, "Empires and Protection: Making Interpolity Law in the Early Modern World," *Journal of Global History* 12, no.1 (2017): 74–92.

34. Fancy, *Mercenary Mediterranean.*

35. Dolores María Pérez Castañera, *Enemigos seculares: Guerra y treguas entre Castilla y Granada (c. 1246—c. 1481)* (Madrid: Silex, 2013), 22. Pérez Castañera's collection of these truces forms the basis for the analysis that follows. See also Luis Suárez Fernández, *Las guerras de Granada (1246–1492): Transformación e incorporación de al-Andalus* (Barcelona: Editorial Planeta, 2017), especially chapter 4, which explains the appeal of truces because they did not signify a cession of sovereignty.

36. Pérez Castañera, *Enemigos seculares,* 142, 143, 145, 146.

37. Pérez Castañera, *Enemigos seculares,* 147, 148; Miguel Angel Ladero Quesada, *La Guerra de Granada (1482–1491)* (Granada: Diputación de Granada, 2007), 16.

38. Pérez Castañera, *Enemigos seculares,* "Apéndice Documental," 130; my translation.

39. Joseph F. O'Callaghan, *Reconquest and Crusade in Medieval Spain* (Philadelphia: University of Pennsylvania Press, 2003), 140. On the capitulation agreements leading up to the conquest of Granada, see Miguel Angel Ladero Quesada, *Castilla y la conquista del reino de Granada* (Granada: Diputación de Granada, 1987), 79–97.

40. For example, as at Almeria, where mass enslavement followed the siege. See O'Callaghan, *Reconquest and Crusade in Medieval Spain,* 140.

41. Thomas W. Barton, *Victory's Shadow: Conquest and Governance in Medieval Catalonia* (Ithaca, NY: Cornell University Press, 2019), 23.

42. Alongside typical acts of capitulation, sponsored settlement, and the grant of *fueros,* or law codes, the crown also maneuvered to strengthen its authority in Granada, insisting on making all ecclesiastical appointments and extending a measure of royal jurisdiction throughout the new territories. This enhanced royal power existed alongside the resurgent power of nobles who were receiving rich grants in lands and offices through the conquest. In contrast to the conquests of Seville and Cordoba, most Muslim residents of the city stayed in place and retained some property rights. The strength of crown authority facilitated in the treaty and its implementation should not be exaggerated; crown policy was reactive and largely driven by petitions from various groups of local notables. See David Coleman, *Creating Christian Granada: Society and Religious Culture in an Old-World Frontier City, 1492–1600* (Ithaca, NY: Cornell University Press, 2003), 74. On the importance of viewing the conquest of Granada not as the end of conflict but as an inflection point in a complex of raiding and plunder that extended to North Africa, see Jocelyn Hendrickson, *Leaving Iberia: Islamic Law and Christian Conquest in North West Africa* (Cambridge, MA: Harvard University Press, 2021); and Andrew W. Devereux, *The Other Side of Empire: Just War in the Mediterranean and the Rise of Early Modern Spain* (Ithaca, NY: Cornell University Press, 2020), 8, 99, 113.

43. On iterations of this claim in both Christian and Islamic traditions of political thought, see Murad Idris, *War for Peace: Genealogies of a Violent Ideal in Western and Islamic Thought* (New York: Oxford University Press, 2019).

44. Katherine Ludwig Jansen, *Peace and Penance in Late Medieval Italy* (Princeton, NJ: Princeton University Press, 2018), 2.

45. Jansen, *Peace and Penance*, 19, 15.

46. Jansen, *Peace and Penance*, 31–35.

47. My argument is consistent with, though somewhat different from, the thrust of several excellent recent studies that analyze the legal context that produced the requerimiento and ordered ritual performance. See especially Faudree, "Reading the *Requerimiento* Performatively"; Yanay Israeli, "The *Requerimiento* in the Old World: Making Demands and Keeping Records in the Legal Culture of Late Medieval Castile," *Law and History Review* 40, no. 1 (2022): 37–62; and Andrew W. Devereux, *The Other Side of Empire: Just War in the Mediterranean and the Rise of Early Modern Spain* (Ithaca, NY, and London: Cornell University Press, 2020). I am grateful to Jorge Díaz Ceballos for sharing insights and sources on the requerimiento; see his book *Poder compartido: Repúblicas urbanas, Monarquía y conversación en Castilla del Oro, 1508–1573* (Madrid: Marcial Pons Ediciones de Historia, S.A., 2020), 69, 85.

48. On the legal capacities and responsibilities of *adelantados* in Castile, see Robert Mac-Donald, "Introduction: Part II," *Leyes de los adelantados mayors: Regulations, Attributed to Alfonso X of Castile, Concerning the King's Vicar in the Judiciary and in Territorial Administration*, ed. Robert A. MacDonald (New York: Hispanic Seminary of Medieval Studies, 2000), 5–29. And on the legal meaning and context of claims of discovery and settlement, see Lauren Benton and Benjamin Straumann, "Acquiring Empire by Law: From Roman Doctrine to Early Modern European Practice," *Law and History Review* 28, no. 1 (2010): 1–38; Lauren Benton, *A Search for Sovereignty: Law and Geography in European Empires, 1400–1900* (New York: Cambridge University Press, 2010), chapter 1, especially 22–23; and Santiago Olmedo Bernal, *El dominio del Atlántico en la baja Edad Media: Los títulos jurídicos de la expansion peninsular hasta el Tratado de Tordesillas* (Valladolid: Sociedad V Centenario del Tratado de Tordesillas, 1995), 420–422.

49. John E. Worth, ed. and trans., *Discovering Florida: First Contact Narratives from Spanish Expeditions along the Lower Gulf Coast* (Gainesville: University Press of Florida, 2014), 73–74.

50. Worth, *Discovering Florida*, 80. The full text of the requerimiento is in Bartolomé de las Casas, *Historia de las Indias*, 3: 26–27.

51. Anthony Pagden, trans. and ed., *Letters from Mexico* (New Haven, CT: Yale University Press, 2001), 12.

52. *Letters from Mexico*, 20. Cortés's actions were not yet styled as conquest because, he recounted, Moctezuma was inviting him to Tenochtitlan; as Pagden notes, he characterized as his "only acts of warfare . . . the subjugation of Tlaxcala—which was in some sense an independent city—and the massacre at Cholula." Anthony Pagden, preface to *Letters from Mexico*, lxix.

53. It is unclear how or whether anyone had extended that promise. *Letters from Mexico*, 21.

54. Spaniards in this case had an interpreter, and they explained that they "did not desire war but only peace and love between us"—whereupon the *indios* "replied not in words but with a shower of arrows." *Letters from Mexico*, 21.

55. *Letters from Mexico*, 54.

56. On the likelihood that Mexica gifts to Spaniards were signs of dominance rather than submission, see Inga Clendinnen, "Fierce and Unnatural Cruelty: Cortés and the Conquest of Mexico," in *New World Encounters*, ed. Stephen Greenblatt (Berkeley: University of California Press, 1993), 12–47, 17. For the argument that Cortés emphasized vassalage in various ways to reinforce his legitimacy as conqueror, see José Valero Silva, *El legalismo de Hernán Cortés como instrumento de su conquista* (México: Universidad Nacional Autónoma de México, 1965), 44–47.

57. See, for example, Camilla Townsend, *Fifth Sun: A New History of the Aztecs* (New York: Oxford University Press, 2021), 88, 104.

58. Cortés is explicit in connecting the rationale for war to Moctezuma's "treachery": "I could scarcely believe that such a great lord should . . . say that he was my friend, and meanwhile should be seeking a way to attack me by another's hand. . . . But since it was true that he did not keep his word or speak the truth, I had changed my plans: whereas, before, I had been going to his land with the intention of seeing him and speaking with him in order to have him as a friend and to converse with him in harmony, now I intended to enter his land at war doing all the harm I could as an enemy, though I regretted it very much, for I had always wished rather to be his friend and ask his advice on all the things that must be done in this land." *Letters from Mexico*, 75.

59. See chapter 3 in this volume for a discussion of the construction of a local right to make war in empires.

60. *Letters from Mexico*, 89.

61. Cortés's strategy in founding a new town is paradigmatic of a broader process that set off jurisdictional conflicts in the course of conquest and colonization. For a clear and fascinating analysis of this dynamic, see Jorge Díaz Ceballos, "New World *Civitas*, Contested Jurisdictions, and Inter-cultural Conversation in the Construction of the Spanish Monarchy," *Colonial Latin American Review* 27, no. 1 (2018): 30–51.

62. Fray Bernardino de Sahagún, *Florentine Codex: General History of the Things of New Spain*, ed. Arthur J. O. Anderson and Charles E. Dibble (Santa Fe, NM: School of American Research), book 12, chapter 11. Townsend contends that Moctezuma gave orders to the Cholulans to withhold food and might also have urged them to ambush Spaniards as they left the city. Townsend, *Fifth Sun*, 104.

63. Bernal Díaz del Castillo, *The True History of the Conquest of New Spain, Vol. II* (New York: Cambridge University Press, 2010), 15. The fact that the requerimiento was not read became a point of criticism during the *residencia* (formal review) of Cortés. *Letters from Mexico*, 454, n. 27.

64. Fray Bernardino de Sahagún, *Florentine Codex*, book 12, chapter 11.

65. Townsend points out that the logic of punishing rebellion, so prominent in Cortés's time, became less salient later because chroniclers "often forgot what they were supposed to say" and mixed in other rationales. Townsend, *Fifth Sun*, 109.

66. The group quickly capitulated and offered cotton cloth, hides, pine nuts, fowl, and some turquoise. Pedro de Castañeda de Nájara, *Relación de la Jornada de Cíbola/Narrative of the Coronado Expedition*, ed. John Miller Morris (Chicago: R. R. Donnelley & Sons, 2002), 106, 108.

67. Castañeda, *Relación*, 125.

68. Castañeda, *Relación*, 125.

69. Castañeda, *Relación*, 136–137, 153–155.

70. Castañeda, *Relación*, 175.

71. Castañeda, *Relación*, 374–376. Similarly, in the early sixteenth-century conquest and settlement of Castilla del Oro, a region in Central America, one agent of Spanish conquest observed that the reading of the requerimiento was counterproductive. Indigenous groups presented with the statement evaded Spaniards by fleeing to the hills. Spaniards' "remedy" was to attack them "without observing any formalities." Archivo General de Indias (AGI), Patronato 193, R. 13. My thanks to Jorge Díaz Ceballos for this source; on conquest and colonization in Castilla del Oro, see his *Poder compartido*.

72. Castañeda, *Relación*, 353.

73. As with the label "Spaniards" in the Americas, the category "English" obscures enormous variety—of terms of settlement, interests, and religion. On Boston's rise and recognition as a powerful "nation" against other "English" political projects, see Mark Peterson, *The City-State of Boston: The Rise and Fall of an Atlantic Power, 1630–1865* (Princeton, NJ: Princeton University Press, 2020), 5–6, 16–18, 35.

74. Alfred A. Cave, *The Pequot War* (Amherst: University of Massachusetts Press, 1996), 170.

75. John Mason, *A Brief History of the Pequot War* (Boston, 1736); John Underhill, *News from America* (London, 1638); Lion Gardiner, *Relation of the Pequot Warres* (Hartford, CT: Acorn Club of Connecticut, 1901 [1660]).

76. Recent historical accounts of the massacre and war improve on Cave's interpretation of the causes of the conflict offered by Alfred Cave in *The Pequot War* and mainly align with my interpretation in the discussion that follows, although Jenny Pulsipher finds greater coherence than I do in English reliance on just war doctrine. Jenny Pulsipher, *Swindler Sachem: The American Indian Who Sold His Birthright, Dropped Out of Harvard, and Conned the King of England* (New Haven, CT: Yale University Press, 2018). For an illuminating analysis of the significance of the war for regional trade, see Peterson, *The City-State of Boston*, 43–54. Cave's book remains invaluable for its details on raids and negotiations, and I have relied on it heavily in my own account.

77. Peterson, *The City-State of Boston*, 48.

78. Disputes about justice and punishment in frontier murders occurred across the continent, and historians have analyzed their political ramifications. See especially Nicole Eustace, *Covered with Night: A Story of Murder and Indigenous Justice in Early America* (New York: Liveright, 2021). Richard White regards such incidents as an opportunity for culturally hybrid juridical processes (*The Middle Ground: Indians, Empires, and Republics in the Great Lakes Region, 1650–1815* [Cambridge, UK: Cambridge University Press, 2011], 75–82). Lisa Ford analyzes them as focal points of jurisdictional politics (*Settler Sovereignty: Jurisdiction and Indigenous People in America and Australia, 1788–1836* [Cambridge, UK: Harvard University Press, 2010]. For debates about mutual intelligibility, see Brian P. Owensby and Richard J. Ross, "Making Law Intelligible in Comparative Context," in Brian P. Owensby and Richard J. Ross, eds., *Justice in a New World: Negotiating Legal Intelligibility in British, Iberian, and Indigenous America* (New York: New York University Press, 2018), 1–58, and Lauren Benton, "In Defense of Ignorance: Frameworks for Legal Politics in the Atlantic World," in Owensby and Ross, *Justice in a New World*, 273–290.

79. John Winthrop, *Winthrop's Journal, "History of New England,"1630–1649, Vol. I.* (New York: Charles Scribner's Sons, 1908), 139.

80. Gardiner, *Relation of the Pequot Warres*; Pulsipher, *Swindler Sachem*, 35. Pulsipher points out that negotiations took a different turn when English soldiers chased and cornered a group

of Pequots after the massacre. After a parley with an English interpreter, Thomas Stanton, the Pequots sent women and children out of the swamp where they had taken refuge. The captives were enslaved; in the ensuing fight, several scores of Pequot men escaped, and those who did not escape were killed (Pulsipher, 38–41).

81. On European perceptions of Indian savagery in warfare and savagery in later contexts, see Peter Silver, *Our Savage Neighbors: How Indian War Transformed Early America* (New York: W. W. Norton, 2008); Christian Crouch, *Nobility Lost: French and Canadian Martial Cultures, Indians, and the End of New France* (Ithaca, NY: Cornell University Press, 2014); and chapter 4 in this volume.

82. Boston magistrates even cited just war doctrine in one instance to favor Indigenous rights to violence. Edward Johnson, *Johnson's Wonder-Working Providence, 1628–1651*, J. Franklin Jameson, ed. (New York: Barnes & Noble, 1952), 166.

83. Pulsipher characterizes the behavior of the Massachusetts Bay Colony as an application of just war theory that would have been known to them through Hugo Grotius's *De Iure Belli ac Pacis* (Pulsipher, *Swindler Sachem*, 42). But there is insufficient evidence of settlers' specific knowledge of Grotius's writings. *De Iure Belli ac Pacis* first appeared in English translation in 1682, well after the Pequot War.

84. Russell, *Just War in the Middle Ages*, 34–36; H.E.J. Cowdrey, "The Peace and the Truce of God in the Eleventh Century," *Past & Present* 46 (1970): 42–67; Randall Lesaffer, Erik-Jan Broers, and Joanna Waelkens, "From Antwerp to Munster (1609/1648)," in *The Twelve Years Truce (1609): Peace Truce, War and Law in the Low Counties at the Turn of the 17th Century*, ed. Randall Lesaffer (Boston: Brill, 2014), 233–255, 235.

85. Russell, *Just War in the Middle Ages*, 70, 244.

86. Russell, *Just War in the Middle Ages*, 183.

87. Idris suggests similarities in Islamic and Christian writers' approaches to the truce. Idris, *War for Peace*, 129.

88. On this point and more generally on late medieval and early modern debates about the nature of truces, see Lesaffer et al., "From Antwerp to Munster," 240–243.

89. Lesaffer et al., "From Antwerp to Munster," 241; Georg Schwarzenberger, "Jus Pacis ac Belli?: Prolegomena to a Sociology of International Law," *American Journal of International Law* 37, no. 3 (1943): 460–479.

90. Alberico Gentili, *De iure belli libri tres*, 2 vols. (New York: Clarendon Press; London: Humphrey Milford, 1933), vol. 2, book II, chapter XII, 186.

91. Hugo Grotius, *The Rights of War and Peace*, book III, ed. Richard Tuck (Indianapolis: Liberty Fund, 2005), chapter XXI, 1596.

92. Grotius, *The Rights of War and Peace*, book III, chapter XXI, 1599. Grotius also commented on the actions permitted during a truce. He noted that although it was not permitted to seize enemy possessions, the ban did not apply to taking places that had been truly "deserted . . . with a Design not to possess them again" (1603). If we think of the fluid give-and-take in ragged contact zones, the difficulties of discerning legitimate from illegitimate seizures become clear.

93. Gentili, *De iure belli libri tres*, book II, chapter XII, 186.

94. Randall Lesaffer, "Alberico Gentili's *ius post bellum* and Early Modern Peace Treaties," in *The Roman Foundations of the Law of Nations*, ed. Benedict Kingsbury and Benjamin Straumann

(New York: Oxford University Press, 2011), 228. Idris notes that Gentili's and Grotius's approach to the truce is that it "freezes, stores away, or defers hostile intentions" and emphasizes the way this association of truces with war reifies peace as a fixed and "even impossible" end to war. Idris, *War for Peace*, 190.

95. Gentili, *De iure belli libri tres*, book II, chapter IV, 147.

96. Gentili, *De iure belli libri tres*, book II, chapter XII, 189.

97. Gentili, *De iure belli libri tres*, book II, chapter VIII, 192.

98. Gentili, *De iure belli libri tres*, book II, chapter XIV, 365; book II, chapter XII, 189.

99. Grotius, *The Rights of War and Peace*, book III, chapter XXI, 1599–1603.

100. Gentili, *De iure belli libri tres*, book I, chapter II, 13.

101. Gentili, *De iure belli libri tres*, book I, chapter II, 14.

102. Alberico Gentili, *The Wars of the Romans: A Critical Edition and Translation of De Armis Romanis*, Benedict Kingsbury and Benjamin Straumann, eds.; trans. David Lupher (New York: Oxford University Press, 2011), 217–218.

103. Gentili, *The Wars of the Romans*, 227.

104. Hugo Grotius, *The Free Sea*, David Armitage, ed. (Indianapolis: Liberty Fund, 2004).

105. On Gentili's involvement with the Earl of Essex, see Diego Panizza, "Alberico Gentili's De Armis Romanis: The Roman Model of the Just Empire," in *Roman Foundations*, 57.

106. Such connections continued. Justifications for violence against peace breaking transitioned into rationales for repression under imperial rule against those who violated "the king's peace." See Lisa Ford, *The King's Peace: Law and Order in the British Empire* (Cambridge, MA: Harvard University Press, 2021).

Chapter 3: Private Booty, Public War

1. We know little about this captive other than that he was soon freed under Isabela's laws for the protection of *indios*.

2. Bernat Hernández, *Bartolomé de las Casas* (New York: Penguin, 2015), 82–83, 85–87.

3. Bartolomé de las Casas, *Brevísima Relación de la Destrucción de la Indias* (Madrid: Alianza editorial, 2014 [2005]), 14, 85, 108; my translation.

4. For example, in an attack on Santo Domingo, Spaniards had chased Native people who had retreated to the hills for their safety. Spanish soldiers killed most of the Indigenous men and seized "70 or 80 maidens and women." Las Casas, *Brevísima Relación*, 106; my translation.

5. Las Casas, *Brevísima Relación*, 85, 105; my translation.

6. Las Casas, *Brevísima Relación*, 110; my translation.

7. Studies of medieval and early modern slavery in Iberia work to break down this distinction while still recognizing differences. See William D. Phillips Jr., *Slavery in Medieval and Early Modern Iberia* (Philadelphia: University of Pennsylvania Press, 2013); and A.C. de C.M. Saunders, *A Social History of Black Slaves and Freedmen in Portugal, 1441–1555* (New York: Cambridge University Press, 1982). Other recent studies make a concerted effort to place Iberian slavery in the context of interpolity relations in the Mediterranean world and Africa. See especially Debra Blumenthal, *Enemies and Familiars: Slavery and Mastery in Fifteenth-Century Valencia* (Ithaca, NY: Cornell University Press, 2009); and Daniel Hershenzon, *The Captive Sea: Slavery,*

Communication, and Commerce in Early Modern Spain and the Mediterranean (Philadelphia: University of Pennsylvania Press, 2018); and Herman L. Bennett, *African Kings and Black Slaves: Sovereignty and Dispossession in the Early Modern Atlantic* (Philadelphia: University of Pennsylvania Press, 2020).

8. For a nuanced analysis of *indios* in households in Castile and the authority of masters over them, see Nancy E. van Deusen, *Global Indios: The Indigenous Struggle for Justice in Sixteenth-Century Spain* (Durham, NC: Duke University Press, 2015), chapter 2.

9. Blumenthal, *Enemies and Familiars*, chapter 1.

10. Vincent Cornell, "Socioeconomic Dimensions of Reconquista and Jihad in Morocco: Portuguese Dukkala and the Sa'did Sus, 1450–1557," *International Journal of Middle East Studies* 22 (1990): 379–418, 393; Jocelyn Hendrickson, *Leaving Iberia: Islamic Law and Christian Conquest in North West Africa* (Cambridge, MA: Harvard University Press, 2021), 41.

11. The efforts of enslaved people to make, retain, and reconstruct households have been detailed in multiple historical studies. A poignant and telling example recounts the legal struggle, over three decades, by Furcy, an enslaved man in the French Indian Ocean, whose quest for freedom was inextricably bound with his struggle to "assert himself as a father and husband." Sue Peabody, *Madeleine's Children: Family, Freedom Secrets, and Lies in France's Indian Ocean Colonies* (New York: Oxford University Press, 2017), 10. Historians have also analyzed the plight of enslaved people in planter households defined as political and legal units. See, for example, Thavolia Glymph, *Out of the House of Bondage: The Transformation of the Plantation Household* (New York: Cambridge University Press, 2008). The struggle of enslaved people in households is the focus of studies in other regions and periods. For example, Laura Culbertson, *Slaves and Households in the Near East* (Chicago: Oriental Institute of the University of Chicago, 2011); and, significant for its argument about slave belonging rather than freedom as an objective for enslaved people in Africa, see Suzanne Miers and Igor Kopytoff, *Slavery in Africa: Historical and Anthropological Perspectives* (Madison: University of Wisconsin Press, 1977). Numerous studies highlight the character of households as sites of politics. For example, for South Asia, Indrani Chatterjee, *Unfamiliar Relations: Family and History in South Asia* (New Brunswick, NJ: Rutgers University Press, 2004); and in the history of political thought, Anna Becker, *Gendering the Renaissance Commonwealth* (New York: Cambridge University Press, 2019). Last, important recent work casts Atlantic slaving and slavery as projects of control over women captives' reproductive capacities and rights. See especially Jennifer Morgan, *Laboring Women: Reproduction and Gender in New World Slavery* (Philadelphia: University of Pennsylvania Press, 2004); and Jennifer Morgan, *Reckoning with Slavery: Gender, Kinship, and Capitalism in the Early Black Atlantic* (Durham, NC: Duke University Press, 2021). I cannot do justice to all aspects of this literature in this chapter but reference key ideas as they relate to households and war in garrison empires.

12. Marriage of European men to local women was foundational to all early European empires, including those not discussed in this chapter. On its importance in the Dutch empire, see Charles H. Parker, *Global Calvinism: Conversion and Commerce in the Dutch Empire, 1600–1800* (New Haven, CT: Yale University Press, 2022), 143. In tracing Calvinists' efforts to promote marriages in the Dutch empire, Parker underscores the importance of religious authorities' jurisdiction over marriage. This chapter does not focus on tensions between secular and

religious authorities in tracing marriage policies in early empires. On the influence of those jurisdictional tensions to the institutional contours of empires, see Lauren Benton, *Law and Colonial Cultures: Legal Regimes in World History* (New York: Cambridge University Press, 2002), chapters 3 and 4.

13. Brett Rushforth, *Bonds of Alliance: Indigenous and Atlantic Slaveries in New France* (Chapel Hill: University of North Carolina Press, 2012); Vincent Brown, *Tacky's Revolt: The Story of an Atlantic Slave War* (Cambridge, MA: Harvard University Press, 2020).

14. Anna Becker points out that Hannah Arendt influenced a generation of scholars when she stated with misplaced confidence that Aristotle had separated a sphere of politics from the world of the household and its preoccupations with "natural life." Anna Becker, *Gendering the Renaissance Commonwealth*, 2.

15. See Becker, *Gendering the Renaissance Commonwealth*, 4.

16. Becker, *Gendering the Renaissance Commonwealth*, 9. This political dimensions of households has been explored in the literature on households in the Atlantic world. See especially Kathleen M. Brown, *Good Wives, Nasty Wenches, and Anxious Patriarchs: Gender, Race, and Power in Colonial Virginia* (Chapel Hill: University of North Carolina Press, 1996); Glymph, *Out of the House of Bondage*; Michelle A. McKinley, *Fractional Freedoms: Slavery, Intimacy, and Legal Mobilization in Colonial Lima 1600–1700* (New York: Cambridge University Press, 2018); María Elena Martínez, *Genealogical Fictions: Limpieza de Sangre, Religion, and Gender in Colonial Mexico* (Stanford, CA: Stanford University Press, 2011); and Ann Twinam, *Public Lives, Private Secrets: Gender, Honor, Sexuality, and Illegitimacy in Colonial Spanish America* (Stanford, CA: Stanford University Press, 1999).

17. Francisco Suárez, *Selections from Three Works*, ed. Thomas Pink (Indianapolis: Liberty Fund, 2015), 99–101, 528.

18. Suárez, *Selections from Three Works*, 431, and see 105.

19. Suárez, *Selections from Three Works*, 105.

20. War can only be legitimately declared by "a sovereign prince who has no superior in temporal affairs, or a state which has retained for itself a like jurisdiction" (Suárez, *Selections from Three Works*, 917). There can only be one party in a war with a just cause, and "there can be no just war without an underlying cause of a legitimate and necessary nature" (929). Suárez's positions on these matters were consistent with those of other scholastics.

21. This position rooted servitude in human volition but also begged the question—much taken up by other scholastics—of whether all slaves, under all conditions, could lawfully consent to their enslavement; on the natural qualities of authority, see Juan Cruz Crus, "El Derecho de Gentes en Suárez: La Constumbre como Plebiscito Permanente," 29–47 in *Suárez em Lisboa 1617–2017: Actos do Congresso*, ed. Pedro Caridade de Freitas, Margarida Seixas, and Ana Caldeira Fouto (Lisbon: AAFDL Editora, 2018), 31–32; André Santos Campos, "O Contratualismo de Francisco Suárez," 111–126 in *Suárez em Lisboa*, 122–123; on voluntary enslavement, see Daniel Severin Allemann, "Slavery and Empire in Iberian Scholastic Thought, c. 1539–1682," Ph.D. Dissertation, University of Cambridge, 2020; and Suárez, *Selections from Three Works*, 420–421. For an interesting discussion of the uses of consent in assigning coerced labor to masters in a different context, see Sonia Tycko, "The Legality of Prisoner of War Labour in England, 1648–1655," *Past & Present* 246, no. 1 (2020): 35–68.

22. Suárez, *Selections from Three Works*, 101. Suárez distinguished between natural law and the *ius gentium* (law of nations), which he identified as human law but also distinguished from civil law. He grouped the law of war, slavery, and treaties of peace and truces under the law of nations. These laws were not directly derived from or necessary under natural reason, though they existed "in harmony with natural reason."

23. Suárez, *Selections from Three Works*, 403, 527. On the subordination of private good to public good, see Suárez, *Selections from Three Works*, 205, 401–402.

24. Suárez, *Selections from Three Works*, 412, 532–533.

25. Rushforth, *Bonds of Alliance*, chapter 1; Brown, *Tacky's Revolt*, 4, 6.

26. Allemann, "Slavery and Empire in Iberian Scholastic Thought."

27. Suárez, *Selections from Three Works*, 986. Emphasis added. The difference between a duel and a conflict with "the true character of war" was that the latter is undertaken "under public authority and for a public cause" (Suárez, *Selections from Three Works*, 987).

28. Suárez, *Selections from Three Works*, 987.

29. Suárez, *Selections from Three Works*, 987–988.

30. Sanjay Subrahmanyam, *The Portuguese Empire in Asia, 1500–1700: A Political and Economic History* (Hoboken, NJ: John Wiley & Sons, 2012), 52, 60. To be sure, the crown did express a preference for peace in its instructions and even exhorted captains to ignore "affronts," but the king also gave broad authorization for captains to respond to any acts of aggression in kind. For example, in his instructions to Diogo Lopes de Sequeira, the king affirmed his wish for "peace and friendship" but also instructed Sequeira that if he came under "armed attack" or was "betrayed" by parties wishing to disarm the fleet, "then you shall cause all the damage and hurt you can upon whomsoever should try to do this." "Instructions to Diogo Lopes de Sequeira Almeirim, 1508 February 13," *Documentos sobre os Portugueses em Moçambique e Na África Central, 1497–1840, Vol II* (Lisboa: Centro de Estudos Históricos Ultramarinos, 1963), 267. High officials in the Estado da Índia carried full authorization to make peace treaties as well as to wage war. See, for example, "Letters Patent Delegating the Powers of Captain-Major to D. Francisco de Almeida," Lisbon, 1505 February 27," *Documentos sobre os Portugueses em Moçambique e Na África Central, 1497–1840, Vol I* (Lisboa: Centro de Estudos Históricos Ultramarinos, 1962), 151. Almeida's instructions included detailed orders to lull "Moors" at Sofala into thinking that the Portuguese had come to trade peacefully while preparing to "leap ashore" and seize all the traders and their goods. "Instructions to the Captain-Major D. Francisco de Almeida, Lisbon, 1505 March 5," *Documentos sobre os Portugueses Vol I*, 181.

31. Their use of violence at sea was not original in the region, as older histories used to claim in contrasting European militarism and peaceful Indian Ocean and Pacific regions. See Sebastian R. Prange, "A Trade of No Dishonor: Piracy, Commerce, and Community in the Western Indian Ocean, Twelfth to Sixteenth Century," *American Historical Review* 116, no. 5 (2011): 1269–1293. And on similarities in Asian and European strategies for casting power over sea space, see Adam Clulow, "Determining the Law of the Sea: The Long History of the Breukelen Case, 1657–1662," in Tonio Andrade, Xing Hang, Anand A. Yang and Kieko Matteson, eds., *Sea Rovers, Silver, and Samurai: Maritime East Asia in Global History, 1550–1700*, ed. Tonio Andrade, Xing Hang, Anand A. Yang, and Kieko Matteson (Honolulu: University of Hawaii Press, 2016), 181–201.

32. In his instructions to the first viceroy, Francisco de Almeida, King Manuel described the terms to be exacted from vanquished rulers Asia as both tribute and agreement to trade with the Portuguese and provide their fortresses with provisions. "Instructions to the Captain-Major D. Francisco de Almeida, Lisbon, 1505 March 5," *Documentos sobre os Portugueses Vol I*, 237.

33. Luis F.F.R. Thomaz, "Precedents and Parallels of the Portuguese Cartaz System," in *The Portuguese, Indian Ocean, and European Bridgeheads, 1500–1800: Festschrift in Honour of Professor K. S. Mathew*, ed. Pius Malekandathil and Jamal Mohammed (Tellicherry, India: Fundação Oriente and Institute for Research in Social Sciences and Humanities of MESHAR, 2001), 67–85; Prange, "A Trade of No Dishonor"; Lauren Benton and Adam Clulow, "Empires and Protection: Making Interpolity Law in the Early Modern World," *Journal of Global History* 12, no. 1 (2017): 74–92.

34. In 1509, the Council of Officials of the Straits Fleet met at Mozambique to debate whether they should let pass a vessel captained by a subject of the King of Malindi that was sailing with two safe-conduct passes. The fact that they were having the debate indicated that seizures of ships carrying Portuguese passes were common. "Minutes of the Council of Officials of the straits Fleet [Mozambique, 1509 January 25]," *Documentos sobre os Portugueses, Vol II*, 327.

35. Captains and crews also siphoned off goods (and probably also captives) from prizes taken with official backing. The king exhorted the first viceroy, Francisco de Almeida, to be vigilant against men concealing prizes. "Instructions to the Captain-Major D. Francisco de Almeida, Lisbon, 1505 March 5," *Documentos sobre os Portugueses Vol I*, 193. And a letter to the king in 1510 complains of "much stealing from the prizes taken by the fleet of Duarte de Lemos" and recommends an inquiry. "Summary by Antonio Carneiro, Secretary of State, of a Letter from Lourenço Moreno and Diogo Pereira to the King, 1510 December 20," *Documentos sobre os Portugueses, Vol II*, 561.

36. "Instructions to the Captain-Major D. Francisco de Almeida, Lisbon, 1505 March 5," *Documentos sobre os Portugueses Vol I*, 183.

37. Albuquerque was not of the same high noble status as Almeida, and so he was not given the title of viceroy.

38. "Treaty between Spain and Portugal Concluded at Tordesillas, June 7, 1494," Document 9 in Frances Davenport and C. O. Paullin, *European Treaties Bearing on the History of the United States and Its Dependencies* (Washington, DC: Carnegie Institute of Washington, 1917), 99. Neither the Treaty of Tordesillas nor the papal donations preceding it characterized lands beyond Europe as unoccupied or unclaimed. They instead bestowed the right to possess newly discovered territories, including acquiring them by conquest or cession. See Lauren Benton and Benjamin Straumann, "Acquiring Empire by Law: From Roman Doctrine to Early Modern European Practice," *Law and History Review* 28, no. 1 (2010): 1–38; and Sharon Korman, *The Right of Conquest: The Acquisition of Territory by Force in International Law and Practice* (New York: Oxford University Press, 1996), 44–45.

39. Portuguese captains erected wooden crosses and stone pillars (*padrões*), often at the mouths of rivers, to mark their "discoveries" and signal inchoate claims at selected points along the West African coast. In the western Indian Ocean, where the Portuguese encountered vibrant commercial networks and powerful coastal communities, the practice of erecting *padrões* became more difficult. In East Africa, Vasco da Gama watched from his ship while locals dismantled a wooden cross his men had erected two days before, and at Calicut, he was reduced

to imploring emissaries who visited his ship to take a *padrão* on shore and place it there. See Benton, *A Search for Sovereignty*, 55–59; Sanjay Subrahmanyam, *The Career and Legend of Vasco Da Gama* (New York: Cambridge University Press, 1997), 144. On European legal discourses about claiming possession, see Benton and Straumann, "Acquiring Empire by Law"; Ken MacMillan, *Sovereignty and Possession in the English New World: The Legal Foundations of Empire, 1576–1640* (New York: Cambridge University Press, 2006); and Lauren Benton, "Possessing Empire: Iberian Claims and Interpolity Law," in *Native Claims: Indigenous Law against Empire, 1500–1920*, ed. Saliha Bellmessous (New York: Oxford University Press, 2011), 19–40, 25.

40. Moroccan forts were more military garrisons than trading posts, but that pattern changed on the West African coast, where the Portuguese negotiated for the right to fortify their factory at El Mina as the central node of their West African trade. Early leaders in the Estado da Índia had served in garrisons in Morocco—including Afonso de Albuquerque. On the episode in Calicut as a turning point in the Portuguese policy of fortification, see Disney, *A History of Portugal and the Portuguese Empire*, 147.

41. Letter from Albuquerque to D. Manuel, November 1507 (estimated), in Afonso de Albuquerque, *Albuquerque, Caesar of the East: Selected Texts by Afonso de Albuquerque and His Son*, trans. and ed. T. F. Earle and John Villiers (Warminster, UK: Aris & Phillips, 1990), 51–64, 59. The fortress was still incomplete when Albuquerque returned to Hormuz in 1515; he died soon after at Goa.

42. *Comentarios do Grande Afonso de Albuquerque*, chapter 44 in Albuquerque, *Albuquerque*, 155.

43. *Comentarios do Grande Afonso de Albuquerque*, 2nd edition (Lisbon, 1576), part III, chapters 22–28, in Albuquerque, *Albuquerque*, 65–91, 79.

44. *Comentarios do Grande Afonso de Albuquerque*, 2nd edition (Lisbon, 1576), part III, chapters 22–28, in Albuquerque, *Albuquerque*, 65–91, 81.

45. Letter from Albuquerque to King Manuel, 1 April 1512, in Albuquerque, *Albuquerque*, 93–150, 95.

46. Letter from Albuquerque to King Manuel, 1 April 1512, in Albuquerque, *Albuquerque*, 93–150, 99.

47. Sebastian Prange, *Monsoon Islam: Trade and Faith on the Medieval Malabar Coast* (New York: Cambridge University Press, 2018), 132.

48. The phrase is from S. F. Dale, "Islamic Architecture in Kerala: A Preface to Future Study," in *Islam and Indian Regions*, 2 vols., ed. A. L. Dallapiccola and S. Zingel-Avé Lallemant (Stuttgart: Steiner, 1993), 491–495, quoted in Prange, *Monsoon Islam*, 126.

49. Subrahmanyam, *The Portuguese Empire in Asia*, 88.

50. Letter from Albuquerque to D. Manuel, November 1507 (estimated), in Albuquerque, *Albuquerque*, 51–64, 57.

51. Letter from Afonso de Albuquerque to the King, 6 February 1507, *Documentos sobre os Portugueses, Vol II*, 121. Almeida recounted that during the raid by his fleet at Mombasa (where "everyone set to loot"), "Many people were taken captive, women, some white, and children and some merchants from Cambay." "Account of the Voyage of D. Francisco de Almeida, Viceroy of India, Along the East Coast of Africa [1506 May 22]," *Documentos sobre os Portugueses, Vol I*, 533, 535.

52. Letter from Albuquerque to King Manuel, 1 April 1512, in Albuquerque, *Albuquerque*, 93–150, 103–105.

53. Instructions to Diogo Lopes de Sequeira, Almeirim, 1508 February 13, *Documentos sobre os Portugueses, Vol II*, 259.

54. He lamented that "these people" had stolen "five hundred men, the best in India, and a further two hundred who were in hiding and concealed." Letter from Albuquerque to King Manuel, 1 April 1512, in Albuquerque, *Albuquerque*, 93–150, 119.

55. Some men also joined Hindu and Buddhist communities, but they tended to be classed as mercenaries rather than *renegados* (apostates). The Portuguese reserved the harshest condemnation for Christians who converted to Islam and often referred to these converts as traitors; former *renegados* "always bore a certain stigma of suspicion." Stuart Schwartz, *Blood and Boundaries: The Limits of Religious and Racial Exclusion in Early Modern Latin America* (Waltham, MA: Brandeis University Press, 2020), 27–28; and see Maria Augusta Lima Cruz, "Exiles and Renegades in Early Sixteenth-Century Portuguese India," *Indian Economic and Social History Review* 23, no. 3 (1986): 250–262.

56. Maria Augusta Lima Cruz, "As andanças de um degredado em Terras Perdidas—João Machado," *Mare Liberum* 5 (1995).

57. "Instructions to the Captain-Major D. Francisco de Almeida, Lisbon, 1505 March 5," *Documentos sobre os Portugueses Vol I*, 233.

58. "Letter from Afonso de Albuquerque to the King [1513]," *Documentos sobre os Portugueses, Vol III*, 403.

59. Francisco Paulo Mendes da Luz, ed., *Livro das cidades, e fortalezas, que a coroa de Portugal tem nas partes da India, e das capitanias* (Lisboa: Centro de Estudos Históricos Ultramarinos, 1960). Originally published in about 1580.

60. The fortress views appear in this order: Mozambique, Mombasa, Hormuz, Diu, Daman, Baçaim (Visai), Chaul, Goa, Barcalor, Caninor, Cunhale, Coulan, Colombo, Cananor, Achem, Malacca, Gale, Mangdor, Isla de Marar, Onor, Muscat, Canganore, Cochin. Through Malacca, the progression is from west to east.

61. "Instructions to the Captain-Major D. Francisco de Almeida, Lisbon, 1505 March 5," *Documentos sobre os Portugueses Vol I*, 239.

62. "Letter from the King to Pero Ferreira Fogaça, Captain of Kilwa [1507]," in *Documentos sobre os Portugueses, Vol II*, 28.

63. Ângela Barreto Xavier points out that the legal status of the *casados* was intimately bound up with the categories "farm," "house," "land," and "marriage," as well as with ideas about the authority of household heads ("Reducing Difference in the Portuguese Empire? A Case Study from Early-Modern Goa," in *Changing Societies: Legacies and Challenges, Vol. 1, Ambiguous Inclusions: Inside Out, Outside In*, ed. S. Aboim, P. Granjo, and A. Ramos [Lisboa: Imprensa de Ciências Sociais, 2018] 241–261, 244). See also Andréa Doré, "Os *casados* na Índia portuguesa: a mobilidade social de homens úteis," in *Raízes do privilégio: mobilidade social no mundo ibérico do Antogo Regime*, ed. Rodrigo Bentes Monteiro, Bruno Feitler, Daniela Buono Calainho, and Jorge Flores (Rio de Janeiro: Editora Civilizaçâo Brasileira, 2011), 510–533; and Subrahmanyam, *The Portuguese Empire in Asia*, 231–234.

64. Christianized slaves were also regarded as potential soldiers. See Stephanie Hassell, "Religious Identity and Imperial Security: Arming Catholic Slaves in Sixteenth- and Seventeenth-Century Portuguese India," *Journal of Early Modern History* 26, no. 5 (2022): 403–428.

65. Letter from Albuquerque to King Manuel, 1 April 1512, in Albuquerque, *Albuquerque*, 93–150, 103–105, 99.

66. Letter from Albuquerque to King Manuel, 1 April 1512, in Albuquerque, *Albuquerque*, 93–150, 103–105.

67. Letter from Albuquerque to King Manuel, 1 April 1512, in Albuquerque, *Albuquerque*, 93–150, 103–105, 137.

68. Albuquerque goes on to say that Master Afonso later "married a woman whom he did not deserve." Letter from Albuquerque to King Manuel, 1 April 1512, in Albuquerque, *Albuquerque*, 93–150, 97.

69. Letter from Albuquerque to King Manuel, 1 April 1512, in Albuquerque, *Albuquerque*, 97.

70. The process continued. Albuquerque reported, "When this person died, the friar at once married her off to someone else." Letter from Albuquerque to King Manuel, 1 April 1512, in Early and Villiers, *Albuquerque*, 93–150, 99.

71. Letter from Albuquerque to King Manuel, 1 April 1512, in Early and Villiers, *Albuquerque*, 93–150, 115.

72. Letter from Albuquerque to King Manuel, 1 April 1512, in Early and Villiers, *Albuquerque*, 93–150, 117.

73. Letter from Albuquerque to King Manuel, 1 April 1512, in Albuquerque, *Albuquerque*, 93–150, 117.

74. Letter from Albuquerque to King Manuel, 1 April 1512, in Albuquerque, *Albuquerque*, 93–150, 147.

75. Letter from Albuquerque to King Manuel, 1 April 1512, in Albuquerque, *Albuquerque*, 93–150, 117.

76. See Letter from Albuquerque to King Manuel, 1 April 1512, in Albuquerque, *Albuquerque*, 93–150, 99; and discussion earlier.

77. Subrahmanyam, *The Portuguese Empire in Asia*, 20–24.

78. Indrani Chatterjee, "Renewed and Connected Histories: Slavery and the Historiography of South Asia," in *Slavery and South Asian History*, ed. Indrani Chatterjee and Richard M. Eaton (Bloomington: Indiana University Press, 2006); see also Daud Ali, "War, Servitude, and the Imperial Household: A Study of Palace Women in the Chola Empire," in *Slavery and South Asian History*, ed. Chatterjee and Eaton. On widespread practices of maritime raiding, some involving captive taking, see Prange, "A Trade of No Dishonor."

79. Indrani Chatterjee, *Gender, Slavery and Law in Colonial India* (New York: Oxford University Press, 1999), 23. Royal chronicles in interior Rajasthan refer to the practice of making gifts of high-status war captives to wealthy households. Ramya Sreenivasan, "Drudges, Dancing Girls, Concubines: Female Slaves in Rajput Polity, 1500–1850," in *Slavery and South Asian History*, ed. Chatterjee and Eaton, 139, 144.

80. Chatterjee, *Gender, Slavery and Law*, 24. Chatterjee shows that exploitation of women as captives occurred alongside structured possibilities for captive women to enhance their positions by transitioning to the status of insiders.

81. Chatterjee, "Renewed and Connected Histories," 21. Note that elsewhere Chatterjee draws a sharper distinction between European and South Asian households, suggesting that the private-public distinction was more salient among Europeans and that this difference led to

misunderstandings of Indian slavery (*Gender, Slavery and Law,* 20, 37). Joseph Miller argued for regional continuities through an emphasis on slaving rather than slavery, although he also pointed to different regional patterns in the way debt was attached to the acquisition of captives. (Joseph C. Miller, *The Problem of Slavery as History: A Global Approach* [New Haven, CT: Yale University Press, 2012]). None of these insights about continuities in slaving and the incorporation of captives in households contradicts arguments about the uniqueness of the Atlantic slave trade in the sheer numbers of captives, their demographic makeup, and systemic innovations in moving, terrorizing, and classifying enslaved people. On the commodification of women in the Atlantic slave trade, see Jennifer L. Morgan, *Reckoning with Slavery: Gender, Kinship, and Capitalism in the Early Black Atlantic* (Durham, NC: Duke University Press, 2021).

82. Goa held about 2,000 *casados* in the mid-sixteenth century. There were smaller communities in other garrison towns. Subrahmanyam estimates that the total population of *casados* in the Estado da Índia was between 5,500 and 6,000 by 1600. These were *casados brancos* ("white" *casados* who were Portuguese or Portuguese descendents). There was another, more numerous group of *casados pretos* ("black" *casados*) who were Christianized locals awarded similar privileges because they lived in Portuguese towns (*The Portuguese Empire in Asia,* 232–234).

83. Letter from Albuquerque to King Manuel, 1 April 1512, in Albuquerque, *Albuquerque,* 93–150, 147.

84. Letter from Albuquerque to King Manuel, 1 April 1512, in Albuquerque, *Albuquerque,* 109, 113.

85. Letter from Albuquerque to King Manuel, 1 April 1512, in Albuquerque, *Albuquerque,* 109.

86. Letter from Albuquerque to King Manuel, 1 April 1512, in Albuquerque, *Albuquerque,* 101.

87. Flores, *Unwanted Neighbors: The Mughals, the Portuguese, and Their Frontier Zones* (New York: Oxford University Press, 2018), chapter 6.

88. Jorge Flores, *Unwanted Neighbors,* 88–101.

89. Already in Albuquerque's time, *casados* were accused of shirking responsibilities to help defend the city and maintain fortifications. During the union with Spain (1580–1640), anxieties about the religious and racial purity of *casados* intensified (Barreto Xavier, "Reducing Difference in the Portuguese Empire?" 246–247; Subrahmanyam, *The Portuguese Empire in Asia,* 238). *Casados* also composed a network of private trade that came into tension with Estado da Índia customs officials. See Pius Malekandathil, "The Portuguese Casados and the Intra-Asian Trade: 1500–1663," *Proceedings in the Indian History Congress,* vol. 61, part 1 (2000–2001): 385–406.

90. On informal versus formal empire, see A. R. Disney, *A History of Portugal and the Portuguese Empire,* vol. II (New York: Cambridge University Press, 2009), chapter 21; Malyn Newitt, "Formal and Informal Empire in the History of Portuguese Expansion," *Portuguese Studies* 17 (2001): 2–21. On the "shadow" empire, see George Winius, "The 'Shadow Empire' of Goa in the Bay of Bengal," *Itinerario* 7, no. 2, (1983): 83–101. In *Unwanted Neighbors,* Flores discusses these models and argues for diversification in frontier zones.

91. Erik Lars Myrup, *Power and Corruption in the Early Modern Portuguese World* (Baton Rouge: Louisiana State University Press, 2015), 4–6; Prange, *Monsoon Islam,* 224; the phrase "networks of nobility" is from Victoria Garcia, "From Plunder to Crusade: Networks of Nobility and Negotiations of Empire in the Estado da Índia 1505–1515," senior thesis, Wesleyan University, 2012.

92. On the multiplicity of images of empire—and the confirmation, by the 1530s and 1540s, that the Estado da Índia *was* being built on an imperial model, see Ângela Barreto Xavier, *A Invenção de Goa: Poder Imperial e Conversões Culturais nos Séculos XVI e XVII* (Lisbon: Imprensa de Ciências Sociais, 2008). On raiding, captive taking, and governance in Brazil, see John M. Monteiro, *Blacks of the Land: Indian Slavery, Settler Society, and the Portuguese Colonial Enterprise in South America* (New York: Cambridge University Press, 2018); Alexandre Pelegrino, "From Slaves to Indios: Empire, Slavery, and Race (Maranhâo, Brazil, c. 1740–90)," *Law and History Review* (2022): 1–27; and discussions of slaving in the region in chapters 4 and 5 later.

93. Karen Ordahl Kupperman, *The Jamestown Project* (Cambridge, MA: Belknap Press, 2009).

94. For a general history of the Providence Island Colony, see Karen Ordahl Kupperman, *Providence Island, 1630–1641: The Other Puritan Colony* (New York: Cambridge University Press, 1993). The discussion that follows is drawn from Kupperman's book. Her account is based principally on Records of the Providence Island Company, TNA CO 124/1 and TNA CO 124/2.

95. Kupperman, *Providence Island*, 28–29.

96. Kupperman, *Providence Island*, 42.

97. Kupperman, *Providence Island*, 48.

98. Stephen Saunders Webb, *The Governors-General: The English Army and the Definition of the Empire, 1569–1681* (Chapel Hill: Omohundro Institute and University of North Carolina Press, 1979), 45.

99. As a puritan colony run by a company, Providence Island did not have a royal governor-general. But the demands of regulating property and planting, organizing for defense, and engaging in prize taking strengthened military over civil authority in familiar fashion.

100. "Instructions unto Generall Robert Venables Given by His Highness by Advice of His Council Upon His Expedition to the West Indies," Appendix in Robert Venables, *The narrative of General Venables, with an appendix of papers relating to the expedition to the West Indies and the conquest of Jamaica, 1654–1655*, ed. C. H. Firth (London and New York: Longmans, Green, and Co., 1900), 111–115, 113.

101. Venables, *Narrative*, 5; quoted in C. H. Firth, preface, Venables, *Narrative*, xxiii.

102. C. H. Firth, preface, Venables, *Narrative*, xxiv, xxx.

103. Venables was later criticized for carrying perhaps as many as two hundred women and children with the fleet, including his own wife. Other reports suggested that the presence of his wife weakened Venables's command and softened his resolve to press the attack on Spanish forces at several key moments. In his defense, Venables later asserted that the soldiers' wives were brought along to nurse the sick and wounded, and to support the English intent to make "a Plantation, where Women would be necessary." Venables, *Narrative*, 102.

104. "Instructions," Venables, *Narrative*, 113–114.

105. Venables, *Narrative*, 8.

106. Venables, *Narrative*, 52, 59.

107. Venables, *Narrative*, 17.

108. Venables, *Narrative*, 36.

109. "Extracts from Henry Whistler's Journal of the West India Expedition, Appendix E in Venables, *Narrative*, 166.

110. Men on the ships fared better, and William Penn, in charge of the fleet, was later criticized for withholding rations from the soldiers on shore. An officer requesting bread for his men was told that "the Men must work or rott." Venables, *Narrative*, 47.

111. Venables, *Narrative*, 50. The officers under Venables presented their own plea for "Cloathing for Officers and Soldiers, and all manner of working Tools and Instruments" and for "such Constitutions and Laws as His Highness shall think fit for the Government of this place." Venables, *Narrative*, 63–64.

112. Venables, *Narrative*, 65.

113. CSP vol. 1, 1574–1660, "Orders of the Council of State," 3 October 1655.

114. CSP vol. 1, 1574–1660, "Order of the Council of State," 19 December 1655; TNA SP 25/77, 881–883.

115. Daniel Gookin was instructed to offer New Haven settlers grants of twenty acres for every male older than twelve and ten acres to "every other male and female." TNA SP 25/76, 304–306.

116. Letter from Jamaica, 5 November 1655, in "Letters Concerning the English Expedition," 142.

117. William Beeston, "Journal kept whilst in Jamaica and narrative of descent on the island by the French," BL Add MS 12430, f. 23.

118. Committee of the Council of Foreign Plantations, Minute, 10 January 1660 / 1, BL Egerton 2395, 290. Committee members deliberated about how to make "the perfect conversion of the Army into a Colonie" and decided it was beyond their capacity from so far away. They settled on the one thing they could agree was necessary: sending money for improvement of the fort. Committee of the Council of Foreign Plantations, Minute, 10 January 1660 / 1, BL Egerton 2395, 289.

119. CSP vol. 15, no. 94. The policy had support from London. Soon after the conquest, Cromwell had offered protection, land, and the rights of free denizens to new settlers to Jamaica—who were then regarded with some jealousy by impoverished soldiers and former soldiers (Carla Gardina Pestana, *The English Atlantic in an Age of Revolution, 1640–1661* [Cambridge, MA: Harvard University Press, 2004], 195). The push for resettlement of Englishmen from other colonies brought in migrants from Barbados and Nevis but failed to lure a contingent from New Haven. Land grants continued sporadically. In the fall of 1662, Governor-General Windsor began "to grant out the lands by Patent. . . . & do all things that might encourage people to settle & Plant the country." Beeston, "Journal," 25v. Officers objected to the assignment of land to common soldiers. On early settlement efforts, see Carla Gardina Pestana, *The English Conquest of Jamaica: Cromwell's Bid for Empire* (Cambridge, MA: Harvard University Press, 2017), chapter 9.

120. Pestana, *The English Conquest of Jamaica*, 226.

121. Michael Guasco, *Slaves and Englishmen: Human Bondage in the Early Modern Atlantic World* (Philadelphia: University of Pennsylvania Press, 2014), chapter 3, especially 100, 111; Casey Schmitt, "Centering Spanish Jamaica: Regional Competition, Informal Trade, and the English Invasion, 1620–1662," *William and Mary Quarterly* 76, no. 4 (2019): 697–726. As noted in chapter 2, Europeans were entering a region where raiding and captive taking were already familiar practices. In an unpublished paper that I cite with the author's permission, Ernesto

Mercado-Montero argues that the people called "Caribs" by Europeans were autonomous communities involved in raiding, captive taking, and the making of plantations. (Ernesto Mercado-Montero, "Raiding, Captive-Taking, and the Slave Trade in the Carib Archipelago," 2023.)

122. In 1600, for example, an English ship intercepted a bark off Barbados that was transporting about 100 African captives to Cartagena and sold them for pearls in another Spanish port. Guasco, *Slaves and Englishmen*, 100.

123. Karl Offen, "Mapping Amerindian Captivity in Colonial Mosquitia," *Journal of Latin American Geography* 14, no. 3 (2015): 35–65, 47.

124. Holly Brewer, "Creating a Common Law of Slavery for England and Its New World Empire," *Law and History Review* 39, no. 4 (2021): 765–834, 775–776.

125. Brewer, "Creating a Common Law of Slavery," 777.

126. Holly Brewer, "Slavery, Sovereignty, and 'Inheritable Blood': Reconsidering John Locke and the Origins of American Slavery," *American Historical Review* 122, no. 4 (2017): 1038–1078, 1046.

127. Quoted in Brewer, "Slavery, Sovereignty, and 'Inheritable Blood,'" n. 18.

128. For a recent overview of privateering in Jamaica, see Mark G. Hanna, *Pirate Nests and the Rise of the British Empire, 1570–1740* (Chapel Hill: University of North Carolina Press, 2015), chapter 3. Hanna devotes an opening paragraph to the army's plight.

129. References to "the line" became a set piece of British discourse about violence in the Americas even into the eighteenth century. Eliga H. Gould, "Zones of Law, Zones of Violence: The Legal Geography of the British Atlantic, circa 1772," *William and Mary Quarterly* 60, no. 3 (2003). The historical uses of the phrase encouraged Carl Schmitt to argue that the European juridical order depended on a "bracketing" of annihilating warfare and its relegation to spaces outside Europe. Carl Schmitt, *The Nomos of the Earth in the International Law of the Jus Publicum Europaeum*, trans. G. L. Ulmen (New York: Telos Press, 2006).

130. Beeston, "Journal," 23–23v.

131. Beeston observed that D'Oyley "gave but little Encouragement to the planting or trading part (but the privateering went on & many considerable prizes were brought in." Beeston, "Journal," 24v.

132. Modyford to Sec. Bennett, CSP vol. 5, 1661–1665, no. 767. Modyford also noted that sponsoring privateering would help create a reserve fighting force for future interimperial wars. Modyford to Abermarle, 1 March 1666, CSP vol. 5, 1661–1665, no. 1144. Minutes of the Council of Jamaica, 22 February 1666, CSP vol. 5, 1661–1665, no. 1138.

133. Beeston, "Journal," f. 26.

134. Modyford to Abermarle, 1 March 1666, CSP vol. 5, 1661–1665, no. 1144.

135. Pestana, *The English Atlantic in an Age of Revolution*, 193. Despite official attempts to redirect privateers to Dutch colonies during the Anglo-Dutch War of 1665 to 1667, Spanish colonies remained the main targets of English raiding.

136. Despite the blurred distinction between pirates and privateers, contemporaries insisted on the latter term when describing their own raiders precisely because it legitimated the sale of booty. On the origins of the term, see Hanna, *Pirate Nests*, 106–107. On the legal implications of the fluid boundary between piracy and privateering and on raiders' use of "legal posturing" to code their attacks as lawful, see Benton, *Search for Sovereignty*, chapter 3; and Lauren Benton,

"Legal Spaces of Empire: Piracy and the Origins of Ocean Regionalism," in *Comparative Studies in Society and History* 47, no. 4: 700–724. Hatfield notes that historians who use the word "pirates" for privateers miss the importance of the term for contemporaries as an aid in rendering the sale of booty as lawful (April Hatfield, *Boundaries of Belonging: English Jamaica and the Spanish Caribbean, 1665–1715* [Philadelphia: University of Pennsylvania Press, 2023], 33). Private-public collaboration in raiding was apparent at every level. In Jamaica in 1662 and 1663, a mixture of navy and private ships participated in raids, and the first major raid that was entirely performed by private men-of-war, the seizure by 120 men of St. Marta on the Spanish mainland, took place only in 1664. Soldiers complained that the lion's share of the booty from that raid had gone "to the State," but the profits still nurtured enthusiasm for other ventures like it. Letter from Jamaica, 5 November 1655, in "Letters Concerning the English Expedition," appendix D, in Venables, *Narrative*, 143.

137. CSP vol. 5, 1661–1669, 14 June 1661, no. 106. Three years later, D'Oyley was ordered by London to pay a portion of the prize to the king and to the officers and mariners of the navy frigate that had captured the Dutch ship. CSP vol. 5, 1661–1669, 19 January 1664, no. 641, and 24 February 1664, no. 671. Whether he ever paid, we do not know.

138. Peter Earle, *The Sack of Panamá: Captain Morgan and the Battle for the Caribbean* (London: Thomas Dunne Books, 2007), 12–13. The English practice of coding dark-skinned people as slaves began earlier (Guasco, *Slaves and Englishmen*) and became routine in Jamaican privateer attacks on Spanish ports (Hatfield, *Boundaries of Belonging*, 35).

139. Earle, *The Sack of Panamá*, chapter 6.

140. Hatfield, *Boundaries of Belonging*, 98.

141. Hatfield describes this case in detail in *Boundaries of Belonging*, 95–98. On the Spanish policy of sanctuary, see Jane Landers, "Spanish Sanctuary: Fugitives in Florida, 1687–1790, *Florida Historical Quarterly* 62, no. 3 (1984): 296–313; Fernanda Bretones Lane, "Spain, the Caribbean, and the Making of Religious Sanctuary," Ph.D. Dissertation, Vanderbilt University, 2019.

142. Venables, *Narrative*, 3.

143. D'Oyley to Sec. Nicholas, March 1661, CSP vol. 5, 1661–1665, no. 61. On captive taking across the early Caribbean, see Casey Schmitt, "Bound among Nations: Labor Coercion in the Seventeenth-Century Caribbean," Ph.D. Dissertation, College of William and Mary, 2018.

144. Charles Lyttelton to Henry Bennet, 15 October 1663, CSP vol. 5, 1661–1665, no. 566.

145. Instruction to Lord Windsor, Gov. Jamaica, 8 April 1662, CSP vol. 5, 1661–1665, no. 278. In justifying his declaration of local war, Windsor was careful to cite the refusal by Spanish authorities to allow him the right to trade at Puerto Rico and Santo Domingo. Beeston, "Journal," f. 25.

146. Beeston, "Journal," f. 25.

147. Beeston, "Journal," 26v. Later other raiders took Campeche and returned with plunder and with lurid tales of its destruction.

148. Hatfield, *Boundaries of Belonging*, chapter 1.

149. Minutes of the Council of Jamaica, 22 February 1666, CSP vol. 5, 1661–1665, no. 1138. Modyford layered creative interpretations of instructions that he claimed granted him latitude to continue to give out commissions. Modyford to Abermarle, 1 March 1666, CSP vol. 5, 1661–1665, no. 1144.

150. Modyford to Sec. Arlington, 5 June 1666, CSP vol. 5, 1661–1665, no. 1209.

151. Hanna, *Pirate Nests*, 112–113. Peter Earle, *The Sack of Panamá*.

152. On race as a defining characteristic of Jamaica as an emerging political community, see Hatfield, *Boundaries of Belonging*.

153. Beeston, "Journal," 6.

154. Beeston, "Journal," 6v.

155. Beeston, "Journal," 9–10.

156. David Armitage, "Introduction" in Hugo Grotius, *The Free Sea* (Indianapolis: Liberty Fund, 2004).

157. Hugo Grotius, *The Rights of War and Peace*, book 1, chapter 3 (Indianapolis: Liberty Fund, 2005), 241.

158. Annabel Brett, "The Space of Politics and the Space of War in Hugo Grotius's *De Iure Belli ac Pacis*," *Global Intellectual History* 1, no. 1 (2016): 33–60. My discussion of Grotius relies heavily on Brett's brilliant analysis.

159. Brett points out that this is a problematic formulation since elsewhere Grotius regards humans in family groupings as already composing a *civitas*. Whereas at least one scholastic predecessor, Luis de Molina, argued that household heads could assume the role of sovereigns and therefore hold the public capacity to make war, Grotius "turned the argument around to make the public right a natural right." (Brett, "The Space of Politics and the Space of War," 45). Although Grotius did not move from here to a definite right of imperfect communities to make war, he did recognize the possibility that a magistrate, standing in for the sovereign, might make war lawfully against private parties. Grotius, *The Rights of War and Peace*, book 1, chapter 3, 250.

160. Grotius, *The Rights of War and Peace*, book 1, chapter 3.

161. The phrase is from Brett, "The Space of Politics and the Space of War," 47.

162. Koskenniemi argues persuasively for a reinterpretation of scholastics as imagining an "empire of private rights.'" Koskenniemi, "Empire and International Law," 32.

163. On corporations in the British empire and varieties of "corporate colonialism," see Philip J. Stern, *Empire, Incorporated: The Corporations That Built British Colonialism* (Cambridge, MA: Belknap Press, 2023), 14.

Chapter 4: Bad Conduct in Far Places

1. "Narrative of the Hostilities committed by the French upon the Ohio in No. America, & of the Negotiation with Mr. de Mirepoix from April 1751 to 1755," BL Add MS 33029, f. 276. Contradictory accounts of the skirmish make it impossible to know whether Jumonville died at the hands of the British or of the Indigenous fighters under their leader, Tanaghrisson. The British avoided directly blaming Indigenous fighters for Jumonville's death, but in general, the decade saw an intensification of discourse about the savagery of Native fighters. Peter Silver, *Our Savage Neighbors: How Indian Wars Transformed Early America* (New York: W. W. Norton, 2008); Christian Ayne Crouch, *Nobility Lost: French and Canadian Martial Cultures, Indians, and the End of New France* (Ithaca, NY: Cornell University Press, 2014). And on the legal significance of the Jumonville debate in the U.S. development of the laws of war, see

John Fabian Witt, *Lincoln's Code: The Laws of War in American History* (New York: Free Press, 2012), 13–14, 19.

2. Daniel Baugh, *The Global Seven Years War 1754–1763: Britain and France in a Great Power Contest* (New York: Routledge, 2011). France was asserting a claim to the Ohio Valley based on the location of French possessions at the headwaters of expansive river systems. The British insisted that the Ohio Valley belonged to the Iroquois, who had come under the protection of the British by treaty, in a relationship that gave Britain the right—indeed, the obligation, the British asserted—to keep other powers from asserting claims "upon Lands indisputably belonging to Great Britain by every kind of Right which the Law of Nations has established" (Letter from Lord Halifax, received August 1753, f. 98, BL Add MS 33029). On the European practice of marking possession over unbounded river systems, see Ken MacMillan, *Sovereignty and Possession in the English New World: The Legal Foundations of Empire, 1576–1640* (Cambridge, UK: Cambridge University Press, 2006); Lauren Benton and Benjamin Straumann, "Acquiring Empire by Law: From Roman Doctrine to Early Modern European Practice," *Law and History Review* 28, no. 1 (2010): 1–38.

3. The French had instructed their governor-general, Michel-Ange Duquesne de Menneville (marquis Duquesne), to avoid making war against "rebel" Indians and to focus instead on "expelling the English traders from the Ohio River." British governors in North America received orders to "do their utmost to prevent by force" French settlements in the region, including any "by the Indians in the French interests." Baugh, *Global Seven Years War*, 54–55, 59.

4. "Proposal for building forts," BL Add MS 33029, f. 111. Officials worried that the steady encroachments of the French, including raiding and captive taking by French-allied Indigenous people in the Connecticut River Valley, represented an explicit strategy of peacetime aggression. Baugh, *Global Seven Years War*, 41–43.

5. "Representation of the State of the Colonies in North America," BL Add MS 33029, 160v; on the history of Connecticut Valley raiding, see John Demos, *The Unredeemed Captive: A Family Story from Early America* (New York: Vintage, 1995).

6. See Witt, *Lincoln's Code*, chapter 1.

7. Emer de Vattel, *The Law of Nations*, ed. Béla Kapossy and Richard Whatmore (Indianapolis: Liberty Fund, 2010); Witt, *Lincoln's Code*. Note that Witt explicitly includes debates about conduct in the Ohio Valley as an important preamble to the later project of codification of the laws of war.

8. On the blending of natural law and positive law discourses in the eighteenth century, see especially David Armitage, *The Declaration of Independence: A Global History* (Cambridge, MA: Harvard University Press, 2007), 89. On the problems of sovereignty, statehood, and regionalism, see Lauren Benton and Lisa Ford, *Rage for Order: The British Empire and the Origins of International Law, 1800–1850* (Cambridge, MA: Harvard University Press, 2016), chapter 6; and Jennifer Pitts, "Law of Nations, World of Empires: The Politics of Law's Conceptual Frames," in *History, Politics, Law: Thinking through the International*, ed. Annabel Brett, Megan Donaldson, and Martti Koskenniemi (Cambridge, UK: Cambridge University Press, 2021), 191–207.

9. On empires as systems of states, and on the projection of imperial power in regions not under direct European rule, see Lauren Benton and Lisa Ford, *Rage for Order*, chapters 6 and 7.

10. The president and council at Fort St. David received a letter from the president and council of Bombay in late November 1748 ordering a cessation of fighting by land and sea. This was a provisional cease-fire; European powers were still negotiating the Treaty of Aix-la-Chapelle. Consultation of 20 November 1748, BL IOR/G/18/6.

11. The British East India Company (EIC) had little precedent for military success in the wider region, and little to show for it. The EIC had poured money for decades into challenging the Marathas, a campaign that had featured an embarrassing and costly defeat by Maratha naval forces under the "pirate" Kanhoji Angre in 1718, and decades more of grinding violence. Near the southern tip of the subcontinent, an EIC contingent that sallied out of the fortress of Anjengo was brutally massacred in 1721, an event presaging a general weakening of company profits and presence in that region. Jon Wilson, *India Conquered: Britain's Raj and the Chaos of Empire* (London: Simon & Schuster, 2016), chapter 3. On the commercial context of Anglo-French rivalry in the region, see John Shovlin, *Trading with the Enemy: Britain, France, and the 18th-Century Quest for a Peaceful World Order* (New Haven, CT: Yale University Press, 2021); Gregory Mole, "L'Économie politique de Joseph Dupleix: commerce, autorité et deuxième guerre carnatique, 1751–1754," *Outre-mers* 103, no. 388–389 (2015): 79–96; and Elizabeth Cross, *Company Politics: Commerce, Scandal, and French Visions of Indian Empire in the Revolutionary Era* (New York: Oxford University Press, 2023).

12. English East India Company officials were also concerned that diplomacy with the nawabs was not always in their hands and that various merchants were taking up negotiations on their own. In April 1749, the president and council wanted to remind "several persons . . . that it is a standing order of the Company's that none but their President shall have a Correspondence with the Country Government." Consultation of 11 April BL IOR/G/18/6, 21.

13. Consultation 24 July 1749, BL IOR/G/18/6.

14. Jon Wilson, *India Conquered*, 87.

15. See, for example, William Dalrymple, *The Anarchy: The East India Company, Corporate Violence, and the Pillage of an Empire* (New York: Bloomsbury, 2019), 53–57.

16. An important exception is Shovlin, *Trading with the Enemy*. His conclusions about commercial relations complement my analysis of the interimperial regulation of war. The tendency to credit Dupleix with inventing a new style of French empire is discussed in Felicia Gottmann, "Intellectual History as Global History: Voltaire's *Fragments sur l'Inde* and the Problem of Enlightened Commerce," in *India and Europe in the Global Eighteenth Century*, ed. Simon Davies, Daniel Sanjiv Roberts, and Gabriel Sánchez Espinosa (Oxford: Voltaire Foundation, 2014), 141–155; and Anthony Strugnell, "A View from Afar: India in Raynal's *Histoire des deux Indes*," in *India and Europe in the Global Eighteenth Century*, 15–27. Other critical evaluations of the French vision of empire include Danna Agmon, *A Colonial Affair: Commerce, Conversion, and Scandal in French India* (Ithaca, NY: Cornell University Press, 2017); Kenneth Margerison, "French Visions of Empire: Contesting British Power in India after the Seven Years War," *English Historical Review* 130, no. 544 (2015): 583–612; and Elizabeth Cross, *Company Politics*. On French company administration within a wider imperial legal order, see Laurie Wood, *Archipelago of Justice: Law in France's Early Modern Empire* (New Haven, CT: Yale University Press, 2020).

17. Company to Saunders, 23 January 1751, Dodwell, *Calendar Madras Despatches* 130.

18. Louis Hubert de Combault d'Auteuil was Dupleix's brother-in-law. Dupleix to d'Auteuil, 14 June 1751, quoted in Virginia McLean Thompson, *Dupleix and His Letters (1742–1754)* (New York: Robert O. Ballou, 1933), 285.

19. IOR/6/18/6, 399.

20. Quoted in Thompson, *Dupleix and His Letters*, 102.

21. Dupleix to La Bourdonnais, 1 December 1744, quoted in Thompson, *Dupleix and His Letters*, 109. He also recognized his own naivete in assuming that the French Indies Company had already "reached an understanding with the English" and that he was charged with merely keeping the peace. Dupleix to La Bourdonnais, 15 January 1745, quoted in Thompson, *Dupleix and His Letters*, 112.

22. Dupleix to La Bourdonnais, 30 July 1746, quoted in Thompson, *Dupleix and His Letters*, 142–143.

23. Thompson, *Dupleix and His Letters*, 143.

24. East India Company to Saunders, 23 August 1751, Dodwell, *Calendar Madras Despatches*, 154. Emphasis added.

25. Consultation 9 December 1750, IOR/P/240/9.

26. He meant anywhere locally, of course. The sentence continued, "either at Fort St. David or the dependencies of Poonamallee, Truvadi or Devikottai." Dupleix to d'Auteuil, 14 June 1751, quoted in Thompson, *Dupleix and His Letters*, 285.

27. "Colonel Lawrence's Narrative of the War on the Coast of Coromandel from the beginning of the Troubles to the Year 1754," in *An Account of the War in India*, ed. Richard Owen Cambridge (London: T. Jefferys, 1762), 6. Lawrence held the rank of major at the start of the war and was promoted to lieutenant colonel in 1752.

28. Consultation 9 December 1750, IOR/P/240/9.

29. Consultation 4 July 1751, IOR/P/240/9.

30. At one moment, the EIC president and council observed that it was debatable whether the law of nations authorized war against all enemies of an ally, but they concluded that "if this conduct is not strictly conformable to the Law of Nations, it is yet perfectly agreeable to the custom in Europe of which the late war produced many examples." Consultation 3 August 1752, IOR/P/240/9.

31. "Colonel Lawrence's Narrative of the War," in Cambridge, *An Account of the War in India*, 5.

32. Consultation 8 June 1752, IOR/P/240/9.

33. Dupleix to Saunders, 18 February 1752, quoted in Thompson, *Dupleix and His Letters*, 279.

34. Consultation of 2 September 1749, IOR/G/18/6.

35. Consultation of 8 September 1749, IOR/G/18/6.

36. Consultation of 16 October 1749, IOR/G/18/6. Spelling modernized in this sentence.

37. On the legal politics surrounding the definition and treatment of prisoners of war in other imperial settings, see Will Smiley, *From Slaves to Prisoners of War: The Ottoman Empire, Russia, and International Law* (New York: Oxford University Press, 2018); Renaud Morieux, *The Society of Prisoners: Anglo-French Wars and Incarceration in the Eighteenth Century* (New York: Oxford University Press, 2019); and Will Smiley, "Rebellion, Sovereignty, and Islamic Law in the Ottoman Age of Revolutions," *Law and History Review* 40, no. 2 (2022): 229–259.

38. Consultation of 3 March 1749, referencing letter from Dupleix, IOR/G/19/7.

39. Consultation of 17 December 1749, IOR/G/18/6, 437.

40. Consultation of 30 November 1749, IOR/G/18/6, 415; Consultation 17 December 1749, IOR/G/18/6, 441.

41. Consultation of 16 October 1749, quoting from Dupleix's letter and also including a copy of the letter by Dupleix of 26 August 1749, IOR/G/18/6, 338.

42. Consultation of 16 October 1749, IOR/G/18/6, 338.

43. Consultation of 16 October 1749, IOR/G/18/6, 364.

44. Consultation of 3 January 1749, IOR/G/18/7, 10.

45. Consultation of 3 January 1749, IOR/G/18/7, 2.

46. Consultation of 3 January 1749, IOR/G.18/7, 2.

47. Consultation of 25 November 1749, IOR/G/18/6, 407.

48. Consultation of 17 December 1749, IOR/G/18/6, 437.

49. Consultation of 27 April 1752, IOR/P/240/9.

50. Consultation of 30 May 1752, IOR/P/240/9.

51. The council declared its intent to take the prisoners' depositions (presumably they had been released) and send them to Dupleix, along with a stark warning that any similar behavior would meet with reprisals. Consultation of 12 December 1751, IOR/P/240/9.

52. Dodwell, *Calendar Madras Despatches, 1744–1755*, 130.

53. Thompson, *Dupleix and His Letters*, 222; H. Dodwell, ed., *The Private Diary of Ananda Ranga Pillai Vol. 6* (Madras: The Superintendent, Government Press, 1918), 255.

54. Consultation of 30 May 1752, IOR/P/240/9; Consultation of 13 August 1752, IOR/P/240/9. The British repeatedly insisted that this imprisonment of French soldiers by Muhammad Ali Khan sharply contrasted with the illegal French taking of a group of Swiss mercenaries on their way by ship to serve with British-allied forces. Seized directly by the French, the Swiss soldiers were not prisoners of war at all, according to the British, but victims of piracy. Consultation of 13 August 1752; 21 May 1753, IOR/P/240/9, 71.

55. *A Genuine Account of some late Transactions in the East-Indies Containing the most Material Occurrences on the Coast of Coromandel, Since the Death of the late Nabob of Arcot, Who was Killed in Battle in July 1749* (London: Printed for R. Baldwin, 1753), 35.

56. *A Genuine Account of some late Transactions in the East-Indies*, 35.

57. "Colonel Lawrence's Narrative of the War," in Cambridge, *An Account of the War in India*, 7.

58. Dupleix to Busy, 9 April 1752, extract in Thompson, *Dupleix and His Letters*, 349.

59. Pekka Hämäläinen, *The Comanche Empire* (New Haven, CT: Yale University Press, 2008).

60. The best studies note the interconnectedness of Indigenous communities but still use single imperial frameworks: John M. Monteiro, *Blacks of the Land: Indian Slavery, Settler Society, and the Portuguese Colonial Enterprise in South America* (New York: Cambridge University Press, 2018); Hal Langfur, *The Forbidden Lands: Colonial Identity, Frontier Violence, and the Persistence of Brazil's Eastern Indians, 1750–1830* (Stanford, CA: Stanford University Press, 2008); Barbara Ganson, *The Guaraní under Spanish Rule in the Río de la Plata* (Stanford, CA: Stanford University Press, 2003). In a recent study, Herzog focuses on interimperial interactions rather than relations among Indian groups (*Frontiers of Possession: Spain and Portugal in Europe and the Americas* [Cambridge, MA: Harvard University Press, 2015]).

61. Contemporary sources often shorten Colônia do Sacramento to "Colônia," and I sometimes use this shorter name.

62. For example, Ganson, *The Guaraní under Spanish Rule*, 91. Ganson does not limit her analysis to this point but follows this observation with detailed analysis of Guaraní reactions to the treaty.

63. The Jesuit census of 1750 lists 26,362 residents in the seven mission towns to be evacuated: San Nicolás, San Miguel, San Luis, Santo Angelo, San Juan Bautista, San Lorenzo, and San Borja. An unspecified number of Indigenous people lived in the areas around the towns. This figure represented a very sizable proportion of the total population of the mission towns; in 1751, the Jesuits counted 97,582 Indigenous residents in the thirty-two missions (two northern missions had recently been founded). The lands on the east bank also comprised haciendas belonging to several missions not subject to evacuation orders because they were located on the western side of the Uruguay River: La Cruz, Concepción, Santo Tomé, and San Francisco Xavier (Ganson, *The Guaraní under Spanish Rule*, 91).

64. See Herzog, *Frontiers of Possession*.

65. Real Orden, Buen Retiro, 24 August 1751, in Instituto Geográfico Militar (IGM), *Documentos Relativos a la Ejecución del Tratado de Limites de 1750* (Montevideo: El Siglo Ilustrado, 1938), 48. All quotes from this collection are my translation.

66. The practice of accepting such goods by town leaders in Santa Fé, for example, became the subject of minor scandal in the eighteenth century.

67. Eduardo F. Acosta y Lara, *La Guerra de los Charrúas en la Banda Oriental* (Montevideo: Talleres de Loreto Editores, 1998), 29.

68. Acosta y Lara, *La Guerra de los Charrúas*, 32–33.

69. "Testimonio del padre Gerónimo Delfín S.I., Sobre las hostilidades perpetradas por los infieles, y consideraciones a la necesidad de hacerles la Guerra," Loreto, 10 August 1701," Acosta y Lara, *La Guerra de los Charrúas*, 38.

70. "Certificación sobre la batalla del Yi, elevada al Rey por el maestre de campo Alejandro de Aguirre," Candelaria, 9 March 1702, Acosta y Lara, *La Guerra de los Charrúas*, 39; my translation.

71. These lines were blurred across the Americas; see Andrés Reséndez, *The Other Slavery: The Uncovered Story of Indian Enslavement in America* (Boston: Mariner Books, 2016).

72. Diego Bracco, *Con las Armas en La Mano: Charrúas, Guenoa-Minuanos y Guaraníes* (Montevideo: Planeta, 2013).

73. IGM, *Documentos*, 132.

74. IGM, *Documentos*, 134.

75. Quoted in Acosta y Lara, *La Guerra de los Charrúas*, 97; my translation.

76. Acosta y Lara, *La Guerra de los Charrúas*, 98; my translation.

77. Draft of a petition prepared by P. Pedro Lozano, 12 March 1751, IGM, *Documentos*, 19, 22, 23, 25.

78. Acosta y Lara, *La Guerra de los Charrúas*, 32–33.

79. Quoted in Acosta y Lara, *La Guerra de los Charrúas*, 61; my translation.

80. Letter from Francisco Pérez de Saravia, San Lorenzo 22 May 1749, Archivo General de Indias (AGI) Buenos Aires 535.

81. Letter from Francisco Pérez de Saravia, San Lorenzo 22 May 1749, AGI Buenos Aires 535.

82. Letter of José de Andonaegui to the Marqués de la Ensenada, Buenos Aires, 2 September, 1749, quoted in Acosta y Lara, *La Guerra de los Charrúas*, 62; my translation. The letter describes a campaign resulting in the deaths of about thirty "armed Indians" and the capture of thirty-six members of their entourage, including women and children, who were "distributed in this city for their education, and religious instruction"; my translation. The letter used the phrase "piezas de chusma" to describe the thirty-six captives; the use of "piezas" (pieces) indicates that the captives were being thought of as quasi-enslaved, and the word "chusma" had a lightly derogatory meaning, similar to "rabble," although the term was frequently applied to women.

83. "Relación de las paces hechas y requerimientos con los Indios Minuanes," AGI Charcas, 218. Acosta y Lara reproduces an account of another expedition against the Minuanes in October 1752 resulting in the capture of about fifteen women and all the horses except those ridden by men who ran away. Acosta y Lara, *La Guerra de los Charrúas*, 104. See also chapter 2 of this volume on the history of the term and practice of *requerimiento*.

84. "Relación de las paces hechas y requerimientos con los Indios Minuanes," AGI Charcas, 218.

85. Real Orden to the Governor of Buenos Aires, Buen Retiro, 16 February 1753, in IGM, *Documentos*, 100.

86. "Instrucciones," AGI Buenos Aires 535, f. 162; my translation.

87. "Instrucciones," AGI Buenos Aires 535, f. 162; my translation.

88. The meeting brought together the Spanish commissioner, the Marqués de Valdelirios; José de Andonaegui, captain-general of the Río de la Plata; and Gómez Freire de Andrada, captain-general of Rio de Janeiro.

89. Quoted in Philip Caraman, *The Lost Paradise: An Account of the Jesuits in Paraguay 1707– 1768* (London: Sidgwick & Jackson, 1975), 245.

90. Bernardo Nusdorffer, "Breve relación de lo sucedido en la Provincia de la plata sobre la entrega de los siete pueblos de Yndios Guaraníes que el Rey Católico ha mandado hacia la Corona de Portugal . . . Mision Yapeyú," 14 August 1752, BL ADD MS 13979, pt. 1, f. 40.

91. For a powerful analysis of moral possibility in scholastic thought, see Annabel Brett, *The Possibility Condition. Rights, Resistance and the Limits of Law in Early Modern Political Thought* (Oxford: Oxford University Press, forthcoming), chapter 2; and see chapter 7 on its application in early seventeenth-century colonial contexts.

92. "Razones contra la evacuación de los Siete Pueblos de Misiones," 1750, IGM, *Documentos*, 1.

93. Draft of a petition prepared by P. Pedro Lozano, 12 March 1751, IGM, *Documentos*, 15.

94. Draft of a petition prepared by P. Pedro Lozano, 12 March 1751, IGM, *Documentos*, 19.

95. Draft of a petition prepared by P. Pedro Lozano, 12 March 1751, IGM, *Documentos*, 24.

96. Draft of a petition prepared by P. Pedro Lozano, 12 March 1751, IGM, *Documentos*, 24.

97. IGM, *Documentos*, 135.

98. "Letter of the Corregidor Miguel Guaho of Mission San Juan Bautista, 1753?" appendix 2 in Ganson, *The Guaraní under Spanish Rule*, 195.

99. Ganson discusses the Guaraní spiritual attachment to the land but not the claim of ownership. Ganson, *The Guaraní under Spanish Rule*, 100–101.

100. "Letter of Nicolás Ñeengirú, Corregidor of Mission Concepción, to the Governor of Buenos Aires, José de Andonaegui, July 20, 1753," appendix 1, Ganson, *The Guaraní under Spanish Rule*, 191–197, 192. The Spanish commissioner, the Marqués de Valdelirios, doubted the ability of the mission Indians to write such letters without Jesuit assistance. Ganson, *The Guaraní under Spanish Rule*, 101.

101. This association was strengthened by an order from Altamirano to Jesuits in the mission to cease performing the sacraments for Guaraní who refused to move or who fled to the backcountry.

102. Draft of a petition prepared by P. Pedro Lozano, 12 March 1751, IGM, *Documentos*, 17–18; emphasis added.

103. IGM, *Documentos*, 202.

104. Letter to Ricardo Wall, San Juan, 27 August 1757, AGI Buenos Aires 535, 102.

105. The pamphlet was printed in Lisbon without attribution in 1757 under the title *Relação abreviada da república que os religiosos jesuítas das províncias de Portugal e Espanha estabeleceram nos domínios ultramarinos das duas monarquias, e da guerra que neles têm movido e sustentado contra os exércitos espanhóis e portugueses; formado pelos registros das secretarias dos dois respectivos principais comissários e plenipotenciário, e por outros documentos autênticos*. As the title indicates, it was intended to show that the Jesuits had formed a secret republic in the Río de la Plata, as supposedly revealed in correspondence and other documents from the war against the Guaraní. Pombal distributed the pamphlet widely, including through diplomatic circles. It was republished in Lisbon in 1758 and subsequently translated into French, Spanish, German, Italian, and Latin. Pierre-Antoine Fabre, José Eduardo Franco, and Carlos Fiolhais, "The Dynamics of Anti-Jesuitism in the History of the Society of Jesus," Jesuit Historiography Online, Brill, https://referenceworks.brillonline.com/entries/jesuit-historiography-online/the-dynamics-of-anti-jesuitism-in-the-history-of-the-society-of-jesus-COM_192530#note30 (accessed 2 November 2022). Note that in the discussion that follows I reference a later edition of the work, which was by the time of its publication attributed to Pombal.

106. Sebastião José de Carvalho e Melo, Marquês de Pombal, *República Jesuíta Ultramarina* (Lisbon: Gravataí, SMEC; Porto Alegre, Martins Libreiro; Santo Ângelo, Centro de Cultura Missionaeira/FUNDAMES: 1989 [1757]), 11. The original title of this work was *Relação abreviada da república*.

107. Pombal, *República Jesuíta Ultramarina*, 13.

108. Pombal, *República Jesuíta Ultramarina*, 12.

109. Pombal, *República Jesuíta Ultramarina*, 14.

110. Pombal, *República Jesuíta Ultramarina*, 8.

111. Pombal, *República Jesuíta Ultramarina*, 7, 9; emphasis added.

112. Pombal, *República Jesuíta Ultramarina*, 9.

113. Pombal, *República Jesuíta Ultramarina*, 8.

114. D. Gillian Thompson, "French Jesuits 1756–1814," in *The Jesuit Suppression in Global Context: Causes, Events, and Consequences*, ed. Jeffrey D. Burson and Jonathan Wright (New York: Cambridge University Press, 2015), 181–198, 184.

115. Dale K. Van Kley, "Plots and Rumors of Plots: The Role of Conspiracy in the International Campaign against the Society of Jesus, 1758–1768," in *The Jesuit Suppression in Global*

Context: Causes, Events, and Consequences, ed. Jeffrey D. Burson and Jonathan Wright (New York: Cambridge University Press, 2015), 13–39, 38–39.

116. Pitts makes this point clearly and mentions the importance to Vattel of various theaters, including the Carnatic coast and North America, in the lead-up to the Seven Years' War (Pitts, *Boundaries of the International*, 68–69, 72); Walter Rech gives pride of place to Vattel's concern with the Barbary States, though he also points out Vattel's more central preoccupation with Prussian aggression. Walter Rech, *Enemies of Mankind: Vattel's Theory of Collective Security* (Leiden: Martinus Nijhoff, 2013); and see the discussion later.

117. Emer de Vattel, *The Law of Nations*, ed. Béla Kapossy and Richard Whatmore (Indianapolis: Liberty Fund, 2010). On the circulation and influence of Vattel in the American Revolution, see William Ossipow and Dominik Gerber, "The Reception of Vattel's Law of Nations in the American Colonies: From James Otis and John Adams to the Declaration of Independence," *American Journal of Legal History* 57, no. 4, (2017): 521–555; Mark Somos, "Vattel's Reception in British America, 1761–1775," in *Concepts and Contexts of Vattel's Political Thought*, ed. Peter Schröder (Cambridge, UK: Cambridge University Press, 2021), 203–219; and Ian Hunter, "Vattel in Revolutionary America: From the Rules of War to the Rule of Law," in *Between Indigenous and Settler Governance*, ed. Lisa Ford and Tim Rowse (Abingdon, UK: Routledge, 2013), 12–22. On the wider context in which his ideas were circulating, see Peter Onuf and Nicholas Onuf, *Federal Union, Modern World: The Law of Nation in an Age of Revolutions, 1776–1814* (Madison, WI: Madison House, 1993); and Eliga Gould, *Among the Powers of the Earth: The American Revolution and the Making of a New World Empire* (Cambridge, MA: Harvard University Press, 2014). On Vattel in colonial Australia, see Lisa Ford, *Settler Sovereignty: Jurisdiction and Indigenous People in America and Australia, 1788–1836* (Cambridge, MA: Harvard University Press, 2011), 27–28, 198. More generally, see Koen Stapelbroek and Antonio Trampas, eds., *The Legacy of Vattel's Droit des Gens* (Cham, Switzerland: Palgrave Macmillan, 2019).

118. In what follows, I draw heavily on the ideas presented by Ian Hunter in "Vattel's Law of Nations: Diplomatic Casuistry for the Protestant Nation," *Grotiana* 31 (2010): 108–140, 112.

119. Hunter, "Vattel's Law of Nations," 112.

120. Hunter, "Vattel's Law of Nations," 131.

121. Hunter, "Vattel's Law of Nations," 125, 132. Hunter's approach has been criticized as overly contextual and limiting of our ability to appreciate the continuing doctrinal relevance of Vattel's approach. The critique overstates the dichotomy between two scholarly programs, one legal and one historical. See Lauren Benton, "Beyond Anachronism: Histories of International Law and Global Legal Politics," *Journal of the History of International Law* (January 2019), 1–34.

122. On the "practice of judgment" as described by Vattel, see Hunter, "Vattel's Law of Nations," 125, 135.

123. The European export of the balance of power as a centerpiece of international law in the long nineteenth century is a much-told story. Perhaps its clearest expression is in Wilhelm G. Grewe, *The Epochs of International Law*, trans. Michael Byers (New York: Walter de Gruyter, 2000), 451. Against this view, see Benton and Ford, *Rage for Order*, 19–22. On the limited use of the metaphor in international treaties, see Heinz Duchhardt, "The Missing Balance," *Journal of the History of International Law* 2 (2000): 67–72. As Jennifer Pitts writes, it is important to "read the *droit des gens* not as a discourse that originally was understood to apply

only to Western Europe and was later extended, or as one simply assumed to apply universally, but rather as a discourse that was sometimes used to frame questions about the possibility for legally governed relations with states and peoples perceived as potentially very different in laws and mores." Pitts, "Law of Nations, World of Empires," 197. And for an insightful account of an influential, though often overlooked, alternative vision of multistate order within Europe, see Isaac Nakhimovsky, *The Holy Alliance: The History of Liberalism and the Politics of Federation* (Princeton, NJ: Princeton University Press, forthcoming).

124. Here Vattel's view of the balance of power differed from that of Christian Wolff, who associated the balance of power with the existence of an overarching authority, the *civitas maxima*. On the differences in the two views, see Rech, *Enemies of Mankind*, 176–182, 184.

125. Rech, *Enemies of Mankind*, 186.

126. Rech, *Enemies of Mankind*, 126.

127. Vattel, *The Law of Nations*, 301.

128. A careful and useful discussion of this question is in Pitts, *Boundaries of the International*, chapter 3, and, more explicitly in Pitts, "Law of Nations, World of Empires." Pitts discusses the ambiguities in Vattel's universalism, and she also affirms his commitment to some version of it. She characterizes Hunter's interpretation of Vattel as "skeptical" and an obstacle to understanding the nature of his universalism (*Boundaries of the International*, 79). As I try to show here, shifting our gaze to the global context and to diplomacy in interpolity regions outside Europe suggests a way of making Hunter's view of state practice useful beyond the narrow confines of the history of political thought. It opens the possibility of a modular effect of repeated loci of practices around the globe. As Pitts acknowledges in somewhat different terms in describing discourse about the law of nations in Europe as "parochial universalism," the multiplication of European-dominated but distinct regional legal regimes might be seen, paradoxically, as a mechanism of asserting European universalism. Pitts, *Boundaries of the International*, 6. For yet a different perspective, one that takes European "legal imagination" as its object of analysis, see Martti Koskenniemi, *To the Uttermost Parts of the Earth: Legal Imagination and International Power 1300–1870* (New York: Cambridge University Press, 2021).

129. Vattel, *The Law of Nations*, 216.

130. Vattel, *The Law of Nations*, 177, 179.

131. Vattel, *The Law of Nations*, 507. Vattel's definition of groups excluded from the capacity for legitimate warmaking is even more capacious where he notes that groups who execute prisoners place themselves outside the framework of nations that observe the laws of war. Vattel, *The Law of Nations*, 554. On the rhetorical equivalence in Vattel's work of pirates and states or other political communities outside the "civilized" order, see Rech, *Enemies of Mankind*.

132. This statement builds on Rech's reading of Vattel (*Enemies of Mankind*) but is also slightly different. Rech regards Vattel's treatment of different kinds of violators as actual equivalence. I agree with Pitts (*Boundaries of the International*, 88) about the value in preserving the notion of a loose analogy, one that continues to note distinctions between European states that are seen as violating the law of nations and quasi-states that exist outside the international order. Both appear in Vattel, and whereas both call up the impulse to collective security that Rech identifies with such clarity in Vattel's approach, they operate to call into existence enforcement across different and partial political fields.

133. Hunter, "Vattel's Law of Nations," 137.

134. Vattel, *The Law of Nations*, 669–670.

135. Quoted in Hunter, "Vattel's Law of Nations," 139. This reasoning reproduced the logic of Grotius and Gentili regarding truces, discussed in chapter 2 earlier.

136. Pitts, *Boundaries of the International*, 89.

Chapter 5: Saving Subjects, Finding Enemies

1. Quoted in Jane Sampson, *Imperial Benevolence: Making British Authority in the Pacific Islands* (Honolulu: University of Hawaii Press, 1998), 13. The year after his visit to the Cocos-Keeling Islands, Captain Sandilands sailed the *Comet* to Pitcairn, where he managed the resettlement of islanders on Tahiti, another example of naval intervention in the region.

2. TNA ADM 125/131. The history of protection in the Cocos-Keeling Islands is covered in depth in Lauren Benton and Adam Clulow, "Protection Shopping among Empires: Suspended Sovereignty in the Cocos-Keeling Islands," *Past & Present* 257, no. 1 (2022), 209–247.

3. TNA ADM 125/131; Benton and Clulow, "Protection Shopping among Empires."

4. Nick Harkaway, *The Gone-Away World* (New York: Vintage, 2009), 172.

5. Quoted in Li Chen, *Chinese Law in Imperial Eyes: Sovereignty, Justice, and Transcultural Politics* (New York: Columbia University Press, 2016), 221.

6. Bernard Semmel, *The Rise of Free Trade Imperialism: Classical Political Economy, the Empire of Free Trade and Imperialism, 1750–1850* (New York: Cambridge University Press, 1970),153. The events leading up to the second Opium War, the so-called Arrow War, spiraled from another protection emergency. After a small Chinese force was reported to have pulled down the British flag aboard the *Arrow* and arrested its Chinese crew, the plenipotenciary in China, John Bowring, ordered a retaliatory attack on Canton.

7. Lauren Benton and Lisa Ford, *Rage for Order: The British Empire and the Origins of International Law, 1800–1850* (Cambridge, MA: Harvard University Press, 2016), chapter 4.

8. See Benton and Ford, *Rage for Order*, chapter 1.

9. Padraic Scanlan, *Freedom's Debtors: British Antislavery in Sierra Leone in the Age of Empire* (New Haven, CT: Yale University Press, 2017).

10. Benton and Ford, *Rage for Order*, 139–145.

11. Benton and Ford, *Rage for Order*, 112–115.

12. For an interesting argument about the systemic expansion of impunity in the early nineteenth century, see Trevor Jackson, *Impunity and Capitalism: The Afterlives of European Financial Crises, 1690–1830* (Cambridge, UK: Cambridge University Press, 2022).

13. Jennifer Pitts, *A Turn to Empire: The Rise of Imperial Liberalism in Britain and France* (Princeton, NJ: Princeton University Press, 2009).

14. David Kenneth Fieldhouse, *Select Documents on the Constitutional History of the British Empire and Commonwealth*, vol. 1 (Westport, CT: Greenwood Press, 1985), 423. Stephen was commenting on the Rio Nuñez affair described in Roderick Braithwaite, *Palmerston and Africa: The Rio Nunez Affair, Competition, Diplomacy, and Justice* (New York: I. B. Taurus, 1996).

15. Benton and Ford, *Rage for Order*, chapter 6.

16. Opportunities for profit centered on head payments for liberated slaves and for pirates captured or killed. On naval captains as reformers, see Jane Samson, *Imperial Benevolence*.

17. "George Pritchard to Captain Fremantle Commanding HM Ship Juno," TNA ADM 173/4, f. 50, and "Captain Morshead to Rear Admiral Bruce HM Ship Dido, 7 May 1856," TNA ADM 173/4, f. 46.

18. "Captain Morshead to Rear Admiral Bruce HM Ship Dido, 7 May 1856," TNA ADM 173/4, f. 46.

19. HMS *Dido*'s cruise touched on Honolulu, Kamchatka, Sitka, Vancouver Island, San Francisco, Hawaii, Samoa, Tahiti, Pitcairn Island, Valparaiso in Chile, and Saint Helena. W. J. Walker, "Journal of the Voyage of the Dido," National Library of New Zealand, MS-2213.

20. George Vancouver, *A voyage of discovery to the North Pacific Ocean, and round the world, in which the coast of north-west America has been carefully examined and accurately surveyed*, vol. I (London: Printed for G. G. and J. Robinson, Paternoster-Row; and J. Edwards, Pall-Mall, 1798), 388.

21. Vancouver, *A voyage of discovery*, 394.

22. "Admiralty Instructions to Hillyar, 12 March 1813," TNA ADM 2/1380, ff. 370–375.

23. Black's act of taking possession of the fort after its purchase would cause confusion at the end of the war. By treaty, Britain agreed to return to the status quo ante bellum, requiring the return of territories seized in the war. The Northwest traders argued that its purchase exempted the fort from the requirement. See Barry Gough, *Britannia's Navy on the Northwest Coast of North America, 1812–1914* (Barnsley, UK: Seaforth Publishing, 2016), 53, 58–59. This would not be the last time that British naval captains' ceremonies of possession in remote places caused consternation at home. See later on the declaration of Hawaii as a protectorate. On the accidental annexation of the Cocos-Keeling Islands in 1856, see Benton and Clulow, "Protection Shopping among Empires."

24. Gough, *Britannia's Navy*, 71. 74.

25. Benton and Ford, *Rage for Order*, 139–145.

26. "James Burley to Earl of Aberdeen, January 20, 1845," TNA ADM 172/3, ff. 4–8v.

27. "George Pritchard to Earl of Aberdeen, December 31, 1845," TNA ADM 172/3, ff. 11–15; "George Pritchard to Admiral Sir George Seymour, March 1847," TNA ADM 172/3, ff. 16–17.

28. "Rear Admiral Seymour to George Prichard, HM Consul Navigator Islands, 14 July 1847," TNA ADM 172/3, ff. 18–21.

29. Addington to War, February 4, 1848, TNA ADM 172/3, ff. 24–26v.

30. As American ships came to dominate the coastal trade, the center of imperial tensions had shifted south to the mouth of the Columbia River. Indigenous actions had a good deal to do with this shift. In 1803, the captain of the American ship *Boston* delivered a slight to the chief of the Nuu-chah-nulth people, Chief Maquinna, whom he called a liar for claiming that the rifle given to him did not work. Maquinna returned the next day, and after a friendly interlude his followers massacred twenty-one of the ship's crew, sparing only two men, whom he took captive. The event intensified traders' fears and prompted a search for other trading points along the coast. Information about the episode comes mainly from the captivity narrative of the ship's armorer. John R. Jewitt, *Narrative of the adventures and sufferings of John R. Jewitt, only survivor of the crew of the ship Boston, during a captivity of nearly 3 years among the savages of Nootka sound:*

with an account of the manners, mode of living, and religious opinions of the natives (Ithaca, NY: Andrus, Gauntlett & Co., 1851). For an account of the legal issues at stake in the Oregon crisis, see Andrew Fitzmaurice, *Sovereignty, Property and Empire, 1500–2000* (New York: Cambridge University Press, 2014), 170–71, 211–212.

31. The Admiralty dispatched five ships to the region in the summer of 1846 with pointed instructions to protect British subjects. Rear-Admiral Seymour instructed Captain Duntz of the *Fisgard* "to afford Protection to Her Majesty's Subjects . . . [and] gain intelligence of the State of Affairs in Oregon." F. V. Longstaff and W. K. Lamb, "The Royal Navy on the Northwest Coast, 1813–1850. Part II," *British Columbia Historical Quarterly* IX, no. 2 (1945): 113–129, 114.

32. Stuart Banner, *Possessing the Pacific: Land, Settlers, and Indigenous People from Australia to Alaska* (Cambridge, MA: Harvard University Press, 2007), chapter 6.

33. Captain Kuper to Rear Admiralty Moresby, 20 July 1852, in "Four Letters Relating to the Cruise of the 'Thetis,' 1852–1853," *British Columbia Historical Quarterly* VI, no. 3: 192; Captain Kuper to Rear-Admiral Moresby, 4 February 1853, "Four Letters," 200.

34. Captain Kuper to Rear-Admiral Moresby, 4 February 1853, "Four Letters," 200. The threat to treat them as "enemies" is interesting because it does not recognize them as British subjects (and therefore rebels), despite expansive British claims to sovereignty in the region.

35. James Douglas to Archibald Barclay, 20 January 1853, "Four Letters," 205.

36. The language of the charge was relayed to the Admiralty, along with the 1853 opinion of the law officers, in 1853. "Wodehouse to Rear Admiral Owen, 9 August 1853; Wodehouse to Captain Hamilton, 4 August 1853; and Copy to Earl of Clarendon from J.D. Harding, A.E. Cockburn, Richard Bethell, Doctors Commons, 28 July 1853," TNA ADM 172/3, ff. 29–32v.

37. "Earl of Clarendon from J. D. Harding, A. E. Cockburn, Richard Bethell, Doctors Commons, 28 July 1853," TNA ADM 172/3, ff. 31–32v. Emphasis in original.

38. "Papers relating to Punishment of Natives for Outrages committed by them in the Solomon Islands and other Groups of the Western Pacific," *Parliamentary Papers*, 16 June 1881.

39. "H.M.S. 'Opal' against Natives of Solomon Islands, Sub-Enclosure, No. 8," *Parliamentary Papers*, 16 June 1881.

40. Tracey Banivanua Mar, "Consolidating Violence and Colonial Rule: Discipline and Protection in Colonial Queensland," *Postcolonial Studies* 8, no. 3 (2005): 303–319, 308.

41. In a letter from viceroy Avilés to Jorge Pacheco, 1 February 1800, quoted in Bracco, *Con Las Armas en La Mano*, 111; my translation.

42. "Diario de Juan Bentura Ifrán, con lo acontecido a su expedición desde 10 de marzo hasta 10 de junio de 1800," Archivo General de la Nación (AGN), Colección Pivel Devoto, Tomo I, Caja 3, Carpeta 10. All subsequent quotes from Ifrán's diary, on unnumbered pages, are from this source; all translations are mine. This document had been stored among the personal papers of the historian Juan Pivel Devoto and was incorporated into the Archivo General de la Nación, Uruguay (AGN) in 2010.

43. Letter from Jorge Pacheco to Marqués de Aviléz, in Acosta y Lara, *La Guerra de los Charrúas*, 194–195; my translation.

44. "Causa contra un mulato nombrado Lucas Barrera y un Yndio llamado Ju.n Man.l" in Acosta y Lara, *La Guerra de los Charrúas*, 199–207; my translation.

45. "Causa contra un mulato nombrado Lucas Barrera y un Yndio llamado Ju.n Man.l" in Acosta y Lara, *La Guerra de los Charrúas*, 199–207; my translation.

46. Letter from Jorge Pacheco to Marqués de Aviléz, 24 June 1801, in Acosta y Lara, *La Guerra de los Charrúas*, 196–198, 197; my translation.

47. Letter from Jorge Pacheco to Marqués de Aviléz, 24 June 1801, in Acosta y Lara, *La Guerra de los Charrúas*, 196–198, 198; my translation.

48. Quoted in P. Rivet, "Los últimos charrúas," *Guaraguao* 8, no. 19 (2004): 165–188; see Darío Arce Asenjo, "Nuevos datos sobre el destino de Tacuavé y la hija de Guyunusa," *Antropologia Social y Cultural de Uruguay*, 5 (2007): 51–71. On the fate of other Charrúa prisoners sent to Montevideo after the massacre, see Jeffrey Alan Erbig Jr., *Where Caciques and Mapmakers Met: Border Making in Eighteenth-Century South America* (Chapel Hill: University of North Carolina Press, 2020), 137.

49. Historians' approaches to violence between settlers and Aborigines in Tasmania have varied, but accounts of the violence align closely. My account relies on works by Lyndall Ryan: *Tasmanian Aborigines: A History since 1803* (Sydney and Melbourne: Allen & Unwin, 2012); *The Aboriginal Tasmanians* (Vancouver: University of British Columbia Press, 1981); and "Massacre in the Black War in Tasmania 1823–34: A Case Study of the Meander River Region, June 1827." *Journal of Genocide Research* 10, no. 4 (2008): 479–499. I also draw on Henry Reynolds, "Genocide in Tasmania," in *Genocide and Settler Society: Frontier Violence and Stolen Indigenous Children in Australian History*, ed. Dirk Moses, 127–149 (New York: Berghan, 2004); Nicholas Clements, *The Black War: Fear, Sex and Resistance in Tasmania* (St. Lucia: University of Queensland Press, 2014); and Alan Lester and Fae Duddart, *Colonization and the Origins of Humanitarian Governance: Protecting Aborigines across the Nineteenth-Century British Empire* (Cambridge, UK; New York: Cambridge University Press, 2014).

50. Quoted in Ryan, "Massacre in the Black War in Tasmania," 485. And see Ryan for a balanced discussion of the politically charged debate about whether historians should describe the Black War in Tasmania as genocide.

51. See, for example, *Hobart Town Gazette*, 29 November 1826.

52. "Proclamation Separating the Aborigines from the White Inhabitants," 9 April 1828, *Historical Records of Australia*, series 3, vol. 7, 180–184; "Towards Genocide: Government Policy on the Aborigines, 1827–1833," appendix in James Boyce, *Van Diemen's Land* (Melbourne: Black Inc, 2008), 206–247; and Penelope Edmonds, "'Failing in Every Endeavour to Conciliate': Governor Arthur's Proclamation Boards to the Aborigines, Australian Conciliation Narratives and Their Transnational Connections," *Journal of Australian Studies* 35, no. 2 (2011): 201–218.

53. Boyce, *Van Diemen's Land*, 206.

54. Lyndall Ryan notes that the conflict amounted to a "guerrilla war with the Aborigines," one that encompassed both settlers' and Tasmanians' tactics (*Aboriginal Tasmanians*, 124).

55. Boyce, *Van Diemen's Land*, 210. Efforts to contain white violence were cited elsewhere, too, as rationales for reinforcing and extending imperial legal authority. See, for example, Elizabeth Kolsky, *Colonial Justice in British India: White Violence and the Rule of Law* (Cambridge, UK; New York: Cambridge University Press, 2010).

56. Quoted in Boyce, *Van Diemen's Land*, 211. Boyce notes that this view was challenged by officials in London, who criticized the report on this point. Lester and Duddart place the

Aborigines Report at the center of a wider discourse in London that sought to reconcile forceful incorporation of Indigenous populations with humanitarianism under the banner of "protection" (*Colonization and the Origins of Humanitarian Governance*, chapter 6). On the ambiguities of protection talk in the early nineteenth-century British Empire, see Benton and Ford, *Rage for Order*, chapter 4.

57. Soldiers and bushrangers could not be criticized, of course, for responding to the reward established for the capture of Tasmanians: five pounds for every adult and two for every child. This 1830 provision did not distinguish between Tasmanians living in "settled" districts or elsewhere. Boyce, *Van Diemen's Land*, 212.

58. As Boyce points out, colonial officials concluded that the Colonial Office would approve resettlement only if it resulted from a treaty or was a voluntary migration. They opted for ambiguity by describing Tasmanians as "voluntary exiles." Boyce, *Van Diemen's Land*, 218. Boyce proposes that the lack of an "economic or security justification" for the removal made it unique among actions against Indigenous communities (231). But alternating between recognizing the interpolitical character of relations with Indigenous peoples and claiming them as subjects was common. See Smiley, "Rebellion, Sovereignty, and Islamic Law." For Tasmania, Lester and Duggart describe the tension between tolerance of settler violence and the official discourse of "conciliation" (*Colonization and the Origins of Humanitarian Governance*, 61–66).

59. Some historians continue to represent the wave of violence on settler colonial frontiers in the nineteenth century as functioning to establish imperial (or national) governmentality. For example, Benjamin D. Hopkins, *Ruling the Savage Periphery: Frontier Governance and the Making of the Modern State* (Cambridge, MA: Harvard University Press, 2020).

60. My account of protection emergencies and discourse about the protection of British interests supplements a vast literature on nineteenth-century British imperial projects aimed at sheltering Indigenous subjects and enslaved people from extreme colonial violence. That literature centers on the question of whether and to what degree such projects constituted humanitarianism. I am intentionally setting this question aside here because even though the discourse of protection connected reform projects with debates about the use of force, the latter also had some distinctive qualities and I want to emphasize them here. On discourses of protection in colonial Australia and New Zealand, see Bain Attwood, *Empire and the Making of Native Title: Sovereignty, Property and Indigenous People* (Cambridge, UK; New York: Cambridge University Press, 2020), especially introduction and chapter 4. On protection in the nineteenth-century British Empire, see especially Lester and Dussart, *Colonization and the Origins of Humanitarian Governance*; Amanda Nettelbeck, *Indigenous Rights and Colonial Subjecthood: Protection and Reform in the Nineteenth-Century British Empire* (New York: Cambridge University Press, 2019); Zoë Laidlaw, *Protecting the Empire's Humanity: Thomas Hodgkin and British Colonial Activism, 1830–1870* (New York: Cambridge University Press, 2021); and Benton and Ford, *Rage for Order*, chapter 4. On protection and empires in comparative context, see Lauren Benton, Adam Clulow, and Bain Attwood, eds., *Protection and Empire: A Global History* (New York: Cambridge University Press, 2018).

61. John Gallagher and Ronald Robinson, "The Imperialism of Free Trade," *Economic History Review* 6, no. 1 (1953): 1–15.

62. Bentham's views are summarized in the essay *A Plan for an Universal and Perpetual Peace*, which appears in the Bentham works edited by his contemporary and friend John Bowring

(Jeremy Bentham, *The Works of Jeremy Bentham*, edited by John Bowring. Edinburgh: W. Tait; Simpkin, Marshall, 1843). The essay is an amalgam of other Bentham essays, two of which dealt with Bentham's preoccupation with security and with the problem of empire: *Pacification and Emancipation* and *Colonies and Navy*. Gunhild Hoogensen, *International Relations, Security and Jeremy Bentham* (New York: Routledge, 2005), 43. Hoogensen argues that the result of splicing Bentham's writings together in this essay results in "a purposefully contrived and distorted picture" of his views on security, yet those views also compose "the key to understanding Bentham" (Hoogensen, *International Relations*, 43, 11).

63. Bentham, *A Plan for an Universal and Perpetual Peace*, 547, 546.

64. Bentham, *A Plan for an Universal and Perpetual Peace*, 556.

65. Bentham, *A Plan for an Universal and Perpetual Peace*, 550. Like other philosophical radicals and reformers, Bentham came to endorse Wakefield's projects of "systematic colonization."

66. Quoted in Hoogensen, *International Relations*, 137.

67. Edward Gibbon Wakefield, *A Letter from Sydney, The Principal Town of Australasia*, ed. Robert Gouger (London: Joseph Cross, 1829), 221–222; emphasis in original.

68. Quoted in Semmel, *The Rise of Free Trade Imperialism*, 105.

69. *Sir William Molesworth's Speech: In the House of Commons, March 6, 1838, on the State of the Colonies* (London: T. Cooper, 1838), 57; "Extract from Speech at Leeds on the State of the Nation, February 5, 1840," *Selected Speeches of Sir W. Molesworth on questions relating to colonial policy*, ed. H. Edward Egerton (London, J. Murray, 1903), 83.

70. *Molesworth's Speech, House of Commons, March 6, 1838*, 6.

71. Semmel, *The Rise of Free Trade Imperialism*, 151.

72. Duncan Bell, "Before the Democratic Peace: Racial Utopianism, Empire and the Abolition of War," *European Journal of International Relations* 20, no. 3 (2014): 647–670.

73. Quoted in Bell, "Before the Democratic Peace," 651.

74. Bell, "Before the Democratic Peace," 650. Duncan Bell, *Dreamworlds of Race: Empire and the Utopian Destiny of Anglo-America* (Princeton, NJ: Princeton University Press, 2020).

75. The usual centerpiece of histories of protection as a discourse of empire is the speech by British Foreign Secretary Lord Palmerston in the Don Pacifico affair in 1850. Palmerston declared it the duty of the British Empire to protect its subjects, and he famously compared British rights to protection to the rights of Roman citizens to protection. Often overlooked are parts of Palmerston's speech in which he discussed ambiguities and complexities of managing protection in pluripolitical regions, and outlined conditions for the exercise of protection. For analysis of the imperial context of the Don Pacifico affair, see Benton and Ford, *Rage for Order*, 113–115.

76. Pablo Kalmanovitz, *The Laws of War in International Thought* (New York: Oxford University Press, 2020), 89.

77. Oona A. Hathaway and Scott J. Shapiro, *The Internationalists: How a Radical Plan to Outlaw War Remade the World* (New York: Simon & Schuster, 2017); Kalmanovitz, *The Laws of War in International Thought*, 86–89.

78. Kalmonovitz, *The Laws of War in International Thought*, chapter 5; John Fabian Witt, *Lincoln's Code: The Laws of War in American History* (New York: Free Press, 2012).

79. Neff places measures short of war into these three categories. He defines interventions as having a mostly positive connotation and as being associated with peacekeeping and collective

punishments for unwarranted violence. Reprisals carried forward some characteristics of just war responses to injuries but more consistently involved public authorization. And emergency actions activated claims, often generalized, of self-defense. Stephen C. Neff, *War and the Law of Nations: A General History* (New York: Cambridge University Press, 2008), chapter 6.

80. Neff, *War and the Law of Nations*, chapter 6.

81. Neff, *War and the Law of Nations*, 215, 216.

82. But this was not a case of law operating in Europe but not outside it. A strand of discourse in Europe about the contrast of lawful and lawless zones was just that—a discourse. "Zones of Law, Zones of Violence: The Legal Geography of the British Atlantic, circa 1772." *William and Mary Quarterly* 60, no. 3 (2003): 471–510.

83. See, for example, Catherine S. Arnold, "Affairs of Humanity: Arguments for Humanitarian Intervention in England and Europe, 1698–1715," *English Historical Review* 133, no. 563 (2018), 835–865.

84. For critical analyses of protection in the history of international law, see Anne Orford, *International Authority and the Responsibility to Protect* (New York: Cambridge University Press, 2011), and Lauren Benton, Adam Clulow, and Bain Atwood, eds., *Protection and Empire: A Global History* (New York: Cambridge University Press, 2017).

Conclusion: Specters of Imperial Violence

1. On the postwar British public's dearth of knowledge about imperial violence, see Erik Linstrum, *Age of Emergency: Living with Violence at the End of the British Empire* (New York: Oxford University Press, 2023). The systematization of violence in the twentieth century British Empire is traced by Elkins, *Legacy of Imperial Violence*. For a critique of parts of that analysis, see Benton, "Evil Empires? The Long Shadow of British Colonialism," *Foreign Affairs* 101, no. 4 (2022): 190–196.

2. Dave Phillips, Eric Schmitt, and Mark Mazzetti, "Civilian Deaths Mounted as Secret Unit Pounded ISIS," *New York Times*, 12 December 2021.

3. Phillips et al. "Civilian Deaths Mounted as Secret Unit Pounded ISIS"; on the history of justifying drone strikes, see Tara McKelvey, "Defending the Drones: Harold Koh and the Evolution of U.S. Policy," in *Drone Wars: Transforming Conflict, Law, and Policy*, ed. Peter L. Bergen and Daniel Rothenberg (New York: Cambridge University Press, 2015), 185–205; Moyn, *Humane*. The Biden administration adopted a more restrictive policy on drone strikes and commando raids.

4. "Transcript: Putin's Televised Address on Ukraine," Bloomberg News, 24 February 2022, https://www.bloomberg.com/news/articles/2022-02-24/full-transcript-vladimir-putin-s -televised-address-to-russia-on-ukraine-feb-24 (accessed 31 March 2022).

5. John Fabian Witt, *Lincoln's Code: The Laws of War in American History* (New York: Free Press, 2013).

6. Oona A. Hathaway and Scott J. Shapiro, *The Internationalists: How a Radical Plan to Outlaw War Remade the World* (New York: Simon & Schuster, 2017).

7. In *Humane*, Moyn (164–166, 173–179) points to the Vietnam War as a pivotal moment when the United States endorsed and accepted the view of international lawyers that the Geneva Conventions should be applied in the conflict.

8. Witt, *Lincoln's Code*; on the contradictory effects of distinguishing war from measures short of war, see Stephen C. Neff, *War and the Law of Nations: A General History* (New York: Cambridge University Press, 2008), chapter 8; on the paradoxical effects of late twentieth-century U.S. efforts to make war more "humane," see Moyn, *Humane*.

9. On the influence of trajectories of empires on international institutions in the twentieth century, see Susan Pedersen, *The Guardians: The League of Nations and the Crisis of Empire* (Oxford: Oxford University Press, 2017); and Mark Mazower, *No Enchanted Palace: The End of Empire and the Ideological Origins of the United Nations* (Princeton, NJ: Princeton University Press, 2013).

10. Moyn's argument that the United States, in seeking to humanize war, unleashed greater destructiveness fits historically much longer patterns, but he errs in portraying modalities in the U.S. "war on terror" as in part a return to the lawless violence of nineteenth-century Indian Wars. See *Humane*, 20. On small wars as the centerpiece of British decolonization, see Erik Linstrum, *Age of Emergency*. Linstrum sticks with the labels of the time: insurgency and counterinsurgency. A longer historical framework suggests the need for other categories.

11. Recognizing the salience and instabilities of these categories poses a challenge to Carl Schmitt's focus on friends and enemies as foundational categories of politics, as Schmitt himself came to realize. Carl Schmitt, *The Concept of the Political: Expanded Edition* (Chicago: University of Chicago Press, 1996, 2007). In *Theory of the Partisan*, which was based on two lectures he delivered in Spain in 1962, Schmitt indicated in the subtitle ("An Interjection to the Concept of the Political") his aim of revising the theory to take account of postwar geopolitical change, including anti-imperial revolutions. The analysis suffered from Schmitt's thin knowledge of imperial violence and his ideological commitments. On *Theory of the Partisan*, see Jan-Werner Müller, *A Dangerous Mind: Carl Schmitt in Post-War European Thought* (New Haven, CT: Yale University Press, 2003), 133–155; and Daniel Clayton, "Partisan Space," in *Spatiality, Sovereignty and Carl Schmitt*, ed. Stephen Legg (New York: Routledge, 2011), 211–219.

12. These categories were unstable in both imperial and international law. Rather than operating outside the law, pirates and brigands rarely claimed outsider status. On pirates, see Benton, "Legal Spaces of Piracy," and Lauren Benton, "Toward a New Legal History of Piracy: Maritime Legalities and the Myth of Universal Jurisdiction," *International Journal of Maritime History* XXIII, no. 1 (2011), 1–15. And on the redefinition of rebels as belligerents without the standing of sovereign enemies in the nineteenth century, see Smiley, "Rebellion, Sovereignty, and Islamic Law," 252–255.

13. See Lester and Duggart, *Colonization and the Origins of Humanitarian Governance*. I prefer to avoid the term "humanitarianism" because its later meanings cloud our understanding of imperial reform in the nineteenth century. On this point, see Benton and Ford, *Rage for Order*.

14. I am adapting Darryl Li's phrase "horizon of belonging." He helpfully puts historical actors in motion in relation to categories of belonging, but as a metaphor, the phrase is limited since an individual sees only one horizon at a time. Darryl Li, *The Universal Enemy: Jihad, Empire, and the Challenge of Solidarity* (Stanford, CA: Stanford University Press, 2020), 14. Also on fluid categories of legal belonging, see Jessica Marglin, *The Shamama Case: Contesting Citizenship across the Modern Mediterranean* (Princeton: Princeton University Press, 2022), 5–7, 225–231.

15. Natasha Wheatley, *The Life and Death of States: Central Europe and the Transformation of Modern Sovereignty* (Princeton and Oxford: Princeton University Press, 2023).

16. The term is from this book's epigraph, from Nick Harkaway, *The Gone-Away World* (New York: Vintage, 2009), 172.

17. On quasi-sovereignty, see Lauren Benton, "From International Law to Imperial Constitutions: The Problem of Quasi-Sovereignty, 1870–1900," *Law and History Review* 26, no. 3 (2008): 595–620.

18. This is the central point in Richard White, *The Middle Ground: Indians, Empires, and Republics in the Great Lakes Region, 1650–1815* (New York: Cambridge University Press, 2010). See also Lauren Benton, "In Defense of Ignorance: Frameworks for Legal Politics in the Atlantic World," in *Justice in a New World: Negotiating Legal Intelligibility in British, Iberian, and Indigenous America*, ed. Brian Owensby and Richard Ross (New York: New York University Press, 2018), 273–290.

19. For a perceptive analysis of one example of "greater institutional conflict" after victory, see Thomas W. Barton, *Victory's Shadow: Conquest and Governance in Medieval Catalonia* (Ithaca, NY: Cornell University Press, 2019), 22.

20. See chapter 3 in this volume.

21. Mary L. Dudziak, *War Time: An Idea, Its History, Its Consequences* (New York: Oxford University Press, 2013).

22. Other juridical traditions produced ways of representing the lawfulness of violence between war and peace. For an interesting analysis of similarities in Christian and Islamic legal traditions and their definition of "limited," "particular," or "modest" peace, see Murad Idris, *War for Peace: Genealogies of a Violent Ideal in Western and Islamic Thought* (Oxford: Oxford University Press, 2019), 319–321.

23. Frantz Fanon quotes an Algerian policy officer as saying, "Those gentlemen in the government say there's no war in Algeria and that the arm of the law, that's to say the police, ought to restore order. But there *is* a war going on in Algeria, and when they wake up to it it'll be too late." Fanon, *Wretched of the Earth*, 268.

24. Linstrum, *Age of Emergency*.

25. Moyn traces the views of international lawyers on the Vietnam War in *Humane*, 164–166, 173–179, 191.

26. We should not overstate the parallels. The Nazi program of extermination was categorically different from imperial violence in its relation to law. See Lauren Benton, "Evil Empires?"

BIBLIOGRAPHY

Abler, Thomas. "Beavers and Muskets: Iroquois Military Fortunes in the Face of European Colonization." In *War in the Tribal Zone: Expanding States and Indigenous Warfare*, edited by R. Brian Ferguson and Neil L. Whitehead, 151–174. Santa Fe, NM: School of American Research Press, 1992.

Acosta y Lara, Eduardo F. *La Guerra de los Charrúas en la Banda Oriental*. Montevideo: Talleres de Loreto Editores, 1998.

Agmon, Danna. *A Colonial Affair: Commerce, Conversion, and Scandal in French India*. Ithaca, NY: Cornell University Press, 2017.

Albuquerque, Afonso de. *Albuquerque, Caesar of the East: Selected Texts by Afonso de Albuquerque and His Son*. Hispanic Classics. Warminster, UK: Aris & Phillips, 1990.

Ali, Daud. "War, Servitude, and the Imperial Household: A Study of Palace Women in the Chola Empire." In *Slavery and South Asian History*, edited by Indrani Chatterjee and Richard M. Eaton, 17–43. Bloomington: Indiana University Press, 2006.

Allemann, Daniel. "Slavery and Empire in Iberian Scholastic Thought, c. 1539–1682." Ph.D. Dissertation, University of Cambridge, 2020.

Anderson, Clare. *Convicts: A Global History*. New York: Cambridge University Press, 2022.

Ando, Clifford. *Law, Language, and Empire in the Roman Tradition*. Philadelphia: University of Pennsylvania Press, 2011.

Arendt, Hannah. *On Violence*. New York: Harcourt, 1969.

Armitage, David. *Civil Wars: A History in Ideas*. New York: Alfred A. Knopf, 2017.

———. *The Declaration of Independence: A Global History*. Cambridge, MA: Harvard University Press, 2007.

Arnold, Catherine S. "Affairs of Humanity: Arguments for Humanitarian Intervention in England and Europe, 1698–1715." *English Historical Review* 133, no. 563 (2018): 835–865.

Arreguín-Toft, Ivan. *How the Weak Win Wars: A Theory of Asymmetric Conflict*. New York: Cambridge University Press, 2005.

Asenjo, Darío Arce. "Nuevos datos sobre el destino de Tacuavé y la hija de Guyunusa." *Antropología Social y Cultural de Uruguay* 5 (2007): 51–71.

Attwood, Bain. *Empire and the Making of Native Title: Sovereignty, Property and Indigenous People*. Cambridge, UK; New York: Cambridge University Press, 2020.

Banivanua Mar, Tracey. "Consolidating Violence and Colonial Rule: Discipline and Protection in Colonial Queensland." *Postcolonial Studies* 8, no. 3 (2005): 303–319.

Banner, Stuart. *Possessing the Pacific: Land, Settlers, and Indigenous People from Australia to Alaska*. Cambridge, MA: Harvard University Press, 2007.

Barnes, Jonathan. "The Just War." In *The Cambridge History of Later Medieval Philosophy: From the Rediscovery of Aristotle to the Disintegration of Scholasticism, 1100–1600*, edited by Norman Kretzmann, Anthony Kenny, and Jan Pinborg, 771–784. Cambridge, UK: Cambridge University Press, 1982.

Bartelson, Jens. "War and the Turn to History in International Relations." In *The Routledge Handbook of Historical International Relations*, edited by Benjamin de Carvalho, Julia Costa Lopez, and Halvard Leira, 127–137. New York: Routledge, 2021.

———. *War in International Thought*. New York: Cambridge University Press, 2018.

Barton, Thomas W. *Victory's Shadow: Conquest and Governance in Medieval Catalonia*. Ithaca, NY: Cornell University Press, 2019.

Baugh, Daniel A. *The Global Seven Years War 1754–1763: Britain and France in a Great Power Contest*. New York: Routledge, 2011.

Becker, Anna K. *Gendering the Renaissance Commonwealth*. New York: Cambridge University Press, 2020.

Becker Lorca, Arnulf. *Mestizo International Law: A Global Intellectual History, 1842–1933*. Cambridge, UK: Cambridge University Press, 2014.

Bell, Duncan. "Before the Democratic Peace: Racial Utopianism, Empire and the Abolition of War." *European Journal of International Relations* 20, no. 3 (2014): 647–670.

———. *Dreamworlds of Race: Empire and the Utopian Destiny of Anglo-America*. Princeton, NJ: University Press, 2020.

Bennett, Herman L. *African Kings and Black Slaves: Sovereignty and Dispossession in the Early Modern Atlantic*. Philadelphia: University of Pennsylvania Press, 2019.

Bentham, Jeremy. *The Works of Jeremy Bentham*. Edited by John Bowring. Edinburgh: W. Tait; Simpkin, Marshall, 1843.

Benton, Lauren. "Beyond Anachronism: Histories of International Law and Global Legal Politics." *Journal of the History of International Law* 21, no. 1 (2019): 7–40.

———. "In Defense of Ignorance: Frameworks for Legal Politics in the Atlantic World." In *Justice in a New World Negotiating Legal Intelligibility in British, Iberian, and Indigenous America*, edited by Richard J. Ross and Brian P. Owensby. New York: New York University Press, 2018.

———. "Evil Empires? The Long Shadow of British Colonialism." *Foreign Affairs* 101, no. 4 (2022): 190–196.

———. "From International Law to Imperial Constitutions: The Problem of Quasi-Sovereignty, 1870–1900." *Law and History Review* 26, no. 3 (2008): 595–620.

———. *Law and Colonial Cultures: Legal Regimes in World History*. Studies in Comparative World History. New York: Cambridge University Press, 2002.

———. "The Legal Logic of Wars of Conquest: Truces and Betrayal in the Early Modern World." *Duke Journal of Comparative and International Law* 28, no. 3 (2018): 425–448.

———. "Legal Spaces of Empire: Piracy and the Origins of Ocean Regionalism." *Comparative Studies in Society and History* 47, no. 4 (2005): 700–724.

———. "Possessing Empire: Iberian Claims and Interpolity Law." In *Native Claims: Indigenous Law against Empire, 1500–1920*, edited by Saliha Belmessous, 19–40. New York: Oxford University Press, 2011.

———. *A Search for Sovereignty: Law and Geography in European Empires, 1400–1900*. New York: Cambridge University Press, 2010.

Benton, Lauren, and Adam Clulow. "Empires and Protection: Making Interpolity Law in the Early Modern World." *Journal of Global History* 12, no. 1 (2017): 74–92.

———. "Legal Encounters and the Origins of Global Law." In *The Cambridge World History. Volume 6, The Construction of a Global World, 1400–1800 CE. Part 2, Patterns of Change*, edited by Jerry H. Bentley, Sanjay Subrahmanyam, and Merry E. Wiesner, vol. 6, 80–100. New York: Cambridge University Press, 2015.

———. "Protection Shopping among Empires: Suspended Sovereignty in the Cocos-Keeling Islands." *Past & Present* 257, no. 1 (2022): 209–247.

———. "Toward a New Legal History of Piracy: Maritime Legalities and the Myth of Universal Jurisdiction." *International Journal of Maritime History* XXIII, no. 1 (2011): 1–15.

Benton, Lauren, Adam Clulow, and Bain Attwood, eds. *Protection and Empire: A Global History*. New York: Cambridge University Press, 2018.

Benton, Lauren, and Lisa Ford. *Rage for Order: The British Empire and the Origins of International Law, 1800–1850*. Cambridge, MA: Harvard University Press, 2016.

Benton, Lauren, and Benjamin Straumann. "Acquiring Empire by Law: From Roman Doctrine to Early Modern European Practice." *Law and History Review* 28, no. 1 (2010): 1–38.

Berjaeu, Jean Philibert, trans. *Calcoen: A Dutch Narrative of the Second Voyage of Vasco Da Gama to Calicut, Printed at Antwerp Circa 1504*. London: B. M. Pickering, 1874.

Bernardino, de Sahagún. *Florentine Codex: General History of the Things of New Spain*. Edited by Arthur J. O. Anderson and Charles E. Dibble. Santa Fe, NM: School of American Research, 1950.

Blumenthal, Debra. *Enemies and Familiars: Slavery and Mastery in Fifteenth-Century Valencia*. Ithaca, NY: Cornell University Press, 2009.

Boot, Max. *The Savage Wars of Peace: Small Wars and the Rise of American Power*. Revised edition. New York: Basic Books, 2014.

Bowd, Stephen D. *Renaissance Mass Murder: Civilians and Soldiers during the Italian War*. Oxford: Oxford University Press, 2018.

Boyce, James. *Van Diemen's Land*. Melbourne: Black Inc, 2008.

Bracco, Diego. *Con las Armas en La Mano: Charrúas, Guenoa-Minuanos y Guaraníes*. Montevideo: Planeta, 2013.

Brading, D. A. *The First America: The Spanish Monarchy, Creole Patriots and the Liberal State 1492–1867*. New York: Cambridge University Press, 1991.

Bradley, Mark, Mary L. Dudziak, and Andrew J. Bacevich, eds. *Making the Forever War: Marilyn B. Young on the Culture and Politics of American Militarism*. Culture and Politics in the Cold War and Beyond. Amherst: University of Massachusetts Press, 2021.

Braithwaite, Roderick. *Palmerston and Africa: The Rio Nunez Affair, Competition, Diplomacy, and Justice*. New York: L. B. Taurus, 1996.

Bretones Lane, Fernanda. "Spain, the Caribbean, and the Making of Religious Sanctuary." Ph.D. Dissertation, Vanderbilt University, 2019.

Brett, Annabel. *The Possibility Condition. Rights, Resistance and the Limits of Law in Early Modern Political Thought*. Oxford University Press, forthcoming.

———. "The Space of Politics and the Space of War in Hugo Grotius's *De Iure Belli Ac Pacis*." *Global Intellectual History* 1, no. 1 (2016): 33–60.

Brewer, Holly. "Creating a Common Law of Slavery for England and Its New World Empire." *Law and History Review* 39, no. 4 (2021): 765–834.

———. "Slavery, Sovereignty, and 'Inheritable Blood': Reconsidering John Locke and the Origins of American Slavery." *American Historical Review* 122, no. 4 (2017): 1038–1078.

Brock, Lothar, and Hendrik Simon, eds. *The Justification of War and International Order: From Past to Present*. Oxford: Oxford University Press, 2021.

Brodman, James. *Ransoming Captives in Crusader Spain: The Order of the Merced on the Christian-Islamic Frontier*. Philadelphia: University of Pennsylvania Press, 1986.

Brooks, Lisa. *Our Beloved Kin: A New History of King Philip's War*. New Haven, CT: Yale University Press, 2018.

Brown, Kathleen M. *Good Wives, Nasty Wenches, and Anxious Patriarchs: Gender, Race, and Power in Colonial Virginia*. Chapel Hill: University of North Carolina Press, 1996.

Brown, Vincent. *Tacky's Revolt: The Story of an Atlantic Slave War*. Cambridge, MA: Belknap Press, 2020.

Burbank, Jane, and Frederick Cooper. *Empires in World History: Power and the Politics of Difference*. Princeton, NJ: Princeton University Press, 2010.

Burnard, Trevor. "Atlantic Slave Systems and Violence." In *A Global History of Early Modern Violence*, edited by Erica Charters, Marie Houllemare, and Peter H. Wilson, 202–217. Manchester, UK: Manchester University Press, 2020.

Callwell, C. E. *Small Wars: Their Principles and Practice*. 3rd ed. Lincoln: University of Nebraska Press, 1996.

Cambridge, Richard Owen. *An Account of the War in India: Between the English and French, on the Coast of Coromandel, from the Year 1750 to the Year 1761. Together with a Relation of the Late Remarkable Events on the Malabar Coast, and the Expeditions to Golconda and Surat; With the Operations of the Fleet. Illustrated with Maps, Plans, &c. The Whole Compiled from Original Papers. The Second Edition by Richard Owen Cambridge, Esq*. London: T. Jefferys, 1762.

Caraman, Philip. *The Lost Paradise: An Account of the Jesuits in Paraguay 1707–1768*. London: Sidgwick and Jackson, 1975.

Casas, Bartolomé de las. *Brevísima relación de la destrucción de las Indias*. Madrid: Alianza editorial, 2014.

———. *Historia de las Indias*. Edited by Agustín Millares Carlo. México: Fondo de Cultura Económica, 1965.

Castañeda de Nájera, Pedro de. *Narrative of the Coronado Expedition*. Edited by John Miller Morris. Chicago: R. R. Donnelley & Sons, 2002.

Cavallar, Georg. "Vitoria, Grotius, Pufendorf, Wolff and Vattel: Accomplices of European Colonialism and Exploitation or True Cosmopolitans?" *Journal of the History of International Law* 10, no. 2 (2008): 181–209.

Cave, Alfred A. *The Pequot War*. Native Americans of the Northeast. Amherst: University of Massachusetts Press, 1996.

Chagnon, Napoleon A. *Yąnomamö, the Fierce People*. Case Studies in Cultural Anthropology. New York: Holt, Rinehart and Winston, 1968.

Chatterjee, Indrani. *Gender, Slavery, and Law in Colonial India*. New York: Oxford University Press, 1999.

———. "Renewed and Connected Histories: Slavery and the Historiography of South Asia." In *Slavery and South Asian History*, edited by Indrani Chatterjee and Richard M. Eaton, 17–43. Bloomington: Indiana University Press, 2006.

———. *Unfamiliar Relations: Family and History in South Asia*. New Brunswick, NJ: Rutgers University Press, 2004.

Chen, Li. *Chinese Law in Imperial Eyes: Sovereignty, Justice, and Transcultural Politics*. New York: Columbia University Press, 2016.

Clausewitz, Carl von. *Clausewitz on Small War*. Translated by Christopher Daase and James W. Davis. New York: Oxford University Press, 2015.

———. *On War*. Translated by J. J. Graham. New York: Penguin, 1999.

Clayton, Daniel. "Partisan Space." In *Spatiality, Sovereignty and Carl Schmitt: Geographies of the Nomos*, edited by Stephen Legg, 211–219. New York: Routledge, 2011.

Clements, Nicholas. *The Black War: Fear, Sex and Resistance in Tasmania*. St. Lucia: University of Queensland Press, 2014.

Clendinnen, Inga. *Aztecs: An Interpretation*. Canto Classics. New York: Cambridge University Press, 2014.

———. *Dancing with Strangers: Europeans and Australians at First Contact*. New York: Cambridge University Press, 2005.

———. "Fierce and Unnatural Cruelty: Cortés and the Conquest of Mexico." In *New World Encounters*, edited by Stephen Greenblatt, 12–47. Berkeley: University of California Press, 1993.

Clulow, Adam. *Amboina, 1623: Fear and Conspiracy on the Edge of Empire*. New York: Columbia University Press, 2019.

———. "Determining the Law of the Sea: The Long History of the Breukelen Case, 1657–1662." In *Sea Rovers, Silver, and Samurai: Maritime East Asia in Global History, 1550–1700*, edited by Tonio Andrade, Xing Hang, Anand A. Yang, and Kieko Matteson, 181–202. Honolulu: University of Hawaii Press, 2016, 181–201.

Coates, Benjamin Allen. *Legalist Empire: International Law and American Foreign Relations in the Early Twentieth Century*. New York: Oxford University Press, 2016.

Coleman, David. *Creating Christian Granada: Society and Religious Culture in an Old-World Frontier City, 1492–1600*. Ithaca, NY: Cornell University Press, 2013.

Cornell, Vincent. "Socioeconomic Dimensions of Reconquista and Jihad in Morocco: Portuguese Dukkala and the Sa'did Sus, 1450–1557." *International Journal of Middle East Studies* 22 (1990): 379–418.

Cortés, Hernán. *Letters from Mexico*. Edited by Anthony Pagden. New Haven, CT: Yale University Press, 2001.

Cowdrey, H.E.J. "The Peace and the Truce of God in the Eleventh Century." *Past & Present*, no. 46 (1970): 42–67.

Craig, Dylan. *Sovereignty, War, and the Global State*. Cham, Switzerland: Palgrave Macmillan, 2020.

Cross, Elizabeth. *Company Politics: Commerce, Scandal, and French Visions of Indian Empire in the Revolutionary Era*. Oxford: Oxford University Press, 2023.

Crouch, Christian Ayne. *Nobility Lost: French and Canadian Martial Cultures, Indians, and the End of New France*. Ithaca, NY: Cornell University Press, 2014.

Cruz, Maria Augusta Lima. "Exiles and Renegades in Early Sixteenth-Century Portuguese India." *Indian Economic and Social History Review* 23, no. 3 (1986): 250–262.

Cruz Crus, Juan. "El Derecho de Gentes en Suárez: La Constumbre como Plebiscito Permanente." In *Suárez Em Lisboa 1617–2017: Actos Do Congresso*, edited by Pedro Caridade de Freitas, Margarida Seixas, and Ana Caldeira Fouto, 29–47. Lisbon: AAFDL Editora, 2018.

Culbertson, Laura. *Slaves and Households in the Near East*. Chicago: University of Chicago Press, 2011.

Dale, S. F. "Islamic Architecture in Kerala: A Preface to Future Study." In *Islam and Indian Regions*, edited by Anna L. Dallapiccola and Stephanie Zingel-Avé Lallemant, 491–495. Stuttgart: Steiner, 1993.

Dalrymple, William. *The Anarchy: The East India Company, Corporate Violence, and the Pillage of an Empire*. New York: Bloomsbury, 2019.

Davis, James W. "Introduction." In *Clausewitz on Small War*, edited by Christopher Daase and James W. Davis, 1–18. New York: Oxford University Press, 2015.

Demos, John. *The Unredeemed Captive: A Family Story from Early America*. New York: Vintage, 1996.

De Souza, Philip. "Rome's Contribution to the Development of Piracy." *Memoirs of the American Academy in Rome*, supplementary volume 6 (2008): 71–96.

Devereux, Andrew W. *The Other Side of Empire: Just War in the Mediterranean and the Rise of Early Modern Spain*. Ithaca, NY: Cornell University Press, 2020.

Díaz Ceballos, Jorge. "New World *Civitas*, Contested Jurisdictions, and Inter-cultural Conversation in the Construction of the Spanish Monarchy." *Colonial Latin American Review* 27:1 (2018), 30–51.

———. *Poder compartido: Repúblicas urbanas, Monarquía y conversación en Castilla del Oro, 1508–1573*. Madrid: Marcial Pons Ediciones de Historia, S.A., 2020.

Díaz del Castillo, Bernal. *The True History of the Conquest of New Spain Vol. II*. Cambridge, UK: Cambridge University Press, 2010.

Disney, A. R. *A History of Portugal and the Portuguese Empire: From Beginnings to 1807*. New York: Cambridge University Press, 2009.

Documentos Sobre Os Portugueses Em Moçambique e Na Africa Central, 1497–1840. Lisboa: Centro de Estudos Históricos Ultramarinos, 1962.

Dodwell, Henry, ed. *Calendar of the Madras Despatches, 1744–1755*. Madras: Government Press, 1920.

———, ed. *The Private Diary of Ananda Ranga Pillai, Dubash to Joseph François Dupleix, Governor of Pondicherry: A Record of Matters, Political, Historical, Social, and Personal, from 1736–1761*. Vol. 6. Madras: The Superintendent, Government Press, 1918.

Donner, Fred M. *The Early Islamic Conquests*. Princeton Studies on the Near East 1017. Princeton, NJ: Princeton University Press, 2014.

Doré, Andréa. "Os *casados* na Índia portuguesa: a mobilidade social de homens úteis." In *Raízes do privilégio: mobilidade social no mundo ibérico do Antigo Regime*, edited by Rodrigo Bentes Monteiro, Bruno Feitler, Daniela Buono Calainho, and Jorge Flores, 510–533. Rio de Janeiro: Editora Civilização Brasileira, 2011.

Duchhardt, Heinz. "The Missing Balance." *Journal of the History of International Law* 2, no. 1 (2000): 67–72.

Dudziak, Mary L. *War Time: An Idea, Its History, Its Consequences.* New York: Oxford University Press, 2012.

Earle, Peter. *The Sack of Panamá.* London: Thomas Dunne, 2007.

Eckstein, Arthur M. *Mediterranean Anarchy, Interstate War, and the Rise of Rome.* Berkeley: University of California Press, 2007.

Edmonds, Penelope. "'Failing in Every Endeavour to Conciliate': Governor Arthur's Proclamation Boards to the Aborigines, Australian Conciliation Narratives and Their Transnational Connections." *Journal of Australian Studies* 35, no. 2 (2011): 201–218.

Elkins, Caroline. *Legacy of Violence: A History of the British Empire.* New York: Alfred A. Knopf, 2022.

Erbig, Jeffrey Alan. *Where Caciques and Mapmakers Met: Border Making in Eighteenth-Century South America.* Chapel Hill: University of North Carolina Press, 2020.

Eustace, Nicole. *Covered with Night: A Story of Murder and Indigenous Justice in Early America.* New York: Liveright, 2021.

Fancy, Hussein. *The Mercenary Mediterranean: Sovereignty, Religion, and Violence in the Medieval Crown of Aragon.* Chicago: University of Chicago Press, 2016.

Fanon, Frantz. *The Wretched of the Earth.* New York: Grove Press, 1965.

Faudree, Paja. "Reading the Requerimiento Performatively: Speech Acts and the Conquest of the New World." *Colonial Latin American Review* 24, no. 4 (2015): 456–478.

Ferrer i Mallol, Maria Teresa. *La Frontera amb l'Islam en el segle XIV: cristians i sarraïns al País Valencià.* Barcelona: Consell Superiord'Investigacions Científiques, 1988.

Fieldhouse, David Kenneth, ed. *Select Documents on the Constitutional History of the British Empire and Commonwealth.* Vol. 1. Westport, CT: Greenwood Press, 1985.

Fitzmaurice, Andrew. *Sovereignty, Property and Empire, 1500–2000.* Cambridge, UK: Cambridge University Press, 2014.

Fletcher, R. A. "Reconquest and Crusade in Spain c. 1050–1150." In *Spain, Portugal and the Atlantic Frontier of Medieval Europe*, edited by José-Juan López-Portillo, 69–86. Burlington, UK: Ashgate, 2013.

Flores, Jorge Manuel. *Unwanted Neighbours: The Mughals, the Portuguese, and Their Frontier Zones.* New Delhi: Oxford University Press, 2018.

Ford, Lisa. *The King's Peace: Law and Order in the British Empire.* Cambridge, MA: Harvard University Press, 2021.

———. *Settler Sovereignty: Jurisdiction and Indigenous People in America and Australia, 1788–1836.* Cambridge, MA: Harvard University Press, 2010.

Fuente, Alejandro de la, and Ariela Julie Gross. *Becoming Free, Becoming Black: Race, Freedom, and Law in Cuba, Virginia, and Louisiana.* Cambridge, UK: Cambridge University Press, 2020.

Gallagher, John, and Ronald Robinson. "The Imperialism of Free Trade." *Economic History Review* 6, no. 1 (1953): 1–15.

Games, Alison. *Inventing the English Massacre: Amboyna in History and Memory.* New York: Oxford University Press, 2020.

Ganson, Barbara Anne. *The Guaraní under Spanish Rule in the Río de La Plata.* Stanford, CA: Stanford University Press, 2003.

Garcia, Victoria. "From Plunder to Crusade: Networks of Nobility and Negotiations of Empire in the Estado Da Índia 1505–1515." Senior Thesis, Wesleyan University, 2012.

Gardiner, Lion. *Relation of the Pequot Warres*. Hartford, CT: Acorn Club of Connecticut, 1901 [1660].

Gentili, Alberico. *De iure belli libri tres*. Translated by John Carew Rolfe. Vol. 2. Oxford: Clarendon Press, 1933.

———. *The Wars of the Romans: A Critical Edition and Translation of De Armis Romanis*. Edited by Benedict Kingsbury and Benjamin Straumann. Translated by David A. Lupher. New York: Oxford University Press, 2011.

A Genuine Account of Some Transactions in the East Indies, Containing the Most Material Occurrences on the Coast of Coromandel, since the Death of the Late Nabob of Arcot, Who Was Killed in Battle in July 1749. London: Printed for R. Baldwin, 1753.

Getachew, Adom. *Worldmaking after Empire: The Rise and Fall of Self-Determination*. Princeton, NJ: Princeton University Press, 2020.

Glymph, Thavolia. *Out of the House of Bondage: The Transformation of the Plantation Household*. New York: Cambridge University Press, 2003.

Goldsworthy, Adrian Keith. *Pax Romana: War, Peace and Conquest in the Roman World*. London: Weidenfeld & Nicolson, 2016.

———. *Roman Warfare*. New York: Basic Books, 2005.

Gong, Gerrit W. *The Standard of "Civilization" in International Society*. New York: Oxford University Press, 1984.

Gottmann, Felicia. "Intellectual History as Global History: Voltaire's *Fragments sur l'Inde* and the Problem of Enlightened Commerce." In *India and Europe in the Global Eighteenth Century*, edited by Simon Davies, Daniel Sanjiv Roberts, and Gabriel Sánchez Espinosa, 141–155. Oxford: Voltaire Foundation, 2014.

Gough, Barry M. *Britannia's Navy on the West Coast of North America, 1812–1914*. Barnsley, UK: Seaforth Publishing, 2016.

———. *The Royal Navy and the Northwest Coast of North America, 1810–1914: A Study of British Maritime Ascendancy*. Vancouver: University of British Columbia Press, 1971.

Gould, Eliga H. *Among the Powers of the Earth: The American Revolution and the Making of a New World Empire*. Cambridge, MA: Harvard University Press, 2012.

———. "Zones of Law, Zones of Violence: The Legal Geography of the British Atlantic, circa 1772." *William and Mary Quarterly* 60, no. 3 (2003): 471–510.

Greenblatt, Stephen. *Marvelous Possessions: The Wonder of the New World*. Chicago: University of Chicago Press, 1991.

Greenwood, Christopher. "The Concept of War in Modern International Law." *International and Comparative Law Quarterly* 36 (1987): 283–306.

Grewe, Wilhelm G. *The Epochs of International Law*. Translated by Michael Byers. New York: Walter de Gruyter, 2000.

Grotius, Hugo. *The Free Sea*. Edited by David Armitage. Indianapolis: Liberty Fund, 2004.

———. *The Rights of War and Peace*. Edited by Richard Tuck. 3 vols. Indianapolis: Liberty Fund, 2005.

Guasco, Michael. *Slaves and Englishmen: Human Bondage in the Early Modern Atlantic World.* Philadelphia: University of Pennsylvania Press, 2014.

Halikowski-Smith, Stefan. "'The Friendship of Kings Was in the Ambassadors': Portuguese Diplomatic Embassies in Asia and Africa during the Sixteenth and Seventeenth Centuries." *Portuguese Studies* 22, no. 1 (2006): 101–134.

Hämäläinen, Pekka. *The Comanche Empire.* New Haven, CT: Yale University Press, 2008.

Hanna, Mark G. *Pirate Nests and the Rise of the British Empire, 1570–1740.* Chapel Hill: University of North Carolina Press, 2015.

Harkaway, Nick. *The Gone-Away World.* New York: Vintage Books, 2009.

Harris, William V. *War and Imperialism in Republican Rome, 327–70 B.C.* Oxford: Clarendon Press, 1979.

Hassell, Stephanie. "Religious Identity and Imperial Security: Arming Catholic Slaves in Sixteenth- and Seventeenth-Century Portuguese India." *Journal of Early Modern History* 25, no. 5 (2022): 403–428.

Hatfield, April. *Boundaries of Belonging: English Jamaica and the Spanish Caribbean, 1665–1715.* Philadelphia: University of Pennsylvania Press, 2023.

Hathaway, Oona A., and Scott J. Shapiro. *The Internationalists: How a Radical Plan to Outlaw War Remade the World.* New York: Simon & Schuster, 2017.

Hendrickson, Jocelyn. *Leaving Iberia: Islamic Law and Christian Conquest in North West Africa.* Cambridge, MA: Harvard University Press, 2021.

Hernández, Bernat. *Bartolomé de las Casas.* New York: Penguin, 2015.

Hershenzon, Daniel. *The Captive Sea: Slavery, Communication, and Commerce in Early Modern Spain and the Mediterranean.* Philadelphia: University of Pennsylvania Press, 2018.

Herzog, Tamar. *Frontiers of Possession: Spain and Portugal in Europe and the Americas.* Cambridge, MA: Harvard University Press, 2015.

———. *A Short History of European Law: The Last Two and a Half Millennia.* Cambridge, MA: Harvard University Press, 2018.

Hoogensen, Gunhild. *International Relations, Security and Jeremy Bentham.* New York: Routledge, 2005.

Hopkins, Benjamin D. *Ruling the Savage Periphery: Frontier Governance and the Making of the Modern State.* Cambridge, MA: Harvard University Press, 2020.

Hoyland, Robert G. *In God's Path: The Arab Conquests and the Creation of an Islamic Empire.* New York: Oxford University Press, 2015.

Hunter, Ian. "Vattel in Revolutionary America: From the Rules of War to the Rule of Law." In *Between Indigenous and Settler Governance*, edited by Lisa Ford and Tim Rowse, 12–22. New York: Routledge, 2013.

———. "Vattel's Law of Nations: Diplomatic Casuistry for the Protestant Nation." *Grotiana (1980)* 31, no. 1 (2010): 108–140.

Hussain, Nasser. *The Jurisprudence of Emergency: Colonialism and the Rule of Law.* Ann Arbor: University of Michigan Press, 2009.

Idris, Murad. *War for Peace: Genealogies of a Violent Ideal in Western and Islamic Thought.* Oxford: Oxford University Press, 2019.

Instituto Geográfico Militar (IGM), Documentos relativos a la ejecución del Tratado de limites de 1750. Montevideo: El Siglo ilustrado, 1938.

Irigoyen-García, Javier. *The Spanish Arcadia: Sheep Herding, Pastoral Discourse, and Ethnicity in Early Modern Spain*. Toronto: University of Toronto Press, 2014.

Israeli, Yanay. "The *Requerimiento* in the Old World: Making Demands and Keeping Records in the Legal Culture of Late Medieval Castile." *Law and History Review* 40, no. 1 (2022): 37–62.

Jackson, Trevor. *Impunity and Capitalism: The Afterlives of European Financial Crises, 1690–1830*. New York: Cambridge University Press, 2022.

Jansen, Katherine Ludwig. *Peace and Penance in Late Medieval Italy*. Princeton, NJ: Princeton University Press, 2018.

Jewitt, John R. *Narrative of the adventures and sufferings of John R. Jewitt, only survivor of the crew of the ship Boston, during a captivity of nearly 3 years among the savages of Nootka sound: with an account of the manners, mode of living, and religious opinions of the natives*. Ithaca, NY: Andrus, Gauntlett & Co., 1851.

Johnson, Edward. *Johnson's Wonder-Working Providence, 1628–1651*. Edited by J. Franklin Jameson. New York: Barnes & Noble, 1952.

Jones, Martha S. *Birthright Citizens: A History of Race and Rights in Antebellum America*. Studies in Legal History. New York: Cambridge University Press, 2018.

Jouannet, Emmanuelle. *Vattel and the Emergence of Classic International Law*. Oxford: Hart, 2019.

Kalmanovitz, Pablo. *The Laws of War in International Thought*. Oxford: Oxford University Press, 2020.

Kennedy, David. *Of War and Law*. Princeton, NJ: Princeton University Press, 2006.

Kennedy, Hugh. *The Great Arab Conquests: How the Spread of Islam Changed the World We Live In*. London: Weidenfeld & Nicolson, 2007.

Kolsky, Elizabeth. *Colonial Justice in British India: White Violence and the Rule of Law*. Cambridge, UK; New York: Cambridge University Press, 2010.

Korman, Sharon. *The Right of Conquest: The Acquisition of Territory by Force in International Law and Practice*. New York: Oxford University Press, 1996.

Koskenniemi, Martti. "Empire and International Law: The Real Spanish Contribution." *University of Toronto Law Journal* 61, no. 1 (2011): 1–36.

———. *To the Uttermost Parts of the Earth: Legal Imagination and International Power 1300–1870*. New York: Cambridge University Press, 2021.

Kupperman, Karen Ordahl. *The Jamestown Project*. Cambridge, MA: Harvard University Press, 2007.

———. *Providence Island, 1630–1641: The Other Puritan Colony*. New York: Cambridge University Press, 1993.

Laband, John. *The Land Wars: The Dispossession of the Khoisan and AmaXhosa in the Cape Colony*. Cape Town: Penguin, 2020.

Ladero Quesada, Miguel Angel. *La guerra de Granada, 1482–1491*. Granada: Diputación de Granada, 2007.

Laidlaw, Zoë. *Protecting the Empire's Humanity: Thomas Hodgkin and British Colonial Activism, 1830–1870*. New York: Cambridge University Press, 2021.

Landers, Jane. "Spanish Sanctuary: Fugitives in Florida, 1687–1790." *Florida Historical Quarterly* 62, no. 3 (1984): 296–313.

Lamb, W. Kaye, ed. "Four Letters Relating to the Cruise of the 'Thetis,' 1852–1853." *British Columbia Historical Quarterly* VI, no. 3 (1942): 189–206.

Langfur, Hal. *The Forbidden Lands: Colonial Identity, Frontier Violence, and the Persistence of Brazil's Eastern Indians, 1750–1830*. Stanford, CA: Stanford University Press, 2006.

Le Cordeur, Basil Alexander, and Christopher C. Saunders, eds. *The War of the Axe, 1847: Correspondence between the Governor of the Cape Colony, Sir Henry Pottinger, and the Commander of the British Forces at the Cape, Sir George Berkeley, and Others*. Johannesburg: Brenthurst, 1981.

Lesaffer, Randall. "Alberico Gentili's *ius post bellum* and Early Modern Peace Treaties." In *The Roman Foundations of the Law of Nations*, edited by Benedict Kingsbury and Benjamin Straumann, 210–240. Oxford: Oxford University Press, 2010.

Lesaffer, Randall, Erik-Jan Broers, and Johanna Waelkens. "From Antwerp to Munster (1609/1648)." In *The Twelve Years Truce (1609): Peace, Truce, War and Law in the Low Countries at the Turn of the 17th Century*, edited by Randall Lesaffer, 233–255 Boston: Brill, 2014.

Lester, Alan, Kate Boehme, and Peter Mitchell. *Ruling the World: Freedom, Civilisation and Liberalism in the Nineteenth-Century British Empire*. New York: Cambridge University Press, 2021.

Lester, Alan, and Fae Dussart. *Colonization and the Origins of Humanitarian Governance: Protecting Aborigines across the Nineteenth-Century British Empire*. New York: Cambridge University Press, 2014.

Li, Darryl. *The Universal Enemy: Jihad, Empire, and the Challenge of Solidarity*. Stanford, CA: Stanford University Press, 2020.

Lima Cruz, Maria Augusta. "As Andaças de Um Degredado Em Terras Perdidas—João Machado." *Mare Liberum* 5 (1995): 39–47.

Linstrum, Erik. *Age of Emergency: Living with Violence at the End of the British Empire*. New York: Oxford University Press, 2023

Lomax, Derek W. *The Reconquest of Spain*. New York: Longman, 1978.

Longstaff, F. V., and W. Kaye Lamb. "The Royal Navy on the Northwest Coast, 1813–1850. Part II." *British Columbia Historical Quarterly* 9, no. 2 (1945): 113–129.

Lovejoy, Paul E. *Transformations in Slavery: A History of Slavery in Africa*. African Studies. Vol. 117. New York: Cambridge University Press, 2011.

MacDonald, Robert A. "Introduction: Part II." In *Leyes de Los Adelantados Mayores: Regulations, Attributed to Alfonso X of Castile, Concerning the King's Vicar in the Judiciary and in Territorial Administration*, edited by Robert A. MacDonald, 5–29. New York: Hispanic Seminary of Medieval Studies, 2000.

MacMillan, Ken. *Sovereignty and Possession in the English New World: The Legal Foundations of Empire, 1576–1640*. New York: Cambridge University Press, 2006.

Malekandathil, Pius. "The Portuguese Casados and the Intra-Asian Trade: 1500–1663." *Proceedings in the Indian History Congress*, vol. 61, part 1 (2000–2001): 385–406.

Manzano Moreno, Eduardo. *Épocas medievales*. Historia de España. Barcelona: Crítica, Marcial Pons, 2010.

Margerison, Kenneth. "French Visions of Empire: Contesting British Power in India after the Seven Years War." *English Historical Review* 130, no. 544 (2015): 583–612.

Marglin, Jessica. *The Shamana Case: Contesting Citizenship across the Modern Mediterranean.* Princeton: Princeton University Press, 2022.

Martin, John Jeffries. "Cannibalism as a Feuding Ritual in Early Modern Europe." *Acta Histriae* 25, no. 1 (2017): 97–108.

Martínez, María Elena. *Genealogical Fictions: Limpieza de Sangre, Religion, and Gender in Colonial Mexico.* Stanford, CA: Stanford University Press, 2008.

Mason, John. *A Brief History of the Pequot War.* Boston: S. Kneeland & T. Green, 1736.

Mattingly, D. J. "War and Peace in Roman North Africa: Observations and Models of State-Tribe Interaction." In *War in the Tribal Zone: Expanding States and Indigenous Warfare,* edited by R. Brian Ferguson and Neil L. Whitehead, 31–60. Santa Fe, NM: School of American Research Press, 1992.

Mazower, Mark. *No Enchanted Palace: The End of Empire and the Ideological Origins of the United Nations.* Lawrence Stone Lectures. Princeton, NJ: Princeton University Press, 2013.

McGregor, Timo Wouter. "Properties of Empire: Mobility and Vernacular Politics in the Dutch Atlantic World, 1648–1688." Ph.D. Dissertation, New York University, 2020.

McKelvey, Tara. "Defending the Drones: Harold Koh and the Evolution of U.S. Policy." In *Drone Wars: Transforming Conflict, Law, and Policy,* edited by Peter L. Bergen and Daniel Rothenberg, 185–207. New York: Cambridge University Press, 2015.

McKinley, Michelle A. *Fractional Freedoms: Slavery, Intimacy, and Legal Mobilization in Colonial Lima.* Studies in Legal History. New York: Cambridge University Press, 2016.

Melo, J. V. "In Search of a Shared Language: The Goan Diplomatic Protocol." *Journal of Early Modern History* 20, no. 4 (2016): 390–407.

Mendes da Luz, Francisco Paulo, ed. *Livro das cidades, e fortalezas, que a Coroa de Portugal tem nas partes da Índia, e das capitanias, e mais cargos que nelas há, e da importancia delles.* Vol. 6. Lisboa: Centro de Estudos Históricos Ultramarinos, 1960.

Mercado-Montero, Ernesto. "Raiding, Captive-Taking, and the Slave Trade in the Carib Archipelago." Unpublished paper, 2023.

Miers, Suzanne, and Igor Kopytoff. *Slavery in Africa: Historical and Anthropological Perspectives.* Madison: University of Wisconsin Press, 1977.

Miller, Joseph C. *The Problem of Slavery as History: A Global Approach.* New Haven, CT: Yale University Press, 2012.

Mole, Gregory. "L'Économie politique de Joseph Dupleix: commerce, autorité et deuxième guerre carnatique, 1751–1754." *Outre-mers* 103, no. 388–389 (2015): 79–96.

Molesworth, William. *Selected Speeches of Sir W. Molesworth on Questions Relating to Colonial Policy.* London: J. Murray, 1903.

———. *Sir William Molesworth's Speech: In the House of Commons, March 6, 1838, on the State of the Colonies.* London: T. Cooper, 1838.

Monteiro, John M. *Blacks of the Land: Indian Slavery, Settler Society, and the Portuguese Colonial Enterprise in South America.* New York: Cambridge University Press, 2018.

Morgan, Jennifer. *Laboring Women: Reproduction and Gender in New World Slavery.* Philadelphia: University of Pennsylvania Press, 2004.

———. *Reckoning with Slavery: Gender, Kinship, and Capitalism in the Early Black Atlantic.* Durham, NC: Duke University Press, 2021.

Morieux, Renaud. *The Society of Prisoners: Anglo-French Wars and Incarceration in the Eighteenth Century*. New York: Oxford University Press, 2019.

Moyn, Samuel. *Humane: How the United States Abandoned Peace and Reinvented War*. New York: Farrar, Straus and Giroux, 2021.

Muir, Edward. *Mad Blood Stirring: Vendetta in Renaissance Italy*. Baltimore: Johns Hopkins University Press, 1998.

Muldoon, James. *Popes, Lawyers, and Infidels: The Church and the Non-Christian World, 1250–1550*. Philadelphia: University of Pennsylvania Press, 2015.

Müller, Jan-Werner. *A Dangerous Mind: Carl Schmitt in Post-War European Thought*. New Haven, CT: Yale University Press, 2003.

Myrup, Erik. *Power and Corruption in the Early Modern Portuguese World*. Baton Rouge: Louisiana State University Press, 2015.

Najib, Aseel. "Common Wealth: Land Taxation in Early Islam." Ph.D. Dissertation, Columbia University, 2023.

Nakhimovsky, Isaac. *The Holy Alliance: The History of Liberalism and the Politics of Federation*. Princeton, NJ: Princeton University Press, forthcoming.

Neff, Stephen C. *Justice among Nations: A History of International Law*. Cambridge, MA: Harvard University Press, 2014.

———. *War and the Law of Nations: A General History*. New York: Cambridge University Press, 2005.

Nettelbeck, Amanda. *Indigenous Rights and Colonial Subjecthood: Protection and Reform in the Nineteenth-Century British Empire*. New York: Cambridge University Press, 2019.

Newitt, Malyn. "Formal and Informal Empire in the History of Portuguese Expansion." *Portuguese Studies* 17, no. 1 (2001): 1–21.

Nuzzo, Luigi. *El Lenguaje Jurídico de La Conquista: Estrategias de Control en Las Indias Españolas*. Ciudad de México: Editorial Tirant lo Blanch, 2021.

Obregón, Liliana. "Peripheral Histories of International Law." *Annual Review of Law and Social Science* 15, no. 1 (2019): 437–451.

O'Callaghan, Joseph F. *Reconquest and Crusade in Medieval Spain*. Middle Ages. Philadelphia: University of Pennsylvania Press, 2003.

Offen, Karl. "Mapping Amerindian Captivity in Colonial Mosquitia." *Journal of Latin American Geography* 14, no. 3 (2015): 35–65.

Olmedo Bernal, Santiago. *El dominio del Atlántico en la baja Edad Media: los títulos jurídicos de la expansión peninsular hasta el Tratado de Tordesillas*. Valladolid: Sociedad V Centenario del Tratado de Tordesillas, 1995.

Onuf, Peter S., and Nicholas Greenwood Onuf. *Federal Union, Modern World: The Law of Nation in an Age of Revolutions, 1776–1814*. Madison, WI: Madison House, 1993.

Orford, Anne. *International Authority and the Responsibility to Protect*. New York: Cambridge University Press, 2011.

Ossipow, William, and Dominik Gerber. "The Reception of Vattel's Law of Nations in the American Colonies: From James Otis and John Adams to the Declaration of Independence." *American Journal of Legal History* 57, no. 4 (2017): 521–555.

Owensby, Brian P., and Richard J. Ross. *Justice in a New World: Negotiating Legal Intelligibility in British, Iberian, and Indigenous America*. New York: New York University Press, 2018.

———. "Making Law Intelligible in Comparative Context." In *Justice in a New World: Negotiating Legal Intelligibility in British, Iberian, and Indigenous America*, edited by Brian P. Owensby and Richard J. Ross, 273–290. New York: New York University Press, 2018.

Pagden, Anthony. "Conquest and the Just War: The 'School of Salamanca' and the 'Affair of the Indies.'" In *Empire and Modern Political Thought*, edited by Sankar Muthu, 30–60. New York: Cambridge University Press, 2012.

Panizza, Diego. "Alberico Gentili's De Armis Romanis: The Roman Model of the Just Empire." In *The Roman Foundations of the Law of Nations*, edited by Benedict Kingsbury and Benjamin Straumann, 53–84. Oxford: Oxford University Press, 2010.

Parker, Charles H. *Global Calvinism: Conversion and Commerce in the Dutch Empire, 1600–1800.* New Haven, CT: Yale University Press, 2022.

Peabody, Sue. *Madeleine's Children: Family, Freedom Secrets, and Lies in France's Indian Ocean Colonies.* New York: Oxford University Press, 2017.

Pedersen, Susan. *The Guardians: The League of Nations and the Crisis of Empire.* New York: Oxford University Press, 2015.

Pérez Castañera, Dolores María. *Enemigos Seculares: Guerra y Treguas Entre Castilla y Granada, c. 1246–c. 1481.* Madrid: Sílex Ediciones, 2013.

Pestana, Carla Gardina. *The English Atlantic in an Age of Revolution, 1640–1661.* Cambridge, MA: Harvard University Press, 2004.

———. *The English Conquest of Jamaica: Oliver Cromwell's Bid for Empire.* Cambridge, MA: Harvard University Press, 2017.

Peterson, Mark A. *The City-State of Boston: The Rise and Fall of an Atlantic Power, 1630–1865.* Princeton, NJ: Princeton University Press, 2020.

Phillips, Dave, Eric Schmitt, and Mark Mazzetti. "Civilian Deaths Mounted as Secret Unit Pounded ISIS." *New York Times*, 12 December, 2021.

Phillips, William D. *Slavery in Medieval and Early Modern Iberia.* Philadelphia: University of Pennsylvania Press, 2013.

Pitts, Jennifer. *Boundaries of the International: Law and Empire.* Cambridge, MA: Harvard University Press, 2018.

———. "Law of Nations, World of Empires: The Politics of Law's Conceptual Frames." In *History, Politics, Law: Thinking through the International*, edited by Annabel Brett, Megan Donaldson, and Martti Koskenniemi, 191–207. Cambridge, UK: Cambridge University Press, 2021.

———. *A Turn to Empire: The Rise of Imperial Liberalism in Britain and France.* Princeton, NJ: Princeton University Press, 2005.

Plank, Geoffrey Gilbert. *Atlantic Wars: From the Fifteenth Century to the Age of Revolution.* New York: Oxford University Press, 2020.

Pombal, Sebastião José de Carvalho e Melo, Marquês de. *República Jesuíta Ultramarina, que os religiosos jesuítas das províncias de Portugal e Espanha estabbeleceram nos domínios Ultramarinos.* Lisbon: Martins Livreiro Editora; Secretaria Municipal de Educação e Cultura; FUNDAMES, 1989.

Prange, Sebastian R. *Monsoon Islam: Trade and Faith on the Medieval Malabar Coast.* Cambridge Oceanic Histories. New York: Cambridge University Press, 2018.

———. "A Trade of No Dishonor: Piracy, Commerce, and Community in the Western Indian Ocean, Twelfth to Sixteenth Century." *American Historical Review* 116, no. 5 (2011): 1269–1293.

Premo, Bianca, and Yanna Yannakakis. "A Court of Sticks and Branches: Indian Jurisdiction in Colonial Southern Mexico and Beyond." *American Historical Review* 124, no. 1 (2019): 28–55.

Pulsipher, Jenny Hale. *Subjects unto the Same King: Indians, English, and the Contest for Authority in Colonial New England*. Philadelphia: University of Pennsylvania Press, 2007.

———. *Swindler Sachem: The American Indian Who Sold His Birthright, Dropped Out of Harvard, and Conned the King of England*. New Haven, CT: Yale University Press, 2018.

Rech, Walter. *Enemies of Mankind: Vattel's Theory of Collective Security*. Leiden: Martinus Nijhoff Publishers, 2013.

Reséndez, Andrés. *The Other Slavery: The Uncovered Story of Indian Enslavement in America*. Boston: Mariner Books, 2016.

Reynolds, Henry. "Genocide in Tasmania." In *Genocide and Settler Society: Frontier Violence and Stolen Indigenous Children in Australian History*, edited by Dirk Moses, 127–149. New York: Berghan, 2004.

Richter, Daniel K. *Facing East from Indian Country: A Native History of Early America*. Cambridge, MA: Harvard University Press, 2022.

Rivet, Paul. "Los últimos charrúas." *Guaraguao* 8, no. 19 (2004): 165–188.

Rochefort, Charles de. *Histoire naturelle et morale des iles Antilles de l'Amerique. Enrichie d'un grand nombre de belles figures en taille douce . . . Avec un vocabulaire Caraibe*. Rotterdam: Arnould Leers, 1665.

Rubin, Milka Levy. "The Surrender Agreements: Origins and Authenticity." *The Umayyad World*, edited by Andrew Marsham, 196–215. New York: Routledge, 2021.

Rushforth, Brett. *Bonds of Alliance: Indigenous and Atlantic Slaveries in New France*. Chapel Hill: University of North Carolina Press, 2012.

Russell, Frederick H. *The Just War in the Middle Ages*. New York: Cambridge University Press, 1975.

Ryan, Lyndall. *The Aboriginal Tasmanians*. Vancouver: University of British Columbia Press, 1981.

———. "Massacre in the Black War in Tasmania 1823–34: A Case Study of the Meander River Region, June 1827." *Journal of Genocide Research* 10, no. 4 (2008): 479–499.

———. *Tasmanian Aborigines: A History since 1803*. Sydney and Melbourne: Allen & Unwin, 2012.

Sahlins, Marshall. *Islands in History*. Chicago: University of Chicago Press, 1987.

Sainsbury, William Noel, ed. *Calendar of State Papers. Colonial Series, 1574–1660*. Vol. 1. London: Longman, Green, Longman & Roberts, 1860.

Sainsbury, William Noel, and J. W. Fortescue, eds. *Calendar of State Papers: Colonial Series, 1681–1685*. Vol. 5. London: Eyre and Spottiswoode, 1896.

Samson, Jane. *Imperial Benevolence: Making British Authority in the Pacific Islands*. Honolulu: University of Hawaii Press, 1998.

Sandberg, Brian. "Ravages and Depredations: Raiding War and Globalization in the Early Modern World." In *A Global History of Early Modern Violence*, edited by Erica Charters, Marie Houllemare, and Peter H. Wilson, 88–102. Manchester, UK: Manchester University Press, 2020.

———. *War and Conflict in the Early Modern World: 1500–1700*. War and Conflict through the Ages. Malden, UK: Polity Press, 2016.

Santos Campos, André. "O Contratualismo de Francisco Suárez." In *Suárez Em Lisboa 1617–2017: Actos Do Congresso*, edited by Pedro Caridade de Freitas, Margarida Seixas, and Ana Caldeira Fouto, 111–126. Lisbon: AAFDL Editora, 2018.

Saunders, A.C. de C.M. *A Social History of Black Slaves and Freedmen in Portugal, 1441–1555.* New York: Cambridge University Press, 1982.

Scanlan, Padraic X. *Freedom's Debtors: British Antislavery in Sierra Leone in the Age of Revolution.* New Haven, CT: Yale University Press, 2017.

Scarfi, Juan Pablo. *The Hidden History of International Law in the Americas: Empire and Legal Networks.* New York: Oxford University Press, 2017.

Scheipers, Sibylle. *On Small War: Carl von Clausewitz and People's War.* Oxford: University Press, 2018.

Schmitt, Carl. *The Concept of the Political: Expanded Edition.* Chicago: University of Chicago Press, 2007.

———. *The Nomos of the Earth in the International Law of the Jus Publicum Europaeum.* Translated by G. L. Ulmen. New York: Telos Press, 2003.

———. *Theory of the Partisan: Intermediate Commentary on the Concept of the Political.* New York: Telos Press, 2007.

Schmitt, Casey. "Centering Spanish Jamaica: Regional Competition, Informal Trade, and the English Invasion, 1620–62." *William and Mary Quarterly* 76, no. 4 (2019): 697–726.

Schneider, Elena Andrea. *The Occupation of Havana: War, Trade, and Slavery in the Atlantic World.* Chapel Hill: University of North Carolina Press, 2018.

Schwartz, Stuart B. *Blood and Boundaries: The Limits of Religious and Racial Exclusion in Early Modern Latin America.* Waltham, MA: Brandeis University Press, 2020.

Schwarzenberger, Georg. "Jus Pacis Ac Belli? Prolegomena to a Sociology of International Law." *American Journal of International Law* 37, no. 3 (1943): 460–479.

Scott, Rebecca J., and Jean M. Hébrard. *Freedom Papers: An Atlantic Odyssey in the Age of Emancipation.* Cambridge, MA: Harvard University Press, 2012.

Seed, Patricia. *Ceremonies of Possession in Europe's Conquest of the New World, 1492–1640.* New York: Cambridge University Press, 1995.

Semmel, Bernard. *The Rise of Free Trade Imperialism: Classical Political Economy, the Empire of Free Trade and Imperialism, 1750–1850.* Cambridge, UK: Cambridge University Press, 1970.

Shovlin, John. *Trading with the Enemy: Britain, France, and the 18th-Century Quest for a Peaceful World Order.* New Haven, CT: Yale University Press, 2021.

Silver, Peter. *Our Savage Neighbors: How Indian Wars Transformed Early America.* New York: W. W. Norton, 2008.

Sivasundaram, Sujit. *Waves Across the South: A New History of Revolution and Empire.* London: William Collins, 2020.

Sluga, Glenda. *The Invention of International Order: Remaking Europe after Napoleon.* Princeton, NJ: Princeton University Press, 2021.

Smiley, Will. *From Slaves to Prisoners of War: The Ottoman Empire, Russia, and International Law.* Oxford: Oxford University Press, 2018.

———. "Rebellion, Sovereignty, and Islamic Law in the Ottoman Age of Revolutions." *Law and History Review* 40, no. 2 (2022): 229–259.

Somos, Mark. "Vattel's Reception in British America, 1761–1775." In *Concepts and Contexts of Vattel's Political Thought*, edited by Peter Schröder, 203–219. Cambridge, UK: Cambridge University Press, 2021.

Sreenivasan, Ramya. "Drudges, Dancing Girls, Concubines: Female Slaves in Rajput Polity, 1500–1850." In *Slavery and South Asian History*, edited by Indrani Chatterjee and Richard M. Eaton, 17–43. Bloomington: Indiana University Press, 2006.

Stapelbroek, Koen, and Antonio Trampus, eds. *The Legacy of Vattel's Droit Des Gens*. Cham, Switzerland: Palgrave Macmillan, 2019.

Stern, Philip J. *Empire, Incorporated: The Corporations That Built British Colonialism*. Cambridge, MA: Belknap Press, 2023.

Straumann, Benjamin. "The Right to Punish as a Just Cause of War in Hugo Grotius' Natural Law." *Studies in the History of Ethics* 2 (2006), 1–20.

Strugnell, Anthony. "A View from Afar: India in Raynal's *Histoire des deux Indes*." In *India and Europe in the Global Eighteenth Century*, edited by Simon Davies, Daniel Sanjiv Roberts, and Gabriel Sánchez Espinosa, 15–27. Oxford: Voltaire Foundation, 2014.

Suárez, Francisco. *Selections from Three Works*. Edited by Thomas Pink. Natural Law and Enlightenment Classics. Indianapolis: Liberty Fund, 2014.

Suárez Fernández, Luis. *Las guerras de Granada (1246–1492): transformación e incorporación de al-Ándalus*. Barcelona: Ariel, 2017.

Subrahmanyam, Sanjay. *The Career and Legend of Vasco Da Gama*. New York: Cambridge University Press, 1997.

———. *Courtly Encounters: Translating Courtliness and Violence in Early Modern Eurasia*. Cambridge, MA: Harvard University Press, 2012.

———. *The Portuguese Empire in Asia, 1500–1700: A Political and Economic History*. Hoboken, NJ: John Wiley & Sons, 2012.

Tacitus, Cornelius. *The Germany and the Agricola of Tacitus*. Oxford Translation Revised. Chicago: C. M. Barnes Company, 1897.

———. *The History of Tacitus*. Translated by Alfred John Church and William Jackson Brodribb. New York: Macmillan, 1888.

Thomaz, Luís F.F.R. "Precedents and Parallels of the Portuguese Cartaz System." In *The Portuguese, Indian Ocean, and European Bridgeheads, 1500–1800: Festschrift in Honour of Professor K. S. Mathew*, edited by Pius Malekandathil, T. Jamal Mohammed, and Kuzhippalli Skaria Mathew, 67–85. Tellicherry, India: Institute for Research in Social Sciences and Humanities of MESHAR, 2001.

Thompson, D. Gillian. "French Jesuits 1756–1814." In *The Jesuit Suppression in Global Context: Causes, Events, and Consequences*, edited by Jeffrey D. Burson and Jonathan Wright, 181–199. New York: Cambridge University Press, 2015.

Thompson, McLean. *Dupleix and His Letters (1742–1754)*. New York: Robert O. Ballou, 1933.

Thornton, Rod. *Asymmetric Warfare: Threat and Response in the 21st Century*. Malden, MA: Polity Press, 2007.

Tilly, Charles. *The Politics of Collective Violence*. Cambridge Studies in Contentious Politics. New York: Cambridge University Press, 2003.

Townsend, Camilla. *Fifth Sun: A New History of the Aztecs*. New York: Oxford University Press, 2021.

Tuck, Richard. "Introduction." In *The Rights of War and Peace*, edited by Richard Tuck, ix–xxxiv. Natural Law and Enlightenment Classics. Indianapolis: Liberty Fund, 2005.

Twinam, Ann. *Public Lives, Private Secrets: Gender, Honor, Sexuality, and Illegitimacy in Colonial Spanish America*. Stanford, CA: Stanford University Press, 1999.

Tycko, Sonia. "The Legality of Prisoner of War Labour in England, 1648–1655." *Past & Present* 246, no. 1 (2020): 35–68.

Underhill, John. *News From America*. London, 1638.

Valero Silva, José. *El legalismo de Hernán Cortés como instrumento de su conquista*. México: Universidad Nacional Autónoma de México, 1965.

Vancouver, George. *A Voyage of Discovery to the North Pacific Ocean, and Round the World; in Which the Coast of North-West America Has Been Carefully Examined and Accurately Surveyed*. Vol. 1. London: Printed for G. G. and J. Robinson, Paternoster-Row; and J. Edwards, Pall-Mall, 1798.

Van Deusen, Nancy E. *Global Indios: The Indigenous Struggle for Justice in Sixteenth-Century Spain*. Durham, NC: Duke University Press, 2015.

Van Kley, Dale K. "Plots and Rumors of Plots: The Role of Conspiracy in the International Campaign against the Society of Jesus, 1758–1768." In *The Jesuit Suppression in Global Context: Causes, Events, and Consequences*, edited by Jeffrey D. Burson and Jonathan Wright, 13–39. New York: Cambridge University Press, 2015.

Vattel, Emer de. *The Law of Nations, or, Principles of the Law of Nature, Applied to the Conduct and Affairs of Nations and Sovereigns, with Three Early Essays on the Origin and Nature of Natural Law and on Luxury*. Edited by Bela Kapossy and Richard Whatmore. Indianapolis: Liberty Fund, 2010.

Venables, Robert. *The Narrative of General Venables, with an Appendix of Papers Relating to the Expedition to the West Indies and the Conquest of Jamaica, 1654–1655*. Edited by C. H. Firth. New York: Longmans, 1900.

Wakefield, Edward Gibbon. *A Letter from Sydney, The Principal Town of Australia*. Edited by Robert Gouger. London: Joseph Cross, 1829.

Walter, Dierk. *Colonial Violence: European Empires and the Use of Force*. London: Hurst & Company, 2017.

Wansbrough, John E. *Lingua Franca in the Mediterranean*. Richmond, Surrey, UK: Curzon Press, 1996.

Weatherford, J. McIver. *Genghis Khan and the Making of the Modern World*. New York: Crown, 2004.

Webb, Stephen Saunders. *The Governors-General: The English Army and the Definition of the Empire, 1569–1681*. Chapel Hill: University of North Carolina Press, 1979.

Welch, Kimberly M. *Black Litigants in the Antebellum American South*. Chapel Hill: University of North Carolina Press, 2018.

Wheatley, Natasha. *The Life and Death of States: Central Europe and the Transformation of Modern Sovereignty*. Princeton and Oxford: Princeton University Press, 2023.

White, Richard. *The Middle Ground: Indians, Empires, and Republics in the Great Lakes Region, 1650–1815*. Cambridge, UK: Cambridge University Press, 2011.

Whitehead, Neil L. "Tribes Make States and States Make Tribes: Warfare and the Creation of Colonial Tribes and States in Northeastern South America." In *War in the Tribal Zone:*

Expanding States and Indigenous Warfare, edited by R. Brian Ferguson and Neil L. White-head, 127–150. Santa Fe, NM: School of American Research Press, 1992.

Whitman, James Q. *The Verdict of Battle: The Law of Victory and the Making of Modern War.* Cambridge, MA: Harvard University Press, 2012.

Wilmshurst, Elizabeth, ed. *International Law and the Classification of Conflicts.* Oxford: Oxford University Press, 2012.

Wilson, Jon. *India Conquered: Britain's Raj and the Chaos of Empire.* London: Simon & Schuster, 2016.

Winius, George. "The 'Shadow Empire' of Goa in the Bay of Bengal." *Itinerario* 7, no. 2 (1983): 83–101.

Winthrop, John. *Winthrop's Journal: "History of New England," 1630–1649.* New York: Charles Scribner's Sons, 1908.

Wirth, Gerhard. "Rome and Its Germanic Partners in the Fourth Century." In *Kingdoms of the Empire: The Integration of Barbarians in Late Antiquity*, edited by Walter Pohl, 13–56. New York: Brill, 1997.

Witt, John Fabian. *Lincoln's Code: The Laws of War in American History.* New York: Free Press, 2012.

Wood, Laurie. *Archipelago of Justice: Law in France's Early Modern Empire.* New Haven, CT: Yale University Press, 2020.

Worth, John E. *Discovering Florida: First Contact Narratives from Spanish Expeditions along the Lower Gulf Coast.* Gainesville: University Press of Florida, 2014.

Xavier, Ângela Barreto. *A Invenção de Goa: Poder Imperial e Conversões Culturais nos Séculos XVI e XVII.* Lisbon: Imprensa de Ciências Sociais, 2008.

———. "Reducing Difference in the Portuguese Empire? A Case Study from Early-Modern Goa." In *Changing Societies: Legacies and Challenges. Vol. 1. Ambiguous Inclusions: Inside Out, Outside In*, edited by S. Aboim, P. Granjo, and A. Ramos, 141–161. Lisboa: Imprensa de Ciências Sociais, 2018.

INDEX

Aborigines (Australian): in New South
Wales, 171, 175; in Tasmania, 171–74, 190,
242n49, 242n54. *See also* Tasmanians
Abu-I-'Ula (caliph of Seville), 39
Africa: East, 73; North, 33, 62, 70, 145, 175,
211n42; Portuguese captive taking in, 62,
73; Portuguese military garrisons in, 70,
221n40; raiding in, 31, 34–36; southern,
1–2, 201n3; West, 36, 70, 152, 210n25,
220n39, 221n40. *See also* Africans
Africans, 2, 34–35, 67, 82, 90, 98, 210n25,
227n122
Albuquerque, Afonso de, 70–81, 93, 98,
220n37, 221nn40–41
Albuquerque, Francisco de, 71
Alfonso X (king of Castile and León), 40
Algeria, 197, 247n23
Algerian War, 197, 247n23
al-Mansur (ruler of Umayyad caliphate of
Cordoba), 38
Almeida, Francisco de, 70, 72, 75, 219n30,
220n32, 220n35, 221n51
Almeria, 211n40
Altamirano, Cristóbal, 133, 236n101
Americas, the: North (*see* North America);
South (*see* Río de la Plata region [South
America]; South America); Spanish con-
quest of, 11–12, 27–28, 35, 45–50; Tenoch-
titlan, 11–12, 23, 46–48, 212n52
Andonaegui, José de, 235n88
Andrada, Gómez Freire de, 235n88
Angediva, 70
Anglo-Dutch War, 227n135
Anglo-Zulu wars, 2

Angre, Kanhoji, 231n11
Arabs, raiding/conquest by, 33–34, 37–42,
209nn14–15. *See also* Islam; Muslims
Aragon, 29, 31, 38–39
Arcot, 107–108, 110
Arendt, Hannah, 2, 218n14
Aristotle, 65, 218n14
armed peace, global regime of: as fully global,
182; military patrolling in, 148–50; as new
international framework, 99–102; protection emergencies, interventions in response
to, 150–55 (*see also* protection emergencies); regulation by European states of, 147
Arthur, George, 173
Artigas, José Gervasio, 166, 168
Asia: Borneo, 152, 159; China, 151–52; Coromandel Coast (India) (*see* Coromandel
Coast); Indian Ocean region (*see* Indian
Ocean region); Southeast, xi, 152, 159
asymmetric warfare, 4–5. *See also* small wars
atrocities: campaign of extermination
against the Tasmanian Aborigines,
172–74; campaigns of dispossession and
extermination, xiii, 2, 3, 19, 101, 188;
conditions for, small wars producing, 3,
188, 197–98; Jesuit responsibility for
Indigenous, accusation of, 140–41;
"limited" intervention and the potential
for, 150; as necessary to prevent atrocities, 174; regime of armed peace and, 101.
See also massacre(s)
authority, consent as the basis for political,
66–67
Áviles, Gabriel, Marqués de, 166

269